Structured program design with Pascal

Structured program design with Pascal

GWYN JONES and MIKE HEADON

PARADIGM

Paradigm Publishing
Avenue House
131 Holland Park Avenue
London W11 4UT

© Gwyn Jones and Mike Headon, 1988

Set in 10½/12½pt. Linotron Times by
Northern Phototypesetting Co, Bolton.

Printed in Great Britain by
Hollen Street Press Ltd, Slough, Berks.

First published 1988

British Library Cataloguing in Publication Data
Jones, Gwyn, *1940–*
  Structured program design with Pascal.
  1. PASCAL (Computer program language)
  2. Structured programming
  I. Title   II. Headon, Mike
  005.13'3   QA76.73.P2

ISBN 0-948825-95-2

For Pamela

Contents

Preface

This book has been written with the aim of raising the standard c programming. The inclusion of an introduction to the various topics c Jackson Structured Programming (JSP) will allow the book to b useful on courses such as BTEC Higher National level courses i various disciplines, and undergraduate computing and engineerin courses. (For instance Chapter 11, on program inversion, great simplifies some problems such as programming real-time system which are usually only tackled on advanced courses.) The earli chapters will also be suitable for use on courses such as 'A' lev Computer Science and BTEC National level courses in Comput Studies.

The program designs in this book have, with very few exception been implemented in ISO level 1 Pascal so that they can l communicated to the computer in a comparatively straight forwa manner using an increasingly popular language. This is primarily book about program design, not coding in Pascal, and should therefo be useful irrespective of the language the reader wishes to us However, enough Pascal is introduced and explained to allow t reader unfamiliar with Pascal to follow both the text and the example and to tackle the numerous exercises.

It would be convenient if fundamental techniques such as the use procedures, top-down design, and JSP could all be covered in Chap 1. Since this is impractical it is to be hoped that readers with some pri knowledge will soon find their way to these key topics.

Introduction

The need for books of this type is demonstrated by the fact that it is generally accepted in higher education and industry that a systematic method is needed to design cost-effective programs. For example, Professor Edsger Dijkstra, one of the world authorities on programming methods, is quoted as complaining that 'programmers who start on BASIC are mentally mutilated beyond hope of regeneration'. The report of the Alvey Committee[1] says '. . . it is no good just providing schools with microcomputers. This will merely produce a generation of poor BASIC programmers. Universities in fact are having to give remedial education to entrants with 'A' Level computer science. Teachers must be properly trained, and the languages chosen with an eye to the future. Uncorrected, the explosion in home computing with its 1950s and 1960s programming style will make the problem even worse'. In industry, over 25% of programming installations in the UK have already responded to the dangers of bad programming by adopting Jackson's methodology, which is based on making the structure of the program reflect the structure of the data.

The traditional design techniques of flowcharting and inspiration are not satisfactory methods for dealing with large programs as they lead to problems in correcting programs and in altering them to meet changing requirements. This arises from the difficulty of understanding the programs, from their inappropriate structure and from a lack of convenient limited sections of program code relating to the changes required. Often there is a lack of 'cohesion' in the program, as closely related operations are often scattered throughout the program. Corrections and alterations are also made difficult by the high degree of 'coupling' in traditional programs, meaning that there is unnecessary interdependence between different sections of the program. Low correlation between the structure of the data and the structure of the

[1] Report of the Alvey Committee—'A programme for Advanced Information Technology' (1982)

program also leads to serious maintenance problems.

The techniques of top-down stepwise refinement, Jackson Structured Programming and Structured Design go a long way to overcome these problems. The first two of these are described in this book and are largely language independent, and hence can be usefully studied *irrespective* of which languages the reader wishes to use.

There is indeed no excuse for introducing anybody at any level to bad program design techniques when the methods of structured programming are no more difficult to use.

As ever, the drive to improve the situation is economic, but we believe that there is far more satisfaction to be gained from writing robust, well-structured programs than from the fragile efforts which traditional methods lead us to.

The reader with some experience of programming may feel that the use of structure diagrams in great detail prior to coding a simple problem is unnecessary. It should however be appreciated that these represent the 'real' program and that the coded form is merely a way of communicating it to a computer. We make no claim to having originated any of the concepts used in this book. Any novelty is in the presentation. The reader is recommended to develop knowledge and skills by further study of books listed in Appendix 3 and above all by patiently using the techniques described here and therein until they become second nature. The exercises are used at times to develop the points in the main text, and also to integrate the different approaches used in this book. For this reason they should be attempted and the solutions studied.

Our thanks are due to our colleagues at the North East Wales Institute for their help and discussions over the years, and to those numerous students who have taught their teachers. The accuracy and incredible patience of Debbie Moses, who typed the manuscript, have been invaluable.

It is inevitable that a book like this will contain some residual errors. The authors would be grateful to hear of any the reader discovers.

Gwyn Jones
Mike Heade

1 Principles of program design

'The sooner you start to code, the longer it is going to take'.

1.1 Definition of 'good' programs

If we wish to write good programs then we have to use a technique called structured programming. By 'good' programs, we mean programs which
1 give correct results;
2 are easy to understand;
3 are easy to correct;
4 are easy to alter;
5 deal sensibly with unusual data.

We are not particularly concerned about programs which can be executed especially quickly by the computer, or which can be run in a computer with as small a memory as possible, although this may be of legitimate interest to a minority of specialists.

1.2 Aims of structured programming

When an article is to be manufactured, be it a house, car, factory or bridge, a great deal of effort is spent in achieving a suitable design or plan, since any errors in the finished product can be very expensive to correct and may even lead to fatal accidents. The same is true of a good computer program. Structured programming is a method of programming which forces us to concentrate on designing a good program, and makes the writing of the actual instructions, called *coding*, a simple task. It leads us to programs which are comparatively easy to test and to understand, contain few errors and are easy to modify when the need arises.

1.3 Design *v* coding

In one sense, this concentration on program design is a little unfortunate. Most of us have a tendency to want to start coding as soon as we can, so that we feel we are doing something definite, and in order to see something happen on the computer. We must resist this temptation or we will be faced with severe frustration in trying to correct faults in our program, especially as correcting an error in one place may cause two more elsewhere. It may even be difficult to understand what we intended to do at times, and to try to understand a program a year later when a hidden fault appears, or a change is necessary, is even more difficult. If we are landed with the job of doing this to someone else's program, then the problem becomes even greater.

A poet once said of one of his poems 'When I wrote it, only God and I knew what it meant. Now only God knows.' This has all too often been true of programs written without proper design.

1.4 Concept of stepwise-refinement

There are a number of complementary methods of structured program design. Many include the idea of stepwise-refinement, that is, we start off with a major problem which we divide up into a series of smaller problems. We can now take these one at a time, dividing them up as required into still smaller problems until we reach a stage where it is easy to write the code for the computer to carry out the task. By doing this, we can reduce a problem we cannot manage as a whole into a number of smaller problems we can manage one at a time; hence we can produce programs which would otherwise be too difficult for us.

1.5 Fundamental programming components

Another vital technique is to use only certain types of 'building blocks' called *program components*, in our design. There are in fact only three main types of component:

sequences — for operations carried out one after the other,
selections — where we choose what to do next,
iterations — where operations may be repeated.

All programs can be designed using a combination of these.

Once we have the design, we can then convert it into a computer program using the facilities provided in the language we are using to implement our design. Some languages allow structured designs to be implemented more easily than others. The importance of the technique is reflected by the fact that most of the newer languages, such as Pascal, are designed to allow this to be done easily, whilst many of the older languages, such as FORTRAN and COBOL, have been, or are now being, updated to meet the same need. This book will show you how Pascal can help you write good programs.

It is important to study the methods used in the next few chapters very carefully, although the problems may seem trivial to readers with some experience. We will leave a discussion on short cuts until later.

After studying this chapter you should be able to
1   list the qualities of 'good programs' in general;
2   identify the aims of structured programming;
3   recognise the importance of designing before coding;
4   outline the method of top-down design;
5   list the three main program components used in structured programming.

cise   1.1   Carry out the activities listed above.

2 Introduction to Pascal

2.1 Program structure

A Pascal program consists of three parts:
1 a declaration of the program name, and a list of the files that it uses;
2 a description of all the other names used in the program;
3 and the code that manipulates these names.

2.2 The program name

Every Pascal program begins with a statement consisting of the word
PROGRAM, the program name, and a list of any file names that we
will use, thus

```
PROGRAM Ch2P1(input,output);
```

This is the first line of a program called 'Ch2P1' that uses the standard
Pascal files 'input' and 'output'. If you are not going to use any files, the
round brackets may be omitted. We shall use this format of program
name to indicate 'Chapter 2, Program 1'.

2.3 Description of names

Pascal lets us use meaningful names, provided we do not use words
reserved for special meanings (such as BEGIN, END and PRO-
CEDURE). A list of these reserved words is given in Appendix 1,
page 259.

The names of computer memory locations whose contents may vary
when the program runs are called *variables*. Variable names should be
different, but existing Pascal compilers might inspect only the first part
of a name (up to a given number of characters) to check this. We will
ensure that the first eight letters of a name are always distinct.

Variable names should start with a letter, and consist of letters and digits only — no hyphens or other punctuation marks.

We shall follow a well-established convention that reserved Pascal words (like PROGRAM and INTEGER) are written in capitals; types, procedures and functions (these terms are explained below) start with a capital letter, and variables and constants with a small letter. Apart from reserved words, capitals are used also for initial letters of words within indentifier names.

As well as listing a variable's name, we must also state its *type*. There are four basic types defined for us; from them, we can construct more complicated types of our own:

1   a variable that contains a whole number (such as –123) is of type INTEGER;
2   a variable that contains a number with a fractional part (such as 123.456) is of type REAL;
3   a variable that contains a single printable character (such as 'k' or ':') is of type CHAR;
4   and a variable that contains either the value TRUE or the value FALSE is of type BOOLEAN.

An example of a set of variable declarations is

```
VAR
   age,
   points: INTEGER;
   interestRate: REAL;
   keyDepressed: CHAR;
   legal,
   decent,
   honest,
   truthful: BOOLEAN;
```

Another sort of name we will require is a *constant*. This name does not represent a variable location, but stands in place of a particular value, which may be a number or one or more characters. For example, it is a good idea never to use any figures in the code part of a Pascal program other than 0 and 1 without good reason. We can then write a long program referring to (say) 'ageOfRetirement' many times, and if the age of retirement is ever reduced (or increased), we will have only one line to change, and that will be easily found at the start of the program. An example of a set of constant declarations is

```
CONST
   ageOfRetirement = 65;
   pi = 3.14159;
   acceptance = ´Y´;
   space = ´ ´;
   mistakes = ´Fehler´;
```

A set of constant declarations like this generally precedes a set o
variable declarations.

2.4 The code

The main body of the code always has the structure

```
BEGIN

    {Pascal statements.}

END.
```

This may be preceded by definitions of *functions* and *procedures* tha
are used in the Pascal statements; these are described later. Note tha
the program body always end with a full stop.

   Comments may appear anywhere in a Pascal program. They are
enclosed in curly brackets {like this} or between delimiters (* like
this *). They are ignored by the Pascal compiler — provided we
remember to provide a matching closing bracket for each opening
bracket.

2.5 A simple program

Program 2–1 is a trivial program which will give us the 'flavour' o
Pascal. It uses the facilities described so far, and it illustrates some o
the basic arithmetic operators available in Pascal. These are

+   addition;
−   subtraction;
*   multiplication;
/   real division – the result of this is always a real number, with a
       fractional part, so that $14/5 = 2.8$;
DIV integer division — the result of this is always an integer number
       with any fractional part discarded, so that $14 \text{ DIV } 5 = 2$;
MOD modulus division — the result of this is always an integer
       number, representing the arithmetic remainder of the division
       so that $14 \text{ MOD } 5 = 4$.

PROGRAM 2–1

```
PROGRAM Ch2P1(input,output);

{Calculates the weight loss of a
substance over a week, and displays this
in imperial and metric measure - may be
 amended for other periods of time}
```

```
CONST
  ouncesPerPound = 16;
  ozToGrammes = 28.35;
  firstPeriodQuery= 'Weight last week?';
  secondPeriodQuery =
                    'Weight this week?';

VAR
  lastPounds,
  lastOunces,
  thisPounds,
  thisOunces,
  weightLossInOz: INTEGER;

BEGIN

  {Enter old and new weights}
  WriteLn(firstPeriodQuery);
  ReadLn(lastPounds, lastOunces);
  WriteLn(secondPeriodQuery);
  ReadLn(thisPounds, thisOunces);

  {Calculate weight change}
  weightLossInOz:=
    (lastPounds * ouncesPerPound
                + lastOunces) -
    (thisPounds * ouncesPerPound
                + thisOunces);

  {Display weight change}
  WriteLn('Weight loss');
  WriteLn('Imperial: ',
    weightLossInOz DIV ouncesPerPound,
        ' pounds ',
    weightLossInOz MOD ouncesPerPound,
        ' ounces');
  WriteLn('Metric: ',
    weightLossInOz * ozToGrammes,
    ' grammes')

END.
```

2.6 Functions

Sometimes we will write a few lines of code whose sole purpose is to leave us with a calculated value. Suppose we wanted to find the larger of two integer numbers, a and b, and leave the result in an integer variable c. The code might look like Pascal Fragment 2.1.

PASCAL FRAGMENT 2–1

```
ReadLn(a,b);
IF
  a >= b
THEN
  c:= a
ELSE
  c:= b;
{ENDIF}
WriteLn(c, ´ is the larger number´)
```

Later in the program, we might want to perform the same operation using three different variables, p, q and r. This is shown in Pascal Fragment 2.2.

PASCAL FRAGMENT 2–2

```
ReadLn(p,q);
IF
  p >= q
THEN
  r:= p
ELSE
  r:= q;
{ENDIF}
WriteLn(r, ´ is the larger number´)
```

The more we do this, the more inefficient it will appear. The structure of the code is identical. Only the names of the variables have changed. All that we are really interested in is *the value of the larger of two numbers*. Pascal allows us to predefine the code structure that we are using here, so that we do not need to write it all out several times.

In the definition, known as a FUNCTION definition, we tell the Pascal compiler

1 that a FUNCTION is to be defined;
2 by what name it is to be identified;
3 how many data items we will supply to it, and what type of data item these will be; and
4 what type of value we expect the function to leave in its place after it has been called.

In our example, we would define a function called 'Larger' as shown in Pascal Fragment 2.3.

PASCAL FRAGMENT 2–3

```
FUNCTION Larger(x,y:INTEGER):INTEGER;
  BEGIN
    IF
      x >= y
```

```
THEN
    Larger:= x
ELSE
    Larger:= y
{ENDIF}
END
```

The first line of Pascal Fragment 2.3 gives all the information that we specified above. The keyword FUNCTION shows that a function is to be defined, and it will be identified by the name 'Larger'. The list in round brackets shows the number and type of data items that we will specify — two integers. x and y have no independent existence as variables, but merely exist here, in the function definition, to indicate the pattern or form that the code should take when operating on the data items that we will supply when we 'call' the function. They are, therefore, known as 'formal' parameters. (The data items we actually supply with the call will be the 'actual' parameters.)

Finally, the type INTEGER written after the last colon indicates that we expect this function to leave an integer value in its place after we have called it.

Since a function leaves a single value in its place when called, we can put the call anywhere we would write a variable name or constant containing such a value — for example, in the 'WriteLn' statements of Pascal Fragments 2.1 and 2.2. These fragments can be rewritten as Pascal Fragments 2.4 and 2.5 respectively.

PASCAL FRAGMENT 2–4

```
ReadLn(a,b);
WriteLn(Larger(a,b),
          ´ is the larger number´)
```

PASCAL FRAGMENT 2–5

```
ReadLn(p,q);
WriteLn(Larger(p,q),
          ´ is the larger number´)
```

Since a function call represents a single value, we can use it several times in one expression:

```
difference:= Larger(a,b) - Larger(p,q)
```

Exercise 2.1 Assuming the function 'Larger' has been defined as above, what will be the effect of Pascal Fragment 2.6?

PASCAL FRAGMENT 2–6

```
ReadLn(a,b,p,q);
WriteLn(Larger (Larger(a,b),
                 Larger(p,q)) )
```

2.7 Procedures

These are the basic building-blocks of Pascal programs. They resemble functions in that they are defined before being used or 'called' by name, and that they make use of formal and actual parameters. Each procedure could be regarded as a miniature Pascal program; alternatively, a Pascal program could be regarded as a procedure. The structure of a procedure resembles that of a program. This means that a procedure may, and generally does, contain its own constant, type and variable declarations, and indeed its own function and procedure declarations. Any names declared in this way are known as 'local' declarations, since they may only be used inside the procedure where they are declared. In fact, there are three ways in which names can be made available to a procedure or function (the word 'subprogram' is used to represent both procedures and functions):

1 local declarations, as just described;
2 parameter-passing, as described in Section 2.6, 'Functions';
3 global declarations: these are names declared at the start of the program, which are available to any subprograms which follow.

A case can be made for the global declaration of constants and types which may be required in more than one subprogram. Global variables, on the other hand, are generally undesirable, and should be replaced as far as possible by local declarations or passed parameters as appropriate.

In this way, each section of a program can be kept cohesive, self contained and logically complete, and unwanted side-effects can be better avoided. We shall return to this subject in Chapter 7. Meanwhile, we shall proceed one step at a time: in order to avoid over-burdening the reader with additional detail during our discussion of sequences, selections and iterations, and how they fit together in structured programming, we shall continue to use global variables in our small illustrative programs; but the reader should bear in mind that the best acts, the ones we would wish to emulate, generally appear later in the show. When we have more experience, we shall join them.

Meanwhile, suppose we were writing a program, at the beginning of which we wanted to 'initialise' some variables (for example, set them to 0). If we had two integer variables, 'sumWt' and 'sumTotal' to initialise, we might produce Pascal Fragment 2.7.

PASCAL FRAGMENT 2–7

```
sumWt:= 0;
sumTotal:= 0
```

Now, this fragment of code could be recast as a procedure. We would define the procedure before we used it, as shown in Pascal Fragment 2.8.

PASCAL FRAGMENT 2–8

```
PROCEDURE Initialise;
  BEGIN
    sumWt:= 0;
    sumTotal:= 0
  END
```

We would call (or 'invoke') these lines of code by naming the procedure in the place where we want it performed or 'executed', thus:

```
Initialise
```

Any advantage from this may not be immediately apparent — indeed, we seem only to be making extra work for ourselves; but what we are doing here is practising the use of one of the chief tools of good program design. To take another example, let's look again at the code section of Program 2–1. We can rewrite this (from the first 'BEGIN' after the VAR block) using procedures as shown in Pascal Fragment 2.9.

PASCAL FRAGMENT 2–9

```
PROCEDURE EnterOldAndNewWeights;
  BEGIN
    WriteLn(firstPeriodQuery);
    ReadLn(lastPounds, lastOunces);
    WriteLn(secondPeriodQuery);
    ReadLn(thisPounds, thisOunces)
  END;

PROCEDURE CalculateWeightChange;
  BEGIN
    weightLossInOz:=
      (lastPounds * ouncesPerPound
                  + lastOunces) -
      (thisPounds * ouncesPerPound
                  + thisOunces)
  END;

PROCEDURE DisplayWeightChange;
  BEGIN
    WriteLn('Weight Loss');
    WriteLn('Imperial: ',
      weightLossInOz DIV 16, ' pounds ',
      weightLossInOz MOD 16, ' ounces');
    WriteLn('Metric: ',
      weightLossInOz * ozToGrammes,
      ' grammes')
  END;
```

```
BEGIN    {Check weight loss}
  EnterOldAndNewWeights;
  CalculateWeightChange;
  DisplayWeightChange
END.      {Check weight loss}
```

This time we begin to see some advantages. By looking at the main section of Pascal Fragment 2.9, that is, the part right at the end (this is necessary because, in Pascal, any functions and procedures used have to be declared before they are called), we obtain an overview of the stages of the program, consisting entirely of procedure names and unclouded by any syntax or semantics peculiar to Pascal.

2.8 More about program structure

A program generally has the type of structure shown in Pascal Fragment 2.10.

PASCAL FRAGMENT 2–10

```
PROGRAM aaaa(input,output);
CONST
  {....
   ....
   ....}
VAR
  {....
   ....
   ....}
PROCEDURE xxxx;
  BEGIN
    {....
     ....
     ....}
  END;
PROCEDURE yyyy;
  BEGIN
    {....
     ....
     ....}
  END;
PROCEDURE bbbb;
  BEGIN
    {....
     ....
     ....}
  END;
```

```
PROCEDURE cccc;
  BEGIN
    {....
     ....}
    xxxx
    {....
     ....}
    yyyy
    {....
     ....}
  END;
PROCEDURE dddd;
  BEGIN
    {....
     ....
     ....}
  END;
BEGIN      {Main program aaaa}
  bbbb;
  cccc;
  dddd
END.       {Main program aaaa}
```

Note that a procedure can call another procedure. If procedure e contains a call to procedure f, and procedure f contains a call to procedure g, then procedure g must be defined first, since it is required by f; procedure f is defined next (required by e), then procedure e, then the main program. This accords with the general rule in Pascal that a name must be defined before it can be used.

Note also how we use *indentation* — that is, certain lines which belong together are moved towards the right. In this book, we have tried to indent two spaces at a time for typographical reasons, but this has not always been possible. Four spaces would be preferable.

2.9 Input and output

Pascal provides us with four ready-made procedures that enable us to read and write data: Read, ReadLn, Write and WriteLn.

```
Read(hours, rate, taxCode)
```

will read the next three data items it finds into the three variables 'hours', 'rate' and 'taxCode', in that order. This data is assumed to be in the standard input file 'input', which must be declared in the PRO-GRAM statement. The input file may be a file of input data on a batch system, or it may be a microcomputer keyboard.

The procedure 'Read' scans along a line of input, but does not move to the next line. To do this, we can say

```
ReadLn(hours, rate, taxCode)
```

which will read three data items into the named variables and then move to the next line, ignoring anything on the same line. (On a microcomputer, the effects of Read and ReadLn can be different from this: consult your manual if necessary.)

The procedure 'Write' displays a message in the standard output file 'output', likewise declared in the PROGRAM statement. The output file may be a spooled printer file on a batch system, or it may be a microcomputer screen. The statement

```
Write('Gross pay = £', grossPay)
```

will display a message in the form

```
Gross pay = £   234
```

assuming that the contents of 'grossPay' is 234. A subsequent Write (or WriteLn) statement will display its message on the same line.

To display a message and then move to a new line, we can write

```
WriteLn('Gross pay = £', grossPay)
```

where the message displayed is identical, but the next message will appear on the next line. (Again, the effects on a microcomputer may be different.)

Many of the programs in this book are written in 'conversational mode', that is, they display a request and wait for a reply to be typed in

```
WriteLn('Enter part number');
ReadLn(partNumber)
```

In a batch system, the WriteLn statement in this example is obviously redundant.

2.10 Semicolons

In Pascal, semicolons separate statements, or declarations and statements. A statement may be either simple or compound. The statement

```
WriteLn('Enter part number')
```

is a simple statement, and so is

```
ReadLn(partNumber)
```

If the second follows immediately after the first, we separate them with a semicolon;

```
WriteLn('Enter part number');
ReadLn(partNumber)
```

A compound statement contains a number of simple statements with a common aim. It is surrounded by a BEGIN . . . END pair:

```
BEGIN
   WriteLn('Enter part number');
   ReadLn(partNumber)
END
```

The compound statement will be separated from whatever follows it by a semicolon after the END.

We shall return to the subject of semicolons in a later chapter.

After studying this chapter, you should be able to

1 define a variable, and list the four basic variable types in Pascal;
2 define a constant;
3 illustrate the layout of a Pascal program;
4 differentiate between functions and procedures;
5 use the standard input and output procedures;
6 describe the use of semicolons in Pascal.

ises

2.2 Name and declare suitable variables for holding
(a) the day of the month;
(b) the state of being married or unmarried;
(c) the first initial of a name;
(d) a patient's temperature.

2.3 Taking program 2–1 as a model, construct a program which asks for your bank balance on a previous date and the current date, and displays the fall in balance and over what period of time it occurred. You may assume that your bank balance is steadily falling.

2.4 Rewrite your solution to Exercise 2.3 using procedures.

2.5 Identify the errors in Program 2–2.

PROGRAM 2–2

```
      PROGRAM Ch2P2(output);

  CONS
    nextLetter = T;

  VAR
    firstValue,
    secondValue: INTEGER;
    average: REAL;
    nextLetter: CHAR;
    best: BOOL;

  BEGIN

    Initialise;
    Read(nextLetter)
    IF
      nextLetter = ´A´
    THEN
      BEGIN
        firstValue:= 20;
        secondValue:= 28.75;
        WriteLn(Average=, (firstValue +
                secondValue) / 2);
      END
    ELSE
      BEGIN
        WriteLn(´Total is ´, (firstValue
                + secondValue)
      END
    {ENDIF}

  END;
```

3 Sequences

A *sequence* of instructions is one of the building blocks, or *components*, of a structured program and is simply a number of operations which have to be carried out, starting with the first and working through to the last.

3.1 Structure diagrams and use of top-down approach

ple   3.1 Let us consider the problem of ordering equipment for members of a sports club. Suppose we have just one order to deal with which we do by multiplying the quantity ordered by the price for each item to give the value of the order. We will have to enter the quantity and the price into the computer, then multiply them together to give the value, and print this. Suppose we want to buy 5 table tennis bats at £3 each. This forms our sample input data. The expected result is that the value of the order is £15.

We can draw a diagram of this operation as in Figure 3.1. Notice that the overall problem of 'Process an order' has been expressed in more detail, in English, in the second 'row', and that the operations in the second row are needed in order, from left to right. This approach demonstrates the *top-down*, stepwise-refinement method of design. We start at the top with the overall problem, and then work down step by step, refining the design by putting in more detail at each step. You

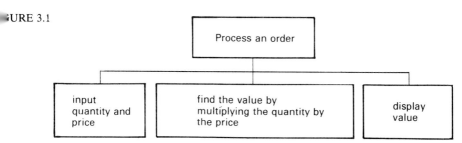

will find, in fact, that many programs have this basic form of Input followed by some operation, followed by an Output or Display section.

This type of diagram is called a *structure diagram*, and was first introduced in this form by Michael Jackson — one of the world authorities on programming — in the early 1970s. It is a good method of describing what you want to do, not only as the eye can often appreciate the shape of a diagram more quickly than it can the written word, but most importantly because sections can be added or removed as the work proceeds, without disturbing the rest of the diagram.

The design of our program is now complete, and the next stage is to convert this into the language we are going to use. In this book, we shall use Pascal, in the version accepted as standard by the ISO (International Standards Organisation). It may be that you are using a different version of Pascal, in which case you should check the sample programs we provide against the facilities available on your machine.

Readers who wish to use other languages might care to convert the structure diagrams to the language of their choice — including assembler code — since the program design expressed as structure diagrams is, in principle, independent of the programming language to be used.

3.2 Pascal variables and simple statements

We need three variables for our program. We will use 'quantity' 'price' and 'value'. What types of variables are they? They are obviously all numbers, but are they integer or real? We can assume 'quantity' is an integer. If we deal in pence or cents, 'price' will be an integer; if we deal in pounds and pence or dollars and cents, 'price' will be a real number. In programming, we should always aim to keep things simple; pence or cents are simpler than pounds or dollars, so we will use the simpler alternative, and make 'price' an integer. This will mean that 'value' must also be an integer. Another aspect of keeping things simple is to avoid mixing integers with real numbers, as far as we can. Our Pascal program will now look like Program 3–1.

PROGRAM 3–1

```
PROGRAM Ch3P1(input,output);

{Process an order:  accepts quantity
sold, and price of article, and displays
value of sale}

VAR
  quantity,
  price,
  value: INTEGER;
```

```
BEGIN    {Process an order}

     Read(quantity);
     Read(price);
     value:= quantity * price;
     WriteLn('Value of sale: ', value)

END.     {Process an order}
```

3.3 Program tracing

When one has a program, or a program design, which is difficult to understand, it is often best to perform a *dry run* or *trace* on it to find out exactly what it does. This means going through the program in the same way as the computer does. It can be tedious, but it is often the quickest way of understanding what is happening.

Table 3.1

step	statement	quantity	price	value	comment
1	Read (quantity)	5			cross out the 5 in the sample data to show it has been input
2	Read (price)	5	3		likewise the 3
3	value: =	5	3	15	the result of the multi-plication is put in "value"
4	WriteLn	5	3	15	underline the 15 to show it has been output.

Table 3.1 is a *trace-table* for Program 3–1, assuming that we wish to order 5 table-tennis bats at £3 each. We go through the program, and the trace-table, line by line, in the same way as a computer would do.

We see that at the end of this program the machine has printed the value and holds numbers in the locations called 'quantity', 'price' and 'value'. Note that when we used the contents of 'quantity' and 'price' in the multiplication, and of 'value' in the WriteLn statement, we did not destroy the data, and it remained available for further use.

It is quite acceptable in a trace-table to put an entry in a column only when the data in that location actually changes, otherwise it is assumed that it stays as it was.

Sample data: 5,3

Example 3.2 The problem this time is to calculate the amount due on an electricity bill. We enter the present meter reading and the previous meter reading and the amount due is the difference between these, multiplied by the cost of a unit of electricity, currently 5 pence per unit.

First, we must get some sample data which we can use to clarify our thoughts on how the required results are to be obtained. Suppose our present meter reading is 20 and the previous reading was 16, so we have used 4 units of electricity, at a cost of 5p each. The amount due to be paid for these units is 4 × 5 = 20p. The *top-level* design is as shown in Figure 3.2. We can now apply the top-down design method to develop this further.

FIGURE 3.2

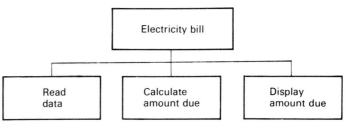

If we ask 'What does Read data consist of?' we arrive at the design of Figure 3.3. Similarly, Calculate amount due consists of operations shown in Figure 3.4. Putting these separate diagrams together, leads to the design of Figure 3.5 which shows the complete design of the program.

FIGURE 3.3

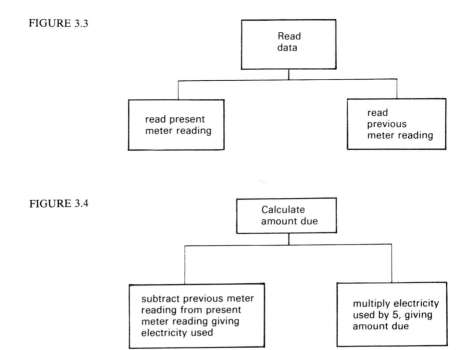

FIGURE 3.4

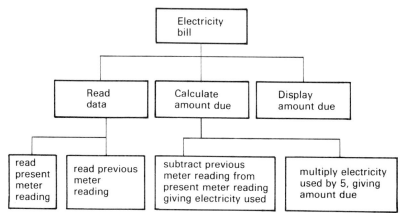

Note that each box forms part of a more detailed explanation of the box it is linked to above. It is *not* an operation to be carried out after the operation above it.

We can now convert our structure diagrams into Program 3–2. Notice that we make use of a Pascal constant 'pencePerUnit' which we set to 5, representing 5 pence per unit (see Section 2.3).

PROGRAM 3–2

```
PROGRAM Ch3P2(input,output);

{Electricity bill:  calculates the
amount due on an electricity bill.}

CONST
  pencePerUnit = 5;

VAR
  presentMeterReading,
  previousMeterReading,
  electricityUsed,
  amountDue: INTEGER;

BEGIN    {Electricity bill}

  BEGIN    {Read data}
    Read(presentMeterReading);
    Read(previousMeterReading)
  END;      {Read data}
```

```
BEGIN    {Calculate amount due}
  electricityUsed:=
    presentMeterReading -
    previousMeterReading;
  amountDue:= electricityUsed *
    pencePerUnit
END;     {Calculate amount due}

BEGIN    {Display amount due}
  WriteLn(´Amount due: ´,
    amountDue, ´ pence´)
END      {Display amount due}

END.    {Electricity bill}
```

Readers already familiar with block-structured languages may protest that, in Program 3–2, we have used far too many BEGIN/END blocks. We should remember, however, that we are studying basic principles: the same principles we can eventually apply to more complicated problems. There are, in fact, two ways in which we can alter the appearance of Program 3–2 to make it more pleasing. The first is by taking into account the fact that three small sequences one after another make one bigger sequence, as in Program 3–3.

PROGRAM 3–3

```
PROGRAM Ch3P3(input,output);

{Electricity bill:  calculates the
amount due on an electricity bill.}

CONST
  pencePerUnit = 5;

VAR
  presentMeterReading,
  previousMeterReading,
  electricityUsed,
  amountDue: INTEGER;

{....
    the above declarations are the same
    as in Program Ch3P2
 ....}
```

```
BEGIN    {Electricity bill}

  {Read data}
  Read(presentMeterReading);
  Read(previousMeterReading);

  {Calculate amount due}
  electricityUsed:=
    presentMeterReading -
    previousMeterReading;
  amountDue:= electricityUsed *
    pencePerUnit;

  {Display amount due}
  WriteLn('Amount due: ',
    amountDue, ' pence')

END.    {Electricity bill}
```

The second way is to use *procedures*; we have done this in Program 3–4.

PROGRAM 3–4

```
PROGRAM Ch3P4(input,output);

{Electricity bill:  calculates the
amount due on an electricity bill.}

CONST
  pencePerUnit = 5;

VAR
  presentMeterReading,
  previousMeterReading,
  electricityUsed,
  amountDue: INTEGER;

{....
    the above declarations are the same
    as in Program Ch3P2
 ....}

PROCEDURE ReadData;
BEGIN
  Read(presentMeterReading);
  Read(previousMeterReading)
END;
```

```
PROCEDURE CalculateAmountDue;
BEGIN
  electricityUsed:=
    presentMeterReading -
    previousMeterReading;
  amountDue:= electricityUsed *
    pencePerUnit
END;

PROCEDURE DisplayAmountDue;
BEGIN
  WriteLn('Amount due: ',
    amountDue, ' pence')
END;

BEGIN   {Electricity bill}

  ReadData;
  CalculateAmountDue;
  DisplayAmountDue

END.    {Electricity bill}
```

We can now trace Program 3–2, using the sample data

Present meter reading: 20
Previous meter reading: 16

The trace table is given as Table 3.2.

Table 3.2

step	statement	present Mtr Rdg	previous Mtr Rdg	elec Used	amount Due	comments
1	Read	20				
2	Read	20	16			
3	elecUsed:=	20	16	4		
4	amount Due:=	20	16	4	20	
5	WriteLn	20	16	4	20	display "amount Due"

It will be seen how easy it has been to do the arithmetic, since the numbers chosen for the sample data were so simple. It can be assumed at present, that if the right answer is obtained with simple numbers, the program will work just as well with awkward ones.

Remember that ':=' should be read as 'becomes' so that in

```
amountDue:= elecUsed * pencePerUnit
```

the previous contents of the variable on the *left* of the 'becomes' sign are replaced by the result of the arithmetic expression on the *right* — which may include the same variable name, as in

```
count:= count + 1
```

where the number stored in 'count' is increased by 1.

After studying this chapter you should be able to
1 define a sequence of operations;
2 represent sequences in structure diagram form;
3 use the top-down stepwise-refinement design approach to developing programs consisting of sequences;
4 encode simple sequences in Pascal;
5 trace the action of a computer in executing a program.

ses

3.1 A meal is to consist of soup, followed by a main course, followed by ice cream. The main course is beef, potatoes, peas, to be served in that order. Draw a structure diagram for the meal.

3.2 A bank charges a flat-rate fee of £1 for changing money from one currency to another, for sums not over £100. There are 11 French francs to the pound on a certain day.
Using
   (a) top-down stepwise-refinement design;
   (b) structure diagrams;
   (c) Pascal
design and write a program which will output the number of francs to be received for a certain number of pounds, assumed to be from £2 to £101.
Trace your solution with suitable sample data.

3.3 The method of converting a temperature from degrees Fahrenheit to degrees Centigrade is to subtract 32 and then multiply this result by 0.5555. Develop, and test, a program to carry out this conversion using the methods of this chapter, as in the last question.

4 Selections and iterations

4.1 Selections

One of the advantages of running a club such as the sports club referre
to in Chapter 3, is to be able to take advantage of discounts that th
supplier offers on orders worth at least a certain value, called the *bul*
order level. To process an order we need to determine its value, an
then decide whether we can deduct a percentage discount or not.

The facility for performing a selection such as this is one of ou
structured programming components, and that is exactly what it
called: *selection*.

4.2 if . . . then . . .

The structure diagram representation of selections is easier to unde
stand if we illustrate it using the above example. This gives us

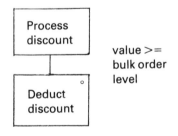

value >=
bulk order
level

We would normally use the Pascal comparison operators rather tha
words; these are

=	is equal to
<>	is not equal to
<	is less than
<=	is less than or equal to
>	is greater than

>= is greater than or equal to

We can code the above fragment in Pascal as

PASCAL FRAGMENT 4–1

```
IF        {Process discount}
   value >= bulkOrderLevel
THEN
   BEGIN    {Deduct discount}
      value:= value - value * discount
                DIV 100
   END        {Deduct discount}
{ENDIF} {Process discount}
```

We have inserted a comment representing the end of the selection — {ENDIF} — this will help us keep the indentation of the lines of our program to a regular scheme, and hence make the meaning stand out clearly from the layout as well as the program text. The name of the selection, 'Process discount', is added to the beginning and end of the Pascal code. Finally, we have enclosed the THEN branch in a BEGIN . . . END pair. This is, of course, not strictly necessary where we only wish to execute a single statement, as here; but it is good practice, since it means that we will have fewer problems if we need to amend the program because the specification has been updated.

The general layout of this type of selection structure in Pascal is

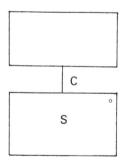

Notice the position of the condition C, and the little circle indicating that the operation S is only carried out if C is true.

Example 4.1 Two items of data are supplied for a person: a reference number, and a code indicating marital state — U for unmarried, M for married, W for widowed, D for divorced. We want a program which reads and displays the reference number and the code, and also displays MARRIED PERSON'S ALLOWANCE in the case where the code is M; if it is any other letter, no additional message is displayed.

Sample data

Sample 1	Input	2864U
	Output	REF 2864 CODE U
Sample 2	Input	2602M
	Output	REF 2602 CODE M
		MARRIED PERSON'S
		ALLOWANCE

The structure diagram is shown as Figure 4.1.

FIGURE 4.1

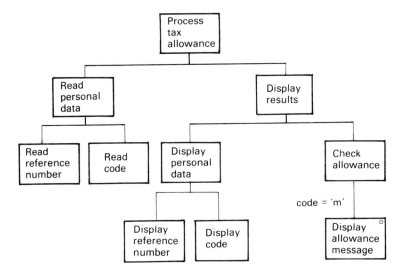

In the above example, we would compare a character variable with the constant 'M' using the equals sign. We can use any comparison operator with characters; the result of the comparison is determined by the method used to represent the characters in the computer.

The commonest method is the ASCII system, in which a space comes first, followed by the digits in the order 0 to 9, then upper-case (capital) letters, and finally lower-case letters. Punctuation marks and other symbols are distributed among various places in the ASCII system, which is given in full in Appendix 2. If strings (described in Chapter 6) are compared, then shorter strings precede longer ones – for example, 'JOAN' precedes 'JOANNA'.

The Pascal code for Program 4–1 would be as shown.

PROGRAM 4–1

```
PROGRAM Ch4P1(input,output);

{This program tests marital status and
may display an appropriate message}
```

```
CONST
  married = 'M';

VAR
  referenceNumber: INTEGER;
  code: CHAR;

BEGIN     {Process tax allowance}

  BEGIN     {Read personal data}
    WriteLn('Enter reference number');
    ReadLn(referenceNumber);
    WriteLn('Enter code');
    ReadLn(code)
  END;       {Read personal data}

  BEGIN     {Display results}
    BEGIN     {Display personal data}
      WriteLn('Reference number: ',
              referenceNumber);
      WriteLn('Code: ', code)
    END;       {Display personal data}

    IF         {Check allowance}
      code = married
    THEN
      BEGIN
        WriteLn('Married person''s ',
                'allowance')
      END
    {ENDIF}   {Check allowance}
  END         {Display results}

END.        {Process tax allowance}
```

4.3 if . . . then . . . else

The selection represented by

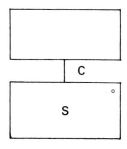

is actually a simplified version of the more powerful

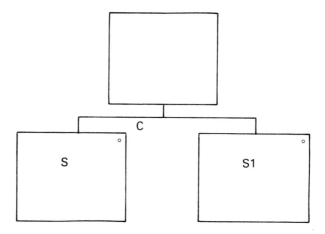

Suppose, for example, we want to read a percentage mark and display 'Mark OK' if it is less than or equal to 100, and 'Mark in error' otherwise. The structure diagram is

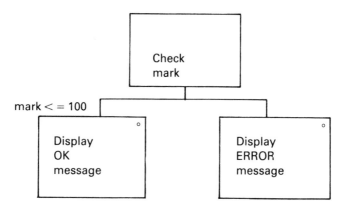

and the Pascal would be as shown in Pascal Fragment 4.2.

PASCAL FRAGMENT 4–2

```
IF       {Check mark}
  mark <= 100
THEN
  BEGIN   {Display OK message}
    WriteLn('Mark OK')
  END       {Display OK message}
ELSE
  BEGIN   {Display error message}
    WriteLn('Mark in error')
  END       {Display error message}
{ENDIF} {Check mark}
```

cise 4.1 Draw the structure diagram, and write the Pascal program to read a student's reference number and examination grade. If the grade is better than 'F' ('A' is the best), display the reference number and the word 'ACCEPT'; if the grade is 'F' or worse, display the reference number and the word 'REJECT'. (Note that we would generally deal with names rather than reference numbers, but reading names in Pascal requires a technique that we will discuss in Chapter 6.)

4.4 Elementary use of AND, OR, NOT

Any selection may include a *compound condition* where more than one test is made. It might be reasonable in the above example to test not only that 'mark' is 100 or less, but also that it is 0 or more. It is simply a matter of combining the conditions using AND or OR as appropriate (NOT may also be used); remember to include brackets around the conditions in the Pascal code. Our example would become

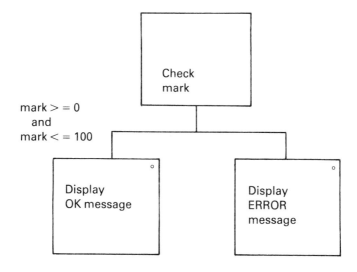

and in Pascal we would write the code shown as Pascal Fragment 4.3.

PASCAL FRAGMENT 4-3

```
IF      {Check mark}
   (mark >= 0)
   AND
   (mark <= 100)
THEN
   {....}
```

Exercise 4.2 Enter a reference number and a code letter as input data. If the code letter is between 'G' and 'M' inclusive, display the reference number and the message 'Access authorised'. Otherwise the message should be 'Code not accepted for access'. Prepare a structure diagram and a Pascal program, which should be tested, to carry out this operation.

Some decisions are more complex than others. Suppose, for example, we want to select one action out of 3 possible ones, as in the following example.

Example 4.2 Design and write a program which will input a percentage mark and output the message 'CREDIT' if the mark is 65% or over, 'PASS' if it is between 40% and 64% inclusive and 'FAIL' if it is less than 40%. Assume that all the input data is between 0 and 100 inclusive.

Sample data
(a) Input 65   Output : CREDIT
(b) Input 64   Output : PASS
(c) Input 40   Output : PASS
(d) Input 39   Output : FAIL
(Note how we make sure we test at the boundaries. We should always include these critical cases in the sample data.)

The mental process for obtaining the output from the input is, for many people, not obvious. One possible method of argument is: if the mark is 65 or over, print 'CREDIT'; otherwise, if it is 40 or over, print 'PASS'; otherwise print 'FAIL'. This is easily represented in a structure diagram as shown in Figure 4.2.

FIGURE 4.2

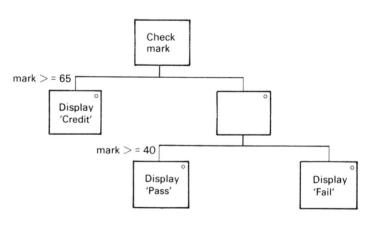

Notice how we only need to specify the condition on one 'leg' of a pair and how we do not *have* to write something in every box.

The Pascal program would be as shown in Program 4–4.

PROGRAM 4–4

```
PROGRAM Ch4P4(input,output);

{This program checks a single mark for
credit, pass or fail}

CONST
  creditLevel = 65;
  passLevel = 40;

VAR
  mark: INTEGER;

BEGIN     {Check mark}

  WriteLn('Enter mark');
  ReadLn(mark);

  IF        {Test for credit}
    mark >= creditLevel
  THEN
    BEGIN
      WriteLn(mark, ' Credit')
    END
  ELSE
    BEGIN     {Test for pass}
      IF
        mark >= passLevel
      THEN
        BEGIN
          WriteLn(mark, ' Pass')
        END
      ELSE
        BEGIN
          WriteLn(mark, ' Fail')
        END
      {ENDIF}
    END        {Test for pass}
  {ENDIF}   {Test for credit}

END.       {Check mark}
```

4.5 Case

When we have a multiple choice situation where we have to choose one
operation out of several, we need the selection type corresponding to
the Pascal CASE statement.

For example, suppose we wish to allow a multiple choice or 'menu' situation such as choosing one action out of three, depending on a value of N, which must be 1, 2 or 3. Our trivial action is to display 'N = 1', 'N = 2' or 'N = 3' as the case may be.

FIGURE 4.3

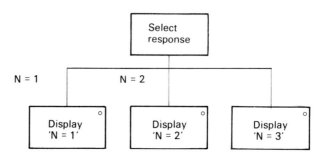

Notice again that we do not write the condition on the right-most selection. If N is not a 1 or 2, then it must be a 3. We can convert this directly into a Pascal CASE statement:

```
CASE          {Select response}
   n
OF
   1:BEGIN
       WriteLn( ´n = 1´)
     END;
   2:BEGIN
       WriteLn( ´n = 2´)
     END;
   3:BEGIN
       WriteLn( ´n = 3´)
     END
END{CASE} {Select response}
```

If N does not contain one of the values we have used as CASE labels (1, 2 and 3), we will generate a run-time error; so, if the contents of N have not been validated, it may be necessary to write

```
IF
   (n >= 1)
   AND
   (n <= 3)
THEN
   BEGIN
     CASE          {Select response}
        n
```

```
        OF
          1:BEGIN
              WriteLn( ´n = 1´)
            END;
          2:BEGIN
              WriteLn( ´n = 2´)
            END;
          3:BEGIN
              WriteLn( ´n = 3´)
            END
        END{CASE} {Select response}
      END
    ELSE
      BEGIN
        WriteLn( ´Contents of n in error:´,
                 n)
      END
    {ENDIF}
```

The following is an important example which shows a combined use
of IF . . . THEN and IF . . . THEN . . . ELSE statements.

le 4.3 Write a program to read 3 numbers representing an account
number, the amount due on an account, and the number of days
by which the payment is overdue, in that order. The account
number is to be printed.

If the amount due is over 10, the message 'Credit limit
exceeded' is also printed. If the number of days the payment is
overdue is greater than 30, the message 'Surcharge payable' is
printed. If neither figure is exceeded then the message 'OK' is to
be printed.

We start with Figure 4.4.

JRE 4.4

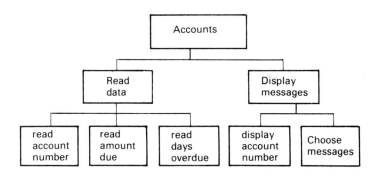

We can develop 'Choose messages', arguing that the message should
be 'OK', or else we will print cautions as appropriate: see Figure 4.5.

FIGURE 4.5

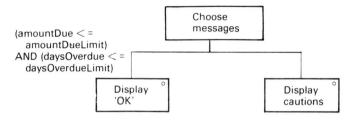

Now we have to be careful. If we try the design of Figure 4.6, we will print either one or the other of these messages — but not both should the amountDue exceed amountDueLimit *and* the daysOverdue exceed daysOverdueLimit.

FIGURE 4.6

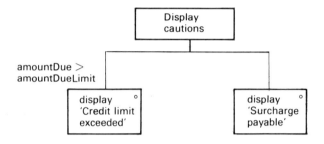

Instead of the above we need to be able to print either the first message, or the second message, or both messages, or neither. This is called the *general OR* condition, as opposed to 'if C then S1 else S2' — which represents *exclusive OR* since carrying out one of the actions S1 or S2 automatically excludes the other.

The easiest way to deal with exclusive OR is to use two separate decisions, as in Figure 4.7.

FIGURE 4.7

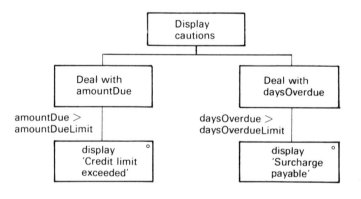

Then the second test is carried out irrespective of the result of the first. The full structure diagram is then as shown in Figure 4.8.

FIGURE 4.8

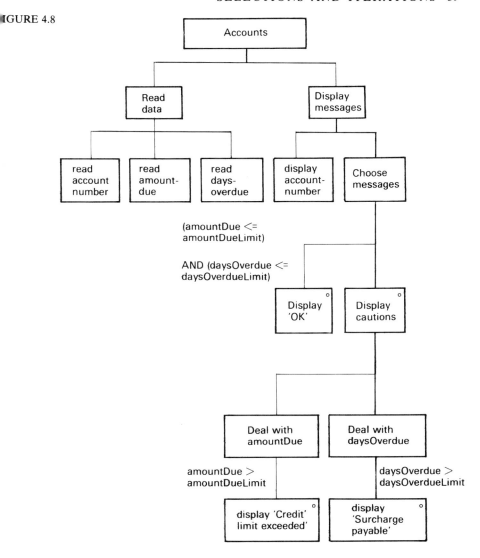

The Pascal coding is shown as Program 4–5.

PROGRAM 4–5

```
PROGRAM Ch4P5(input,output);

{This program tests the details of an
account for exceeded credit limit and/or
overdue payments.}

CONST
  limitAmountDue = 10;
  limitDaysOverdue = 30;
```

```
VAR
  accountNumber,
  amountDue,
  daysOverdue: INTEGER;

BEGIN    {Accounts}

  BEGIN    {Read data}
    WriteLn('Enter account number');
    ReadLn(accountNumber);
    WriteLn('Enter amount due');
    ReadLn(amountDue);
    WriteLn('Enter days overdue');
    ReadLn(daysOverdue)
  END;     {Read data}

  BEGIN    {Display messages}
    WriteLn('Account number: ',
            accountNumber);
    IF       {Choose messages}
      (amountDue <= limitAmountDue)
      AND
      (daysOverdue <= limitDaysOverdue)
    THEN
      BEGIN
        WriteLn('This amount OK')
      END
    ELSE
      BEGIN    {Display cautions}
        IF       {Deal with amount due}
          amountDue > limitAmountDue
        THEN
          BEGIN
            WriteLn(
              'Credit limit exceeded')
          END;
        {ENDIF}  {Deal with amount due}

        IF      {Deal with days overdue}
          daysOverdue > limitDaysOverdue
        THEN
          BEGIN
            WriteLn('Surcharge payable')
          END
        {ENDIF} {Deal with days overdue}
      END        {Display cautions}
    {ENDIF}   {Choose messages}
```

END   {Display messages}

END.   {Accounts}

4.6 Structure diagrams

A word of warning: we have introduced the selection structures shown in Figure 4.9.

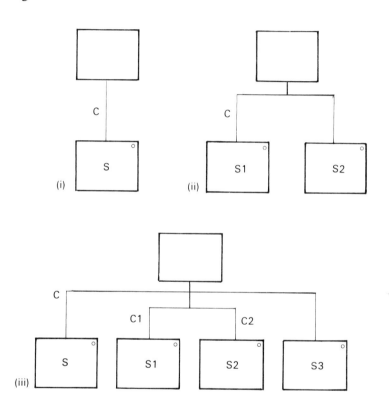

It is incorrect to hang anything but a selected operation with a circle in the top right corner from the upper box, and when we do that, it means we choose only one of the possibilities — although in the case represented by Figure 4.9 (i), we may choose not to carry out the selected operation at all.

FIGURE 4.10

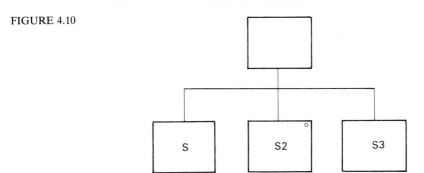

For example, the Figure 4.10 is *wrong*, since S and S3 have no su◄ circles, and hence are not operations which are selected. It must ► drawn as Figure 4.11.

FIGURE 4.11

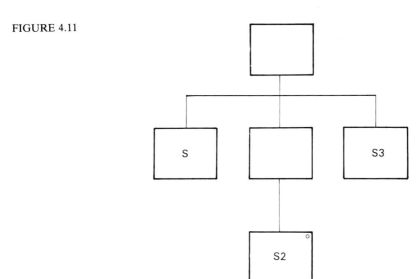

Do not hesitate to put in extra 'dummy' boxes like this—they are of◄ necessary, and are essential to avoid errors.

4.7 Iterations

It is generally necessary to repeat sequences and selections a num► of times in a program. For instance, we need to consider how we co► process the orders for the sports club if there were more than ◄ order.

Let us suppose that there are exactly three:

Order number 1: 5 table tennis bats at £3.00
Order number 2: 3 pairs of boots at £7.50
Order number 3: 4 track suits at £20.25

If we ignore the possibility of discounts for the moment, we could process these by running program 3–1 (which was developed in Chapter 3), three times.

The basic program, 'Process an order', was as in Program 4–6.

PROGRAM 4–6

```
PROGRAM Ch4P6(input,output);

{Process an order:  accepts quantity
sold, and price of article, and displays
value of sale}

VAR
  quantity,
  price,
  value: INTEGER;

BEGIN    {Process an order}

  Read(quantity);
  Read(price);
  value:= quantity * price;
  WriteLn( 'Value of sale: ', value)

END.     {Process an order}
```

The disadvantages of running the program three times, once for each order, is that firstly, it is time-consuming (suppose we had 50 orders), and secondly, should we wish to know the combined total value of all the orders, there is no easy way of finding it out.

To solve this problem, we need *iteration*. Iteration is a way of carrying out some operation a number of times — or, in some cases, missing it out. An iteration is sometimes called a *loop*.

4.8 'FOR' iterations

There are three types of iterations. The first we shall consider is called a 'FOR' loop, and is used when it is known exactly how many times an operation is to be carried out.

ole   4.4   The conventional way of showing an iteration in a structure diagram is illustrated in Example 4.4, Figure 4.12.

FIGURE 4.12

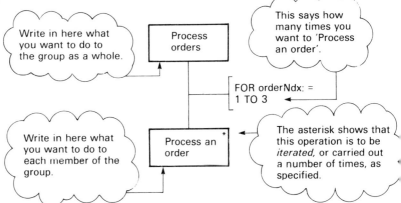

Many people find it easier to construct structure diagrams using the form shown in Figure 4.13, as this rules out some of the common errors which are made.

FIGURE 4.13

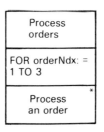

We shall use both forms in this book.

The Pascal version of this particular example is shown as Program 4–6.

```
PROGRAM Ch4P6(input,output);

{Process orders:  accepts number of
orders, quantity sold, and price of
article, and displays value of sale}

VAR
  noOfOrders,
  quantity,
  price,
  value,
  orderNdx: INTEGER;

BEGIN    {Process orders}
```

```
Read (noOfOrders);
FOR
  orderNdx:= 1 TO noOfOrders
DO
  BEGIN    {Process an order}

    Read(quantity);
    Read(price);
    value:= quantity * price;
    WriteLn('Value of sale: ', value)

  END      {Process an order}
 {ENDFOR}

END.    {Process orders}
```

Suppose that the value of the first data item is 3. We start by reading this into 'noOfOrders'. 'orderNdx' is called the *counter* or *index* and is set to 1 to start with. 'Process an order' is then executed for the first time. After this, 'orderNdx' is increased by 1 to 2, and 'Process an order' is then executed for the second time. Next, 'orderNdx' is once more increased (or *incremented*) by 1, so that it is 3, and 'Process an order' is executed for the final time before the program continues, since the value of 'orderNdx' is now equal to the value of 'noOfOrders'. Once 'Process an order' has been executed for the final time, the value of 'orderNdx' is *undefined* and cannot be used.

The general layout of a FOR loop in Pascal is

```
FOR       {Name of iteration}
  counter:= initialValue TO finalValue
DO
  BEGIN

    {....statements to be iterated....}

  END
 {ENDFOR} {Name of iteration}
```

Consistent with our IF statement layout, and for the same reasons, we have included an {END FOR} comment, and will generally enclose the body of the FOR loop in a BEGIN . . . END pair. The counter is a scalar variable whose name you choose. This scalar variable must (in ISO-Pascal) be declared in 'the block closest-containing the FOR statement'. In other words, this means that the counter must be declared as a *local variable* if it is to be used in a procedure or function. A local variable is declared in the declarative-part of a block. A Pascal block consists of a declarative part (defining constants, types, variables, and so on) followed by a compound statement (BEGIN . . . END). So a procedure is a block, and so is a function, and we can make declarations immediately following the PROCEDURE or FUNCTION statements.

Items declared like this are deemed not to exist outside the block in which they are declared, unlike the *global variables* declared at the start of the main program block. This is illustrated in Program 4–7.

The *initial value* and *final value* can be constants (any constants other than 0 and 1 should be declared in the CONST block), variables to which values have been assigned, or expressions that the computer can evaluate. The initial value need not be 1.

In our example, we already know what the 'instructions to be iterated' are. They are simply the instructions for 'Process an order' which we developed earlier.

The full Pascal coding for our program is shown as Program 4–7, and it is traced in Table 4.1.

Table 4.1

Step	Routine	order Ndx	quantity	price	value	Comment
1.1	Process Orders	1				
2.1a	Process An Order		5			
2.1b				3		
2.1c					15	
2.1d						Display
					15	Value = 15
1.2	Process Orders	2				
2.1b	Process An Order		3			
2.2b				7.50		
2.3b					22.50	
2.4b						Display
					22.50	Value = 22.5
1.3	Process Orders	3				
2.1c	Process An Order		4			
2.2c				10.25		
2.3c					41.00	
24c						Display
					41.00	Value = 41

PROGRAM 4–7

```
PROGRAM Ch4P7(input,output);

{This program calculates the value of an
order a given number of times.}

CONST
  noOfOrders = 3;

VAR
  quantity,
  price,
  value,
  orderNdx: INTEGER;

PROCEDURE ProcessAnOrder;
BEGIN
  Read(quantity);
  Read(price);
  value:= quantity * price;
  WriteLn('Value of sale: ', value)
END;

BEGIN    {Process orders}

  FOR
    orderNdx:= 1 TO noOfOrders
  DO
    BEGIN
      ProcessAnOrder
    END
  {ENDFOR}

END.     {Process orders}
```

Sample data
Input : 5   3.00
         3   7.50
         4   10.25
Output : Value = 15
         Value = 22.5
         Value = 41

―――――――
le   4.5   Write a program to read four numbers and display their total. See Figure 4.14.

FIGURE 4.14

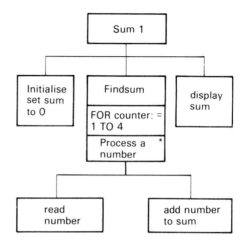

The Pascal is shown as Program 4–8.

PROGRAM 4–8

```
PROGRAM Ch4P8(input,output);

{This program reads four numbers and
displays their total}

CONST
  howMany = 4;

VAR
  sum,
  number,
  counter: INTEGER;

BEGIN     {Sum1}

  BEGIN     {Initialise}
    sum:= 0
  END;      {Initialise}

  FOR       {Find sum}
    counter:= 1 TO howMany
  DO
    BEGIN     {Process a number}
      WriteLn('Enter next number');
      ReadLn(number);
      sum:= sum + number
    END;      {Process a number}
  {ENDFOR} {Find sum}
```

```
WriteLn('Sum is ', sum)

END.       {Sum1}
```

ple   4.6 This shows how to use the counter within the scope of the FOR
statement. The problem is to write a program to add up the whole
numbers from 50 to 55, inclusive, and display the result. See
Figure 4.15.

URE 4.15

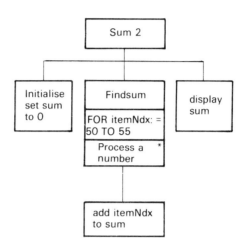

The Pascal code is shown as Program 4–9.

PROGRAM 4–9

```
PROGRAM Ch4P9(input,output);

{Adds a sequence of numbers}
CONST
  lowerLimit = 50;
  higherLimit = 55;

VAR
  sum,
  itemNdx: INTEGER;

BEGIN     {Sum2}

  BEGIN     {Initialise}
    sum:= 0
  END;      {Initialise}

  FOR        {Find sum}
    itemNdx:= lowerLimit TO higherLimit
```

```
DO
   BEGIN      {Process a number}
      sum:= sum + itemNdx
   END;       {Process a number}
   {ENDFOR} {Find sum}

   WriteLn(´Sum is ´, sum)

END.       {Sum2}
```

Example   4.7 This example shows how to control how many times a process is iterated by reading the final value for the counter as data. The problem is to read a student's percentage marks in an unknown number of subjects, and display the average mark for that student. The number of subjects examined is given as the first data item. See Figure 4.16.

FIGURE 4.16

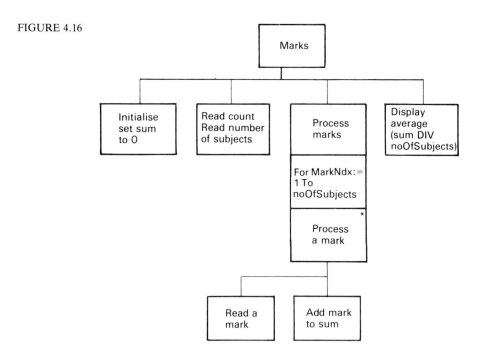

Sample data

Input :   5   75   74   75   0   41
Output :   5 subjects taken
           Average mark is 53
The Pascal is shown as Program 4–10.

PROGRAM 4-10

```
PROGRAM Ch4P10(input,output);

{This program calculates a student's
average mark}

VAR
  sum,
  noOfSubjects,
  mark,
  markNdx: INTEGER;
  average: REAL;

BEGIN     {Marks}

  BEGIN     {Initialise}
    sum:= 0
  END;      {Initialise}

  BEGIN     {Read count}
    WriteLn('Enter number of subjects');
    ReadLn(noOfSubjects)
  END;      {Read count}

  FOR       {Process marks}
    markNdx:= 1 TO noOfSubjects
  DO
    BEGIN     {Process a mark}
      WriteLn('Enter next mark');
      ReadLn(mark);
      sum:= sum + mark
    END;      {Process a mark}
  {ENDFOR} {Process marks}

  WriteLn('Average is ',
          sum / noOfSubjects)

END.      {Marks}
```

While it is easy to set or change the initial and final values for a FOR loop in a program, neither they, nor the counter itself, may ever be changed by the programmer inside the loop. Neither may the value of the counter be used anywhere but inside the loop, as its value elsewhere is undefined. The counter variable itself may be re-used to contain the index to another FOR loop, but its value there will bear no relation to its previous use.

Pascal allows us to decrement the counter, so that (if 'totalSecond' is 10) we can say

```
FOR      {Process seconds}
   secondsNdx:= totalSeconds DOWNTO 1
DO
```

This causes I to go from 10 to 9, to 8, and so on down to 1. The step size cannot be changed inside the loop.

Before tackling some examples on 'FOR' type iterations, there is further point to consider. It is sometimes difficult to decide what to call the counter and the final value in setting up a 'FOR' loop. To avoid mistakes it will often be found to be useful to:

1 use the name given to the 'thing' being processed within the loop followed by 'Ndx', as the counter. For example, 'nameNdx';

2 put 'noOf' (number of) before the plural of the 'thing' to form the final value. For example, 'noOfNames'.

It is essential in producing an intelligible program to use variable names which can be easily understood. This can make it tedious to write out the program, although this is a small price to pay for the benefits gained. Intelligent use of an Editor's *multiple string replacement* facility can be helpful here. It is often possible to abbreviate data names, without loss of meaning.

One method is to leave out letters so that the sound stays more less the same. For example 'Index' becomes 'Ndx'. Another method to first cross out the vowels and then any double letters, and if you like the look of what you finish up with, use that.

Exercise 4.3   Five sets of 'Present' and 'Previous' electricity meter readings are to read in (in the above order) and validated (or checked). If the 'Present' reading is less than the 'Previous' reading, or if either reading negative, print the readings, and the word 'Query!'

4.9 while . . . do . . .

This type of iteration is used when we do not know exactly how many times to carry out an operation; it may be that we don't need to carry out the operation at all.

If C is the condition which controls the number of times that operation S is to be carried out, then the WHILE . . . DO loop can be drawn as

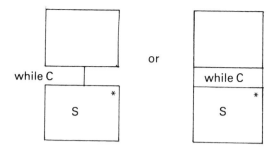

while the Pascal, using the same principles as previously, becomes

```
WHILE        {Name of iteration}
   condition
DO
   BEGIN

      {....statements to be iterated....}

   END
{ENDWHILE} {Name of iteration}
```

Example 4.8 Crates with a maximum weight of 300 kg are loaded on an aircraft in the order in which they are received, until the total weight of the crates exceeds 1000 kg for the first time. Write a program to read in the weights, and display the total weight of the load, assuming that there are enough crates to form a full load.

Sample data
Input: 200   200   300   100   300   200   100
Output: 1100

The weight of the load will be

200 + 200 + 300+ 100+ 300 = 1100.

As the 1000kg may change, we shall set it as a parameter called 'limit'. The structure diagram is shown as Figure 4.17.

FIGURE 4.17

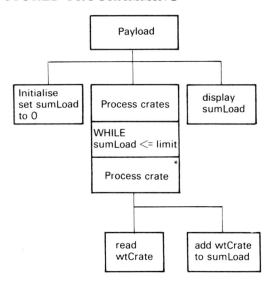

It will be seen that the box called 'Process crates' is refined into 'Process crate', to be repeated as required. This method of naming the boxes used in iteration will be found to be useful in a great many problems.

The Pascal is shown as program 4–11.

PROGRAM 4–11

```
PROGRAM Ch4P11(input,output);

{Aircraft loading}

CONST
  limit = 1000;

VAR
  sumLoad,
  wtCrate: INTEGER;

BEGIN    {Payload}

  BEGIN        {Initialise}
    sumLoad:= 0
  END;         {Initialise}

  WHILE        {Process crates}
    sumLoad <= limit
  DO
    BEGIN        {Process crate}
      WriteLn( ´Enter next crate weight´);
      ReadLn(wtCrate);
```

```
       sumLoad:= sumLoad + wtCrate
         END;          {Process crate}
      {ENDWHILE} {Process crates}

      WriteLn('Payload: ', sumLoad, ' kg')

      END.      {Payload}
```

This should be traced using the sample data suggested to see how it works.

4.10 Read-ahead

Although 'WHILE . . . DO' is probably the most useful of the iterative constructs, it requires a little care in its use. This is because we must set up our condition, C, before we can test it in the first place, and set it up again before we test it again. To cope with this we need a technique called *read-ahead* by Jackson. The idea is shown in Figure 4.18.

RE 4.18

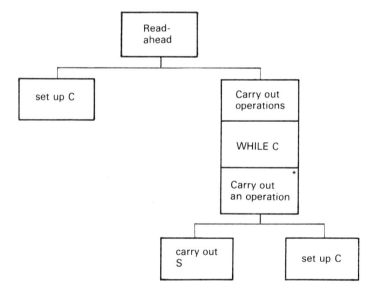

In other words, we set up C initially and then think of our overall operation as being

1   do the main operation, S
2   set C up again.

Note the positions of 'Set up C' in the above structure diagram — it is a pattern which turns up again and again.

This is not really difficult, as the following example will show.

Example   4.8   The problem is to read the value of each of a number of orders, and display the total value. All the values are positive or zero, and the end of the data is indicated by a special *rogue* value, or *sentinel*, which is –1.

Sample data
Input: 5   3   2   -1
Output: 10
The process is just to add them up, until we get to the -1. The structure diagram is shown as Figure 4.19.

FIGURE 4.19

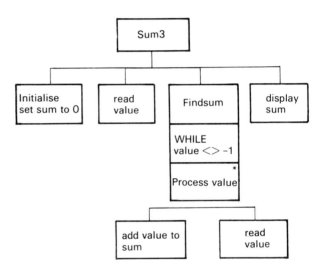

The Pascal is shown as Program 4–12.

PROGRAM 4–12

```
PROGRAM Ch4P12(input,output);

{Find total value of orders}

CONST
  sentinel = -1;

VAR
  sum,
  value: INTEGER;

BEGIN     {Sum3}

  BEGIN        {Initialise}
    sum:= 0
  END;         {Initialise}
```

```
WriteLn( ´Enter next value´);
ReadLn(value);

WHILE        {Find sum}
   value <> sentinel
DO
   BEGIN        {Process value}
      sum:= sum + value;
      WriteLn( ´Enter next value´);
      ReadLn(value)
   END;          {Process value}
   {ENDWHILE} {Find sum}

WriteLn( ´Sum is ´, sum)

END.      {Sum3}
```

4.11 repeat . . . until . . .

The final type of iteration is used when an operation must be repeated an unknown number of times, but at least once. This is called the 'REPEAT . . . UNTIL' loop, and is generally not as useful as the 'WHILE . . DO' loop as it may make it difficult to cope with 'silly' data, such as input data of simply −1 for Example 4.8, where nothing actually has to be done. It is perhaps most useful in mathematical problems which use *iterative* methods in which an approximate answer is repeatedly improved until it is acceptable. Such problems are outside the scope of this book.

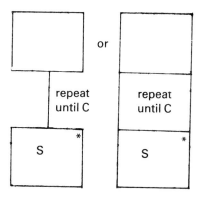

where S is the operation or operations to be repeated until condition C becomes true.

In Pascal this is coded as

```
REPEAT          {Name of iteration}

    {....statements to be iterated....}

UNTIL
   condition
{ENDREPEAT} {Name of iteration}
```

xample   4.9   Write a program which will accept as data the cost of a pint of milk and will print a table under suitable headings showing the numbe of pints and their cost in pence up to (and including) a total of 100 or 6 pints, whichever comes first.

Sample data

Input: 20

Output:	*Pints*	*Cost*
	1	20
	2	40
	3	60
	4	80
	5	100

We shall deal with the maximum cost, and the maximum number of pir as parameters, 'maxCost' and 'maxNmr'.

If we assume that the cost of a pint of milk is less than 100p, we will ha to print at least one line in the table and can therefore use 'REPEAT. UNTIL'. The structure diagram is shown in Figure 4.20.

FIGURE 4.20

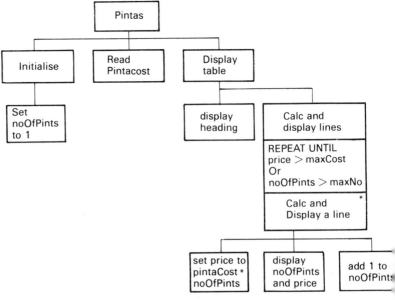

We do not have to initialise 'cost' before we enter the iterated operation 'Calc and display a line', as 'cost' is given a value in that operation, and is not checked until that operation is finished. Note also how 'Display heading' is separated from 'Calc and display lines'.

e   4.4   Encode Figure 4.20 in Pascal, and test it.

e   4.5   Write a program to read a series of four-digit numbers, and to display any number which is 9000 or greater; stop when the last number, which is 9999, has been printed.

We have now covered all the control components needed to write well-structured programs in *any* general computer language, from machine code to COBOL. There are some refinements to come, and there are many details concerning particular languages which will have to be looked up elsewhere. But the reader should now be familiar enough with the fundamentals of sound programming to write good small programs.

4.12 Nested loops

Let us consider some further problems concerning loops. Suppose we want to display the first three values of the 5 times table, as follows
$1 \times 5 = 5$
$2 \times 5 = 10$
$3 \times 5 = 15$
The structure diagram is given as Figure 4.21.

RE 4.21

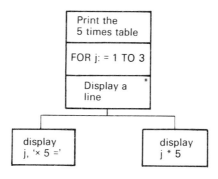

The Pascal is shown as Program 4–13.

PROGRAM 4–13

```
PROGRAM Ch4P13(input,output);

{Display the 5 times table}
```

```
CONST
  table = 5;
  noOfLines = 3;
  times = ´ x ´;
  equals = ´ = ´;

VAR
  j: INTEGER;

BEGIN     {Display the 5 times table}

  FOR
    j:= 1 TO noOfLines
  DO
    BEGIN     {Display a line}
      Write(j, times, table, equals);
      Write(j * table);
      WriteLn
    END       {Display a line}
  {ENDFOR}

END.      {Display the 5 times table}
```

Now, suppose we want to display our 5 times table fragment as above followed by the corresponding 6 times table fragment.

We could repeat our program with suitable changes. A much better system, however, is to use the structure shown in Figure 4.22.

FIGURE 4.22

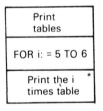

All we need to do is to fit this into our previous program, with I instead of 5, giving the structure shown in Figure 4.23.

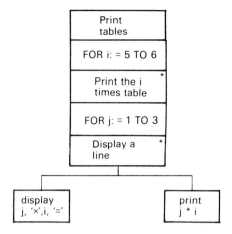

The Pascal is shown as Program 4–14.

PROGRAM 4–14

```
PROGRAM Ch4P14(input,output);

{Display a number of tables}

CONST
  firstTable = 5;
  lastTable = 6;
  limit = 3;
  times = ' x ';
  equals = ' = ';

VAR
  i,j: INTEGER;

BEGIN    {Display tables}

  FOR
    i:= firstTable TO lastTable
  DO
    BEGIN    {Display the i times table}
      FOR
        j:= 1 TO limit
      DO
        BEGIN    {Display a line}
          Write(j, times, i, equals);
          Write(j * i);
          WriteLn
        END    {Display a line}
    {ENDFOR}
```

```
      END        {Display the i times table}
   {ENDFOR}

   END.      {Display tables}
```

The trace table is shown in Table 4.2.

Table 4.2

Step	Routine	i	j	i*j	Comments
1.1	Display tables	5			
2.1a	Display the i		1		
2.2a	times table			5	display 1 x 5 = 5
2.3a			2		
2.4a				10	display 2 x 5 = 10
2.5a			3		
2.6a				15	display 3 x 5 = 15
2.7a			undefined		inner loop complete
1.2	Display tables	6			
2.1b	Display the i		1		
2.2b	times table			6	display 1 x 6 = 6
2.3b			2		
2.4b				12	display 2 x 6 = 12
2.5b			3		
2.6b				18	display 3 x 6 = 18
2.7b			undefined		inner loop complete
1.3	Display tables	undefined			outer loop complete

It can be seen that by placing one loop inside another we have asked t computer to do a great deal of work, and so the programmer shou always check that the terminating conditions, which control how ma times the program loops, are correctly set.

If the program has to carry out the outer loop *i* times, and the inner l *j* times, it will carry out the inner loop *i**j times in all.

After studying this chapter, you should be able to:

1 use the structure diagram representations of the two main selecti components, and of the CASE component;

2 convert these to Pascal for simple comparisons, and comparisons u AND, OR, NOT;

3 use the selection-type program components for more compl selections such as 'one out of three', and 'general OR';

4 name and know when to use each of the three iterative componen

5 express the iterative components in structure diagram and Pascal fc

6 recognise when the read-ahead technique is needed, and use it;

7 design and implement programs using nested loops.

ses

The reader should be prepared to make a number of attempts at the following tasks.

The techniques which should be used include:

1 devising sample data which includes the 'boundary' tests;
2 identifying parameters and using them properly;
3 using top-down design;
4 using structure diagrams and Pascal;
5 displaying messages requesting input;
6 trying to get a neat printout.

In future exercises, these will not be specifically asked for—they should be used as a matter of course.

4.6 Input two unequal positive numbers, and print them in ascending order.

4.7 Input two grades in the range 'A' to 'F' and print only those equal to 'A', 'B' or 'C'.

4.8 Input three positive unequal numbers, and print them in ascending order.

4.9 A sports equipment supplier offers discount of 10% on orders of £10 and over up to £30. On orders of £30 and over, the discount is 20% of the size of the order. After any discount has been allowed, VAT of 15% must be added to the amount to give the total amount due.

The order as printed should have the same approximate layout shown in the example below, or may be an improvement upon it, but should print your own data.

Customer code: 1234
Please supply:

Quantity	Part-number	Price/item	Amount
4	26247	12.50	50.00
		Discount at 20%	10.00
		Net amount, ex VAT	40.00
		Vat at 15%	6.00
		Amount due:	46.00

We enclose cheque for the amount due

The parts underlined should be set up and printed as constants, whereas the other parts will vary from order to order, or from time to time.

If either the quantity or the amount are negative, only the customer code, and the words 'INVALID ORDER' should be printed. This checks or validates the data and tries to ensure that data which is obviously incorrect is dealt with in a sensible manner.

4.10 Write a program which will accept a positive number as input data, and then display that number of minus signs.

4.11 A number of electricity bills are to be produced. In each case, the present meter reading and then the previous meter reading are supplied in that order. The difference between these represents the amount used in the units at a cost of 5 pence a unit. The cost must be calculated and displayed for each bill. Each cost displayed must be separated from the previous one by 10 blank lines.
The final pair of readings are followed by a sentinel of −1, −1.

4.12 The sum of a series of marks is to be found, where each mark is no less than zero. The final mark is a sentinel of −1. Write a program for doing this:
    (a) using a *while . . . do* loop,
    (b) using a *repeat . . . until* loop.
Which is better?

4.13 The sum of a series of marks is to be found, where each mark is no less than zero, and where the marks to be summed are preceded by a number saying how many marks there are. No sentinel is provided. Write a program to do this.

4.14 A group of 5 payments are to be made into an account. To make sure there are no errors in entering the amounts, the total amount (called the checksum) of the 5 payments together is entered first of all. The final payment is followed by −1. Write and test a program which will accept the checksum and the payments as data, and display the actual sum, together with appropriate messages, such as

    'Number of payments and sum correct',
    'Number of payments incorrect',
    'Sum incorrect'.

4.15 A *Fibonacci series* is a series of numbers which sometimes turns up in computing. If such a series starts 0, 1 then from there on the next number is the sum of the two previous ones. For example, in this series we have:
$$0, 1, 1, 2, 3, 5 . . .$$
Write a program to display the numbers in this series, stopping after the first one to exceed 10000 is displayed.

5 Program design

5.1 Top-down stepwise-refinement

Now that a description of the essential components of structured programming has been given, we can look at the approach to program design using top-down stepwise-refinement and structure diagrams in more detail.

Structure diagrams are the class of diagrams called *trees*, since they resemble real trees even if they are upside down.

The names for the parts of such tree diagrams are given in Figure 5.1.

FIGURE 5.1

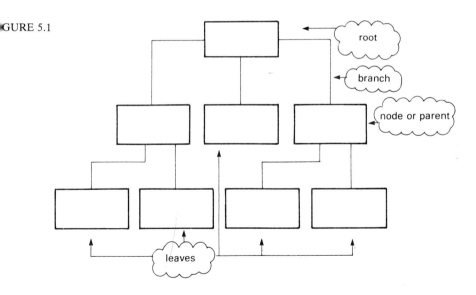

It should be noted that in our structure diagrams a leaf or a node never belongs to more than one branch, so the design shown in Figure 5.2 never happens.

FIGURE 5.2

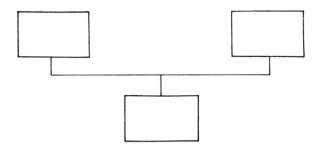

The advantage of using a tree structure to develop a program desig
is that we can start at the root — which will be just the name of th
program — and then by asking 'What does this consist of?' we ca
move down to the next level. Here we will have a number of boxes, bt
probably no more than 5, such as Initialise, Read, Process and Displa
results. For example, a typical program may have a top-level design a
shown in Figure 5.3.

FIGURE 5.3

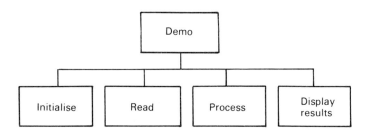

We now proceed, step by step, applying the same process of askii
'What does this consist of?' to each of these boxes in whatever order v
please. This means that we can concentrate our attention on one box
a time, without having to worry too much about the others. We mu
however limit ourselves to the structured programming construc
when we do this by using only the sequences, selections and iteratio
already described.

This process is repeated until the whole problem has been broke
down into a diagram where each of the leaves is an *elementary oper
tion*, which means that it is so basic that it can be easily converted in
our programming language.

It will be found that the boxes which are not leaves are commen
The only exceptions are the iteration controls which appear in di
grams such as Figure 5.4.

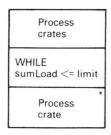

Process crates
WHILE sumLoad <= limit
Process crate *

The tree is an important structure in computing, because it allows leaves, or whole branches, to be grafted on or pruned without difficulty. This means it is a *dynamic* structure and is easy to amend as our ideas develop. In using a structure diagram to develop a program, we are in fact producing an excellent description of the program for somebody else to use in future if they need to work on it.

5.2 Examples

The next example demonstrates this approach to programming on a problem which requires the use of nested loops, and of the read-ahead technique. Just for a change, it is somewhat rustic in flavour.

ple 5.1 In a trial of feed-stuffs for pigs, groups of pigs are weighed and the weight of each pig in a group is recorded. It is necessary to print the number of each group, followed by the average weight of the pigs in that group, and also the average weight of all the pigs.

It is assumed that the number of groups is entered before the rest of the data, and that the end of each group is indicated by a sentinel which is −1.

Write a program to perform this operation.

Sample data
The first task is to try to understand the problem by producing some sample data. For instance, the weights of the pigs in a single group might be, with a sentinel:

10   11   12   13   14   −1

If we have three groups we could have:

3
10   11   12   13   14   −1
 9   10   11 −1
15 −1

where the first '3' gives the number of groups.
The expected output is:

GROUP 1	Average weight is	12
GROUP 2	Average weight is	10
GROUP 3	Average weight is	10
GROUP 3	Average weight is	15

Average of all pigs is 11.67

where the average of each group is found by adding up the weights i
that group, and dividing the sum by the number of pigs in the group
The average of all the pigs is the sum of all their weights, divided by th
total number of pigs. (The average is not the average of the averages c
the separate groups, since they do not all have the same number of pig
in them.)

We can now see if there are any parameters. In this question i
appears that there is nothing which is likely to vary. The top-leve
design is given in Figure 5.5. Developing 'Process groups' we obtai
the design of Figure 5.6.

FIGURE 5.5

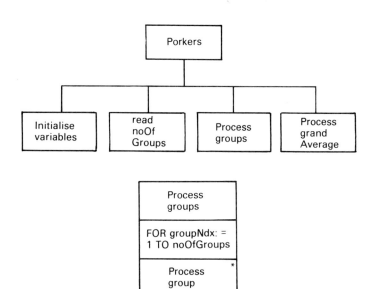

FIGURE 5.6

It will frequently be found that both whole programs and operatio
such as 'Process group' will have three main parts, which correspond
1 prepare or initialise;
2 perform the main process;
3 finish off.
So it is in this case, as we have the design given in Figure 5.7.

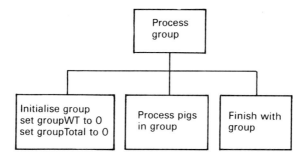

As we are using a sentinel to indicate the end of a group, we have to use the read-ahead technique here. This leads to a structure diagram for 'Process group' as shown in Figure 5.8.

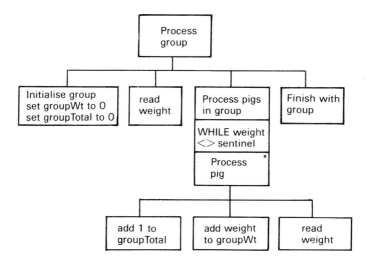

We can add detail to this until we arrive at the stage where each leaf is very simple and easy to turn into the programming language. That is, until each leaf represents an elementary operation.

The full program structure is shown as Figure 5.9. In the Pascal program we write, we could make the data-names more explicit by using fewer abbreviations; for example, groupWeight, numberOfGroups, grandAverage.

FIGURE 5.9

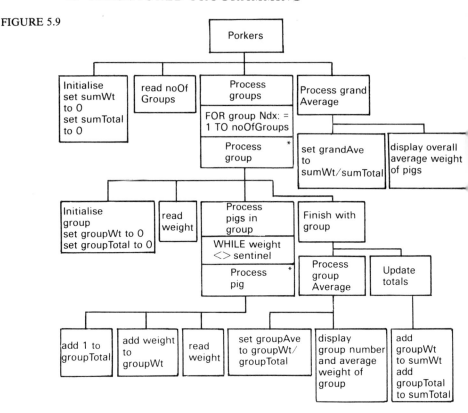

This completes the design of the program. All we have to do now is to convert it into our programming language.

Exercise 5.1   Convert the above design into a program and test it.

The next problem is a little more complex, and demonstrates how a large structure diagram can be broken down into smaller ones.

Example 5.2   The problem is to produce the payslips for the employees of a small firm. The payslip, which is enclosed with a worker's weekly wage, has the following layout, with the standard headings italicised. The parts which vary from one payslip to the next are not italicised.

Name   R. G. Jones   *Week ending:* 13 Feb 88
Reference Number 1212
Pay at flat rate   38 *hours at* 2.10 *per hour*   76.38
Pay at overtime rate   6 *hours at* 3.15 *per hour*   18.90
                            Gross pay   95.28
Deductions
National Insurance   4.50

Income tax	25.72	
	Total Deductions	30.22
	Net Pay	65.06

The data required, including the National Insurance deduction, is read from an input file and the output calculated from it. Income tax is calculated by first subtracting 30% from the gross pay, giving the taxable pay, and then calculating 33% of the taxable pay. Although the date is the same for all the payslips, it varies from week to week, and is supplied as data each week.

First, we must make sure we understand the problem by producing suitable input data and deriving by hand the necessary output data. Let us try:

Name: S. C. Shipway
Reference Number   162426
Hours worked (flat rate)=   25
Hours worked (overtime)=   4
Hourly rate   2.00
National Insurance   4.00

From this we see that the pay for the hours worked at flat rate should be:

$25 \times 2 = 50$

The pay for hours worked at overtime rate should now be found. Here we hit a snag, as we do not know what the overtime rate of pay is. It appears to be 'time and a half' from examination of the sample data, but we cannot be sure. This type of weakness in a specification is very common, and it is part of the work of a program designer to look for it, and then to go back to the person who defined the problem (often called a system designer or analyst) or even the user, to obtain clarification. Let us suppose that the overtime rate in fact is 1.5 times the flat rate, giving:

overtime pay: $2.00 \times 1.5 \times 4 = 12.00$
gross pay: $12.00 + 50 = 62$

To calculate the income tax, we find 30% of 62 which is 18.6, and so

taxable pay: $62 - 18.6 = 43.4$

tax on this is 33%
$43.4 \times 0.33 = 14.32$ (to the nearest penny.)

Adding on the National Insurance we see the total deductions are 19.32 and that S. C. Shipway's net take-home pay is: $62 - 19.32 = 42.68$.

The output we would expect, if trailing zeros after a decimal point are printed, is:

Name   S C Shipway   Week ending   13 June 87

Reference Number
162426
Pay at flat rate   25 hours at 2.00 per hour 50.00
Pay at overtime rate   4 hours at 3.00 per hour 12.00
                                            Gross pay   62.00

Deductions
National Insurance   4.00
Income Tax   14.32
                          Total Deductions   18.3
                          Net Pay   43.6

FIGURE 5.10

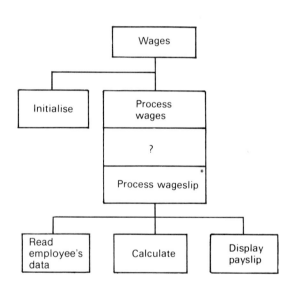

The parameters to be set at the start of this program are the multipliers for calculating the overtime rate of pay, the percentage tax-free pay, and the rate of tax as a percentage.

We may not understand how to do all this at this stage but we can make an initial design as given in Figure 5.10.

Unfortunately, we do not know how many times we have to process a wageslip, as this was omitted from the problem description. Checking with our analyst or user reveals that the final set of data followed by a sentinel of ****

Using the read-ahead technique to examine the first item of data relating to a person — that is, the name — we can detect when we have finished. This leads us to an outline structure diagram which contains all the major operations, as given in Figure 5.11.

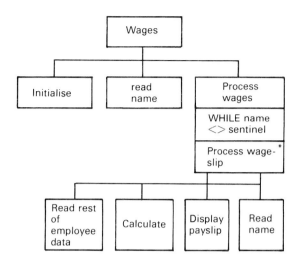

The next stage is to examine each of the boxes drawn, as most need to be expressed in more detail. 'Initialise', 'Enter rest of employee data', and 'Calculate' are shown in Figures 5.12, 5.13 and 5.14 respectively. By developing each of the operations involved in 'Calculate', we obtain the structure diagrams of Figure 5.15 (i), (ii) and (iii). Figure 5.16 represents 'Display payslip', and the associated operations 'Display pay details' and 'Display deductions', are shown in Figures 5.17 and 5.18.

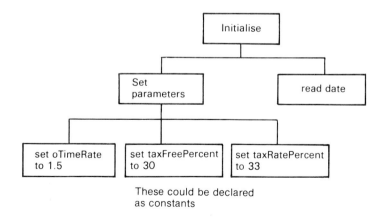

FIGURE 5.13

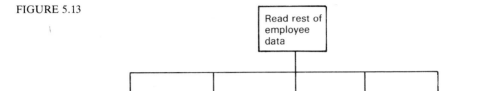

FIGURE 5.14

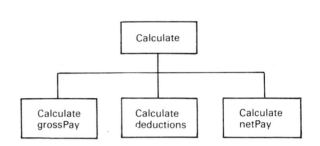

FIGURE 5.15

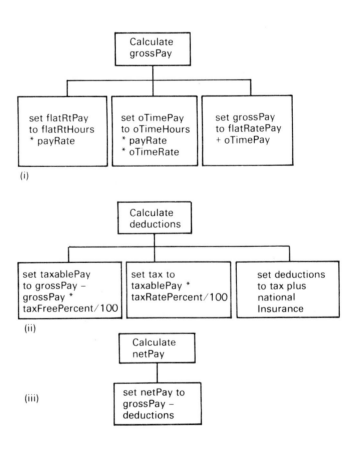

(i)

(ii)

(iii)

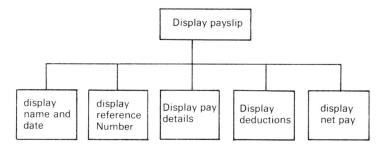

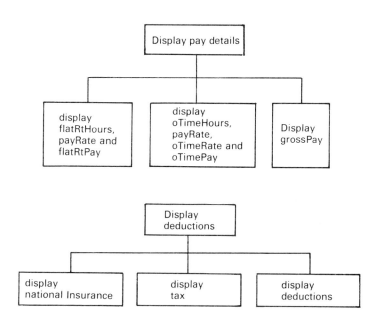

The full print layout is usually supplied as part of the program specification.

___ise 5.2___ Code and test the above design. You will need to find out how to read a name.

By considering the whole problem as a number of smaller problems, and tackling them one at a time, breaking them down further if necessary, we have reduced quite a large problem into one which we can easily deal with. When each of the smaller problems is concerned with a particular operation or function (e.g. 'Read records', 'Calculate'), then the method is sometimes called *functional decomposition*.

5.3 The concept of cohesion

In using this approach to program design, we sometimes have to

choose between several possible methods of making refinements. It
usual to consider the program as being made up of sections of code
called *modules*. Examples of modules in our 'Wages' example above
are 'Initialise', 'Process wageslip', 'Calculate' and so on. Each modul
should ideally consist only of closely related or similar operations. Th
is sometimes called *high cohesion*. For example the 'Calculate' modul
contains all the calculations in the design and hence has high cohesion
If we have to correct or alter any calculations, it is a great help to kno
that they are all in the same module and not scattered throughout th
program.

5.4 Methods of testing

When we have designed and coded a program in this manner the ne
step is to run it and ensure that it works.

It will be found that programs designed in this way have few errors
the logic of their design, although they may well have plenty due to th
unfamiliarity of the programmer with the language, or due to errors
typing the program. The number of such errors can be dishearten in
especially to those who pride themselves on their accuracy. Howeve
this is a stage all would-be programmers have to go through, and it
important not to become demoralised by it.

There are several useful techniques that can be used in trying
debug a program, that is, to rid it of errors.

Pascal programs written for batch systems can be made to 'echo' t
input data, that is, to display the value of each data item as it is rea
Provided that an identifying message accompanies each item, it w
then be clearer what may be the cause of the problem.

A *trace* can be constructed in a Pascal program by inserting Writel
statements at strategic points — for example, wherever a procedure
entered. Great care must be taken with this technique: a procedu
inside an iteration may be executed many times, and the resulti
barrage of output may waste printer paper or flash past the user sittii
at a microcomputer screen. One way round the problem is to count t
messages displayed and stop after a certain number.

5.5 Difficulties and limitations of testing

Once a program runs with our sample data and gives sensible resul
we know little more than that it works with that set of data. In order
be sure our program works properly, we should test it with eve
possible set of input data, so that we can test every possible combir
tion of paths through the program. Unfortunately, this is the counsel
perfection, and is not practical in anything but the simplest progra
In fact, there is no method the ordinary person can use to pro
conclusively that a non-trivial program will always work, althou

mathematically based research is under way with a view to achieving this.

It is generally accepted in the area of quality assurance that testing is not a satisfactory way of ensuring the reliability of a product, and that reliability must be built into a product by good design and careful workmanship. This applies to computer programs as well as to factory-produced articles. To achieve a good design we have in this chapter used the top-down stepwise-refinement method of designing a program built with structured program components only.

This allows us to consider a program as a number of modules consisting of sequences, selections and iterations which are composed of similar components themselves, together with elementary operations. Each module and component has only one beginning and one end. Errors are then less likely when a component is being coded, and the number of paths through the collection of components making up the program is limited. These factors lead to a well-designed program in the sense that it should be reliable with few, if any, logical errors.

You should note that this approach does not, however, necessarily lead to a design which can be easily modified — a method which tackles this need is described in Chapter 8.

In spite of all our care, errors will occur and may lie dormant in apparently good programs for years until they cause trouble due to an unusual set of circumstances.

Thus we have a situation where a well designed, carefully coded program should have no errors, but testing is necessary in case it does. We can have no guarantee, however, that a well-tested program will always work since the number of possible paths through the program is often too high for us to be able to test them all. This means that we must test as best we can. The test data for the program should at least try to ensure that the following are tested:

1 all combinations of classes of input data, including the 'sentinel only' case;

2 all possible types of output;

3 all the program statements in the program;

4 all selections;

5 the number of times each iteration is carried out, including the case where nothing has to be done.

It is in fact good practice to design the test data before the program itself is designed, as this clarifies one's ideas concerning the objectives of the program. However, as it is very difficult to check one's own work effectively, a program should also be tested using data designed by a person other than the programmer, such as the customer, an auditor, or a colleague working on a different project. Some programmers go further by working in a team and conducting *structured walkthroughs*. In these, the work of each individual is explained to the other programmers so that they can help to spot the errors, perhaps even before the program is put on to a computer. Another approach is for programmers always to work in pairs, so that each can continuously check the work of the other.

When we have a design, we must then proceed towards a working program. It is possible in many languages, including Pascal, COBOL, FORTRAN and others, to use a *preprocessor* which accepts a structure diagram displayed on a visual display unit, together with lists of statements and conditions, as input, and which supplies the actual program as output, saving a great deal of time and removing the possibility of mistakes in the coding operation.

After studying this chapter, you should be able to:
1 describe the use of top-down stepwise-refinement and structure diagrams;
2 use top-down stepwise-refinement to develop detailed structure diagrams;
3 use 'comment' and 'elementary operations' in structure diagram boxes;
4 understand the need for, and the limitations of, program testing;
5 describe and use the principles of designing test data.

Exercises

5.3 The **porker** example fails to give an adequate response if the number of groups is zero, or if there are no pigs in a certain group. Amend the program to deal with this.
(Hint: **if . . . then . . . else** components will be useful.)

5.4 The tax system used in the **wages** problem is to be modified as follows: The first £20 of any week's pay is to be tax-free. The next £30 is to be taxed at 25%, whilst the remainder is to be taxed at 35%. Modify the program accordingly, and design appropriate test data. The program should be tested by running it.

5.5 As goods for shipment to a certain destination arrive at an airport their reference number and weight are entered on a form. The goods are then stored. The aircraft type used to ship them has a payload of 1000kg. The goods are shipped strictly in the order in which they arrive.

Write a program which accepts the list as input data and prints a series of load numbers (1, 2, 3 . . .), each followed by the reference number of each item which is to make up that load. Your program should cope with incomplete loads where necessary, and should be thoroughly tested, stating any assumptions made.

Have you ever encountered a similar problem?

6 Arrays

6.1 Definition of an array

Data can of course exist independently of computers and can be defined and described without reference to the way it is to be held in a computer. Such data is said to be *abstract*. One very important type of abstract data structure is the *array*. This is a set number of data elements each of which can be referred to using a reference or index of its own. All the data elements must be of the same type. For example, suppose we have a payroll where each name on the payroll has a reference number which is one of a set of consecutive integers. This can be drawn as:

Reference Number	Name on Payroll
1	Catrin
2	Elin
3	Gareth
4	Martyn
5	Niall
6	Siân

Then, if we want the name of the employee whose reference number is 5, we just look for the fifth name on the list. In this example, the array could be called 'nameOnPayroll' and each element in the array is a string of characters. The elements of an array could be anything we want them to be, but for the moment, we will confine ourselves to numbers and strings.

6.2 Arrays in Pascal

To declare an array in Pascal, we specify the numbers to be used to reference the first and last elements of the array, and the **type** of each element in the array—all elements in an array must be of the same type.

To declare an array capable of holding three part numbers we could use

```
CONST
  numberOfParts = 3;

TYPE
  PartNdxs = 1..numberOfParts;
  Parts = ARRAY[PartNdxs] OF INTEGER;

VAR
  part: Parts;
```

Suppose our part numbers are 012, 678, 345. If we store this data in our array, then we can represent it as

```
element
number:   1      2      3
part:     012    678    345
```

where 012 is called element 1 of the array, 'part', written as part [1] and 678 is called element 2 of the array, written as part [2] and so on. This is called a one-dimensional array. The bracketed quantity is the reference or element number of the element in the array, and is called an *index* or *subscript*.

Example 6.1 Suppose we want to read the part numbers described above, and store them in an array. We could do this as shown in Figure 6.1, but this could get tedious. A far better way is to use the counter of a 'FOR' loop as an index to identify the particular element we are entering and storing. This is expressed in Figure 6.2.

FIGURE 6.1

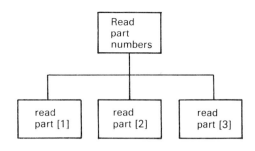

FIGURE 6.2

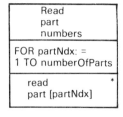

The full coding in Pascal is shown in Program 6–1.

PROGRAM 6–1

```
PROGRAM Ch6P1(input,output);

{Set up an array of part numbers}

CONST
  numberOfParts = 3;

TYPE
  PartNdxs = 1..numberOfParts;
  Parts = ARRAY[PartNdxs]OF INTEGER;

VAR
  part: Parts;
  partNdx: PartNdxs;

BEGIN

  FOR        {Enter part numbers}
    partNdx:= 1 TO numberOfParts
  DO
    BEGIN
      WriteLn('Enter next part number');
      ReadLn(part[partNdx])
    END
  {ENDFOR} {Enter part numbers}

END.
```

Sample data: 012, 678, 345

The action of this can be followed in a trace, shown as Table 6.1.

Table 6.1
Sample data: 012, 678, 345

step	statement	part Ndx	part [1]	part [2]	part [3]	comment
1	part Ndx: =	1				loop initialised
2	read	1	012			part Ndx = 1
3	read	2		678		part Ndx = 2
4	read	3			345	part Ndx = 3
5	(after FOR)	undefined				

If we wanted to display these part numbers in the same order, we could use the design of Figure 6.3 which is coded in Pascal as:

```
FOR        {Display part numbers}
   partNdx:= 1 TO numberOfParts
DO
   BEGIN
      WriteLn('Part ', partNdx, '
              part[partNdx])
   END
{ENDFOR} {Display part numbers}
```

FIGURE 6.3

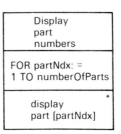

It should be realised that we are doing something fundamentally new in fragments of code such as this. We are in fact changing the effect of statements such as

```
WriteLn('Part ', partNdx, ' : ',
        part[partNdx])
```

in a controlled way *while the program is running*. This allows us to write very versatile programs for processing lists of data items, and in some cases it makes possible operations, such as sorting, which would be nearly impossible by other means.

Frequently, we have to carry out operations on every element of an array. As long as we know the length of the array, this is easily done

Example 6.2 Add up the elements of an array called 'quote' which has three elements.

We can do this as in Figure 6.4, where 'noOfQuotes' is the number of elements in 'quote'.

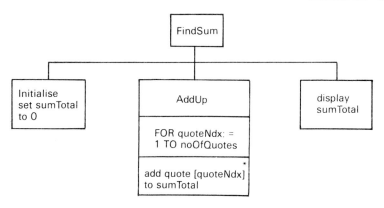

This diagram is easily converted into Pascal, and should be traced with suitable test data.

6.3 Searching an array

le 6.3 A common requirement is to find the lowest (or highest) element in an array, as in the following example. An array called 'quote' contains 'noOfQuotes' elements. Design a fragment of code to display the element of 'quote' with the lowest value.

Sample data
Input (quote): 5 4 6 2 3
Output   : Lowest = 2

This is very easy to process mentally, as here we have a short list. However, if there were 100 elements in the list, we would need a methodical approach. One safe way is to let the first element be the lowest we have found so far ('lowest'). Then we compare 'lowest' with each of the other elements, changing its value when necessary. The structure diagram is given in Figure 6.5.

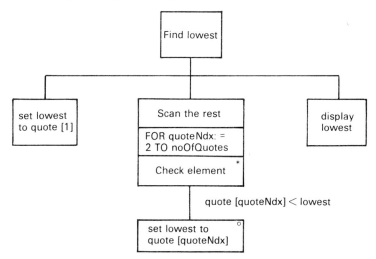

In Pascal this leads to Program 6–2

PROGRAM 6–2

```
PROGRAM Ch6P2(input,output);

{Find lowest quote}

CONST
  numberOfQuotes = 5;

TYPE
  QuoteIndexes = 1..numberOfQuotes;
  Quotes= ARRAY[QuoteIndexes]OF INTEGER;

VAR
  quote: Quotes;
  quoteNdx: QuoteIndexes;
  lowest: INTEGER;

BEGIN    {Find lowest}

  lowest:= quote[1];

  FOR        {Scan the rest}
    quoteNdx:= 2 TO numberOfQuotes
  DO
    BEGIN      {Check element}
      IF
        quote[quoteNdx] < lowest
      THEN
        BEGIN
          lowest:= quote[quoteNdx]
        END
      {ENDIF}
    END;       {Check element
  {ENDFOR} {Scan the rest}

  WriteLn('Lowest quote is ', lowest)

END.      {Find lowest}
```

Example   6.4   A related problem is the slightly more complicated one of ensuri
that the lowest valued quote in the array comes first. Since we a
not concerned with the final position of other elements, we c
simply consider the first element as the lowest to start with, a
perform the appropriate interchanges (or *swaps*) as we scan alo
the rest of the array.

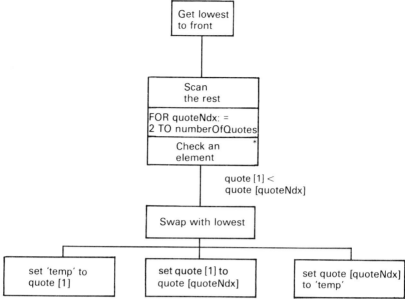

The structure diagram is shown in Figure 6.6, and the Pascal as Program 6–3. This should be traced with the data of Example 6.3.

PROGRAM 6–3

```
PROGRAM Ch6P3(input,output);

{Move lowest quote to first position}

CONST
  numberOfQuotes = 5;

TYPE
  QuoteIndexes = 1..numberOfQuotes;
  Quotes= ARRAY[QuoteIndexes]OF INTEGER;

VAR
  quote: Quotes;
  quoteNdx: QuoteIndexes;
  temp: INTEGER;

BEGIN     {Get lowest to front}

  FOR       {Scan the rest}
    quoteNdx:= 2 TO numberOfQuotes
  DO
    BEGIN     {Check an element}
      IF
        quote[1] > quote[quoteNdx]
```

```
THEN
    BEGIN   {Swop with lowest}
        temp:= quote[l];
        quote[l]:= quote[quoteNdx];
        quote[quoteNdx]:= temp
    END
    {ENDIF}
    END        {Check an element
{ENDFOR} {Scan the rest}

END.      {Get lowest to front}
```

6.4 The use of an array in data logging

The next example is an important one as it is of a type which, in one for
or another, is common in computing. The essential requirement is
count the number of times different types of events occur. As a concre
example of this, let us consider the 'data logging problem'.

Example   6.5 Suppose that we have a computer which is monitoring the per
formance of a system such as a chemical plant. Signals repi
senting the flow of chemicals in different parts of the plant a
made available to the computer in the form of signals where a
means that a tonne of a certain chemical has passed flowmen
number 1, a '2' means that a tonne has passed flowmeter numbe
and so on, for a total of 3 flowmeters. The end of the signals
indicated by a signal of -1.

We want a program to accept the data (assuming there are
error signals and that two signals cannot occur at the same insta
and to output the number of tonnes passing each flowmeter.

Sample data
Input: 2   1   1   2   1 -1
Output: Flowmeter 1 : 3 tonnes
          Flowmeter 2 : 2 tonnes
          Flowmeter 3 : 0 tonnes

We could try a solution similar to that represented in Figure 6.7. T
could be coded using a complicated set of nested *if . . . then . . . (*
statements, or by using a CASE statement.

A far neater method is to use the fact that when the signal is 1, we a
1 to flow [1]; when 'signal' is 2, we add 1 to flow [2] and so on. T
suggests that we can use the value of 'signal' to set the index to poin
the element of 'flow' that we wish to increase.

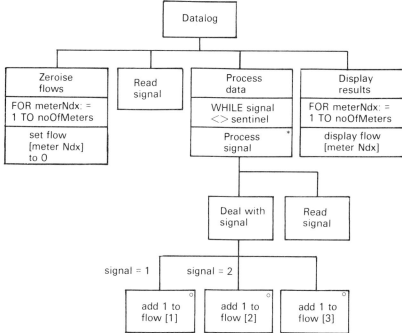

Consider the statement

$$\text{flow[signal]:= flow[signal] + 1}$$

If 'signal' is 1, this means

$$\text{flow[1]:= flow[1] + 1}$$

If 'signal' is 2, it means

$$\text{flow[2]:= flow[2] + 1}$$

and so on. This is exactly what we want, as we are using the value of 'signal' itself to control which element of the array we are referring to. The operation 'Process signal' now becomes as shown in Figure 6.8.

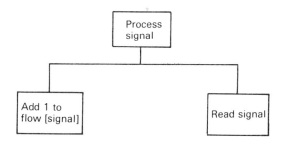

The Pascal code for this is given in Program 6–4. It is worth carrying out a condensed trace on this program to see how it is working. Table 6.2 shows a trace-table with sample data.

Table 6.2

Sample data
Input: 2 1 1 2 1 −1
Output: Flowmeter 1 : 3 tonnes
Flowmeter 2 : 2 tonnes
Flowmeter 3 : 0 tonnes

step	procedure	meter Ndx	signal	flow[1]	flow[2]	flow[3]	commen
1	Initialise	1					
2	Flows	1		0			meter Ndx
3		2			0		meter Ndx
4		3				0	meter Ndx
5		undefined					
6	Read signal		2				
7	Process				1		signal is
8	data		1				
9				1			signal is
10			1				
11				2			signal is
12			2				
13					2		signal is
14			1				
15				3			signal is
16			−1				signal is
17	Display	1					
18	results	1		3			display flo
19		2					
20		2			2		display flo
21		3					
22		3				0	display flo
23		undefined					

This example shows that this method is elegant, and is useful whe the code used takes values which are consecutive integers. If they do n start at 1, this can easily be allowed for in the design, and this is left f the reader.

PROGRAM 6–4

```
PROGRAM Ch6P4(input,output);

{ Collect  & display flowmeter data}

CONST
  noOfMeters = 3;
```

```
      sentinel = -1;

   TYPE
     MeterIndexes = 1..noOfMeters;
     Meters= ARRAY[MeterIndexes]OF INTEGER;

   VAR
     flow: Meters;
     meterNdx: MeterIndexes;
     signal: INTEGER;

   BEGIN    {Datalog}

     FOR          {Zeroise flows}
       meterNdx:= 1 To noOfMeters
     DO
       BEGIN
         flow[meterNdx]:= 0
       END;
     {ENDFOR}    {Zeroise flows}

     Read(signal);

     WHILE       {Process data}
       signal <> sentinel
     DO
       BEGIN         {Process signal}
         flow[signal]:= flow[signal] + 1;
         Read(signal)
       END;          {Process signal}
     {ENDWHILE} {Process data}

     FOR          {Display results}
       meterNdx:= 1 TO noOfMeters
     DO
       BEGIN
         WriteLn('Flowmeter ', meterNdx,
             ' Flow: ', flow[meterNdx])
       END
     {ENDFOR}

   END.    {Datalog}
```

6.5 Strings

We have already encountered *strings* in Pascal. Whenever we have used a statement such as

```
WriteLn('Enter part number')
```

we have used a string. The characters between the quote marks form a string. A string, in Pascal, is a packed array of characters, whose lower subscript *must* always be 1. We can declare the packed array as being of any length, but we cannot change its length once we have declared it. The fact that it is *packed* simply means that the Pascal compiler will arrange that the characters in the array occupy the minimum amount of space required. We could declare our array as follows. Note the similarity betweeen these definitions and the example we gave earlier for the array 'part'.

```
CONST
  stringLength = 17;

TYPE
  StrNdxs = 1..stringLength;
  String = PACKED ARRAY[StrNdxs]OF CHAR;

VAR
  invitation: String;
```

We can manipulate a string in the same way that we can manipulate a single character variable, with one important exception. Firstly, we can display it in a single Write or WriteLn statement. Suppose we had an array 'invitation', containing 17 characters. Its contents might look like this:

invitation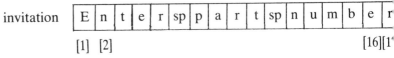

[1] [2]   [16][17]

(where 'sp' indicates a space character). The Pascal statement

```
Writeln(invitation)
```

would be equivalent to

```
WriteLn('Enter part number')
```

The important exception to what we can do with strings is read them in a single statement. Unfortunately, in ISO-Pascal we must read a string one character at a time. If we know in advance the exact length of the string we are reading, we can use a FOR loop:

```
VAR
  invitation: String;
  invNdx: StrNdxs;
```

```
{....
   ....
   ....}

FOR
   invNdx:= 1 TO stringLength
DO
   BEGIN
      Read(invitation[invNdx])
   END
{ENDFOR}
```

le 6.6 It will more often be the case that we wish to read a message whose length we are unaware of, but which is terminated with a recognisable character such as a full stop or the code produced by pressing the 'Return' key on a keyboard. This example takes this problem one step further.

Write a program to read an integer, 'howMany', followed by up to 120 characters, ending with an asterisk. The characters, except for the asterisk, should be stored in an array 'stringA', and the first 'howMany' of these characters should be transferred to another array, 'stringB', and then displayed, followed by the original string. We shall assume that there are more than 'howMany' and fewer than 121 characters in the input string.

Sample data
Input: 8 B l a i s e sp P a s c a l
Output: B l a i s e sp P
('sp' indicates a space)

The top-level design is given in Figure 6.9, and 'Set up StringA', 'Truncate', 'Display stringB' and 'Display stringA' are shown in Figures 6.10, 6.11, 6.12 and 6.13 respectively.

RE 6.9

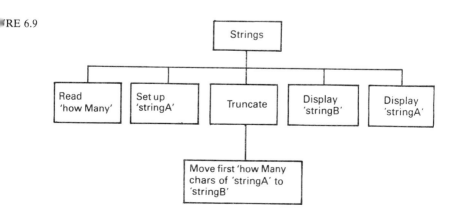

FIGURE 6.10

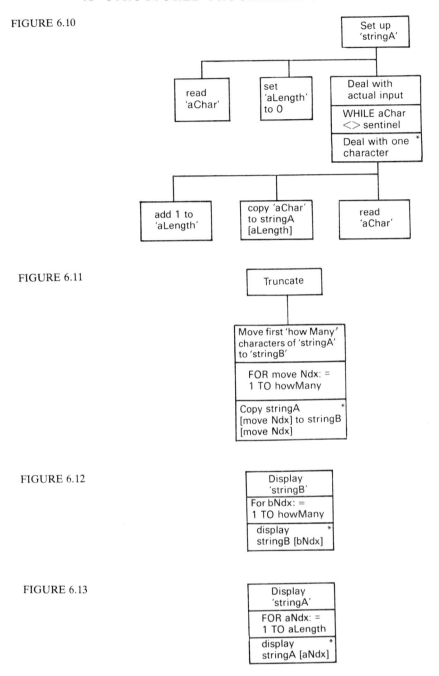

FIGURE 6.11

FIGURE 6.12

FIGURE 6.13

We use a separate character variable, 'aChar', since we want examine the character to see if it is an asterisk before we store it in array; otherwise we could have used

Read(stringA[aLength])

'aLength' has the same value as the number of characters stored in 'stringA'. Converting the structure diagrams directly into Pascal, we obtain Program 6–5.

PROGRAM 6–5

```
PROGRAM Ch6P5(input,output);

{Extract a substring from a string}

CONST
  maxLength = 121;
  sentinel = '*';

TYPE
  StrNdxs = 1..maxLength;
  String = PACKED ARRAY[StrNdxs]OF CHAR;

VAR
  stringA,
  stringB: String;
  howMany,
  aLength: INTEGER;
  aChar: CHAR;

PROCEDURE Initialise;
BEGIN
  WriteLn('Enter substring length');
  ReadLn(howMany)
END;

PROCEDURE SetUpStringA;
BEGIN
  WriteLn('Enter main string');
  Read(aChar);
  aLength:= 0;
  WHILE        {Deal with actual input}
    aChar <> sentinel
  DO
    BEGIN        {Deal with one character}
      aLength:= aLength + 1;
      stringA[aLength]:= aChar;
      Read(aChar)
    END        {Deal with one character}
  {ENDWHILE} {Deal with actual input}
END;
```

```
PROCEDURE Truncate;
VAR
  moveNdx: StrNdxs;
BEGIN
  FOR
    moveNdx:= 1 TO howMany
  DO
    BEGIN
      stringB[moveNdx]:=stringA[moveNdx]
    END
  {ENDFOR}
END;

PROCEDURE BDisplayStringB;
VAR
  bNdx: StrNdxs;
BEGIN
  FOR
    bNdx:= 1 TO howMany
  DO
    BEGIN
      Write(stringB[bNdx])
    END;
  {ENDFOR}
  WriteLn
END;

PROCEDURE ADisplayStringA;
VAR
  aNdx: StrNdxs;
BEGIN
  FOR
    aNdx:= 1 TO aLength
  DO
    BEGIN
      Write(stringA[aNdx])
    END;
  {ENDFOR}
  WriteLn
END;

BEGIN     {Strings}

  Initialise;
  SetUpStringA;
  Truncate;
  BDisplayStringB;
```

```
ADisplayStringA

END.    {Strings}
```

Note that a Pascal program may fail if we attempt to examine or display a named location into which we have not placed a value; so, where there is a danger that it may be necessary to examine or display an element or elements of a string in which no characters have been stored, it is as well to space-fill (that is, to fill with spaces) any such strings at the start of the program.

This can be done with a FOR loop, but we can also make use of the second important attribute of a string: we can assign a value to it in a single statement. This means that we are able to write such statements as

```
invitation:= 'Enter part number'
```

and

```
partRequest:= invitation
```

(provided that 'partRequest' has been declared as an item of the same type—and, in particular, of the same length—as 'invitation') and, if we do wish to set 'invitation' to all spaces, either

```
invitation:= '                '
```

or

```
CONST
   spaces = '                ';

{ ... }
{ ... }
{ ... }

   invitation:= spaces
```

The important point to note is that the lengths must match.

Thirdly, we can compare one string with another string. Again, the lengths must match. It would be meaningless to say

```
IF
   choice = invoice
```

if 'choice' and 'invoice' were defined as being of different lengths, since then it would be impossible for them ever to be equal. We can use the comparison operators $=$, $<>$, $>$, $<$, $>=$ and $<=$ and $<=$, as explained in Section 4.2. Remember that, the farther down the alphabet, the greater the value of the letter.

Exercise   6.1 Design and write a program which will read three strings, and display them in alphabetical order. (Hint: if stringA is greater than stringB, i may or may not be greater than stringC; if stringA is less than stringB stringB may or may not be greater than stringC. You may assume that a three strings are different.)

6.6 Stacks and queues

There are a number of abstract data structures which can be handled using arrays as concrete structures. A *stack* is such a structure, being a li of data items where the next data item to be deleted from the list i always the last one to have been added on.

For example, suppose we have a stack consisting of the reference numbers of seasonal employees. These can be stored in an array as

Index:	1	2	3	4	5	6	7
STACK	123	456	789	012	345	—	—

Such a structure is appropriate if the employer has a policy of '*last in first out*' (LIFO), so that the last employee to join (number 345) will be the first to leave. Stacks are also used in computing in translating algebraic statements such as $A+B*C$ into machine code, and also wit subprograms as used in Chapter 7.

There are two things we need to know about a stack in order to be abl to use it. The first is called the *stack pointer* and is the position of next fre location in the stack (position 6 in the above example as it stands) and t length of the stack, so that we do not try to add an element to a stac which is already full. Similarly, we need to be sure we do not try t remove an element from an empty stack.

Assume we have the stack set up as shown above with 'stackPointe equal to 6 and 'stackLength' equal to 7.

Placing an element (678) on to the stack will leave it as

Index:	1	2	3	4	5	6	7
	123	456	789	012	345	678	—

stackPointer = 7

The structure diagram shown in Figure 6.14 will cope with adding (*pushing*) an element on to the stack.

JRE 6.14

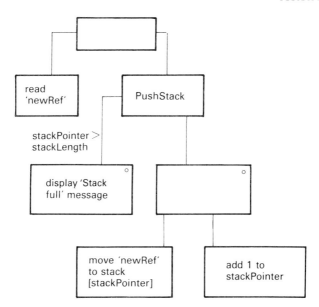

6.2 Code a program to test the structure diagram of Figure 6.14.

6.3 Design, code and test a design for removing (or *popping*) an element from the stack (given the value of stackPointer), and printing that element.

A *queue* is a data structure from which elements are removed in the same order as they are added. This is called *first in, first out* (FIFO). Queues frequently arise due to the need to model a real situation in the computer. Two pointers are needed with a queue. One (front), shows the next free location for an element to be added (or pushed) to a queue. The other (back) points to the next element which is to be removed (or popped). Suppose we have a queue of vans which are queuing for service on a FIFO basis. If we refer to the vans using their registration numbers we could have

(1)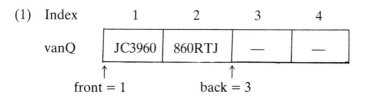

If TUN478J joins the queue, and JC3960 leaves the queue as it goes for service, we obtain

(2) Index

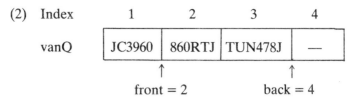

Index	1	2	3	4
vanQ	JC3960	860RTJ	TUN478J	—

front = 2   back = 4

It will be seen that JC3960 remains in location with index 1, but we ar
no longer interested — the 'front' pointer is now to the right of it. Also
the relevant part of the queue now goes from index 2 to index 3, instea
of from 1 to 2. If one more vehicle joins the queue, even though tw
more leave, we shall obtain

(3) Index

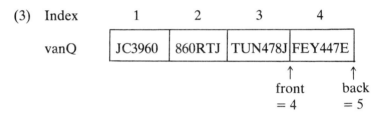

Index	1	2	3	4
vanQ	JC3960	860RTJ	TUN478J	FEY447E

front = 4   back = 5

FIGURE 6.15

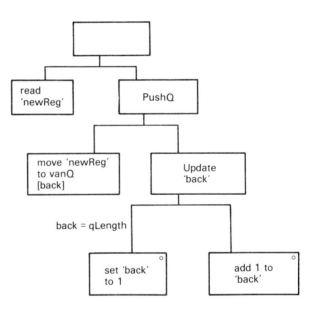

The stack is now full, even though we have three free locations at t
left-hand end. We can make use of these by linking the right-hand end
the left-hand end, as in the design of Figure 6.15 for pushing an eleme
on to the queue. 'qlength' is the number of elements in the arr
holding the queue.

Example   6.7   Trace Figure 6.15 for pushing FEY477E and AJC977 on to the que
as represented in Array (2), and draw the resulting queue.

The result is

(4)   Index   1   2   3   4

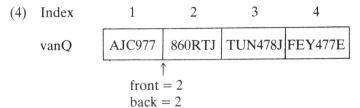

front = 2
back = 2

It appears that we can use the fact that 'front' and 'back' are equal to test for a full queue. The next example demonstrates otherwise.

<u>mple   6.8</u> Develop a design to pop an element from a queue, using 'vanQ', 'front' and 'back' as above. Then starting with the queue as represented by Array (2), pop two elements from the queue.

The structure diagram is given in Figure 6.16.

GURE 6.16

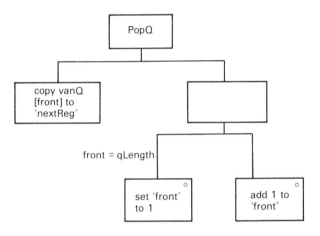

Tracing this leads to

(5)   Index   1   2   3   4

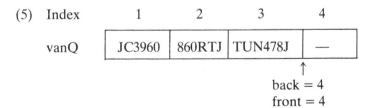

back = 4
front = 4

As can be seen from this example, once again we have 'front' and 'back' equal, but this time it means we have an empty queue, not a full one. Thus we cannot use this to test if we are trying to push on to a full queue, or to pop from an empty one.

There are various ways of dealing with this. Probably the simplest is to keep an empty location, as shown by the hatched box in Array (6), between the 'front' and the 'back' of the queue so that a full queue is one where 'back' points to the location which is logically to the left of 'front' as in

(6) Index

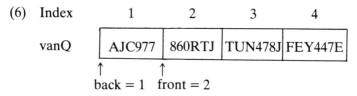

back = 1   front = 2

The queue is from 860RTJ to FEY477E, since 'back' points to the next free location and AJC977 has left the queue. Only an empty queue is then indicated by equal pointers.

The design for pushing on to a queue can now be expressed as in Figure 6.17.

FIGURE 6.17

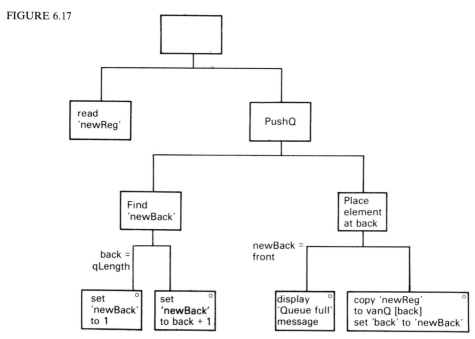

Example   6.9   Trace Figure 6.17 for pushing AXD420M following by AJC977 onto the queue as represented in array (2), with 'qlength' = 4. The initial queue is:

(2) Index

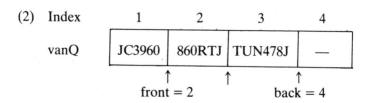

front = 2   back = 4

Solution

Step 1 Push AXD420M. This leads to

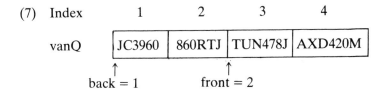

(7)   Index   1   2   3   4

| vanQ | JC3960 | 860RTJ | TUN478J | AXD420M |

back = 1   front = 2

Step 2 Since 'newBack' becomes equal to 'front', AJC977 is not pushed.

___cise   6.4___   Develop, code and test a section of code to pop an element from a queue which may be empty. Use the notation of the above examples.

6.7 Two-dimensional arrays

It is sometimes convenient to look on a list as being made up of sublists. For instance, let us suppose that there are just three pupils in a class, referred to as numbers 1, 2, 3, and their marks in each of 4 subjects are entered, always in the same order, in one list.

For example, consider a table such as Table 6.3. The list can be held as an array, called 'mark' as shown below.

Index   1 2 3 4 5 6 7 8 9 10 11 12

| mark | 10 | 20 | 30 | 40 | 20 | 30 | 40 | 50 | 30 | 40 | 50 | 60 |

Table 6.3

	subject 1	subject 2	subject 3	subject 4
Pupil 1	10	20	30	40
Pupil 2	20	30	40	50
Pupil 3	30	40	50	60

Table 6.4

		Column			
		1	2	3	4
	1	10	20	30	40
Row	2	20	30	40	50
	3	30	40	50	60

It will be seen that the mark of pupil 3 in subject 2 is given by

$$mark[(3-1) * 4 + 2]$$

which equals

$$mark[10]$$

Checking in the list, we find that this has the value 40. In general, i
we want the mark of pupil *i* in subject *j* it can be found using

$$mark[(i-1) * n + j]$$

where *n* is the number of elements relating to one of the subjects of th
array — in this case a pupil.

The need to handle tables of data such as this occurs so frequentl
that there is a mechanism in Pascal to cater for it: the array of arrays, o
two-dimensional array. (Note that Pascal allows us to declare arrays o
arrays of arrays, and so on ad infinitum; but these structures ar
outside the scope of this book.)

To declare an array of arrays, we can use

```
CONST
  noOfPupils = 3;
  noOfSubjects = 4;

TYPE
  Pupils = 1..noOfPupils;
  Subjects = 1..noOfSubjects;
  PupilRows = ARRAY[Subjects]OF INTEGER;
  Marks = ARRAY[Pupils] OF PupilRows;

VAR
  mark: Marks;
```

If we are not going to use the TYPE PupilRows elsewhere, we ca
contract the two lines containing it into

```
Marks = ARRAY[Pupils,Subjects]
        OF INTEGER;
```

To refer to the second column in row three we can use

$$mark[3,2]$$

and, in general, we can refer to element *j* of row *i* as

$$mark[i,j]$$

Now let us consider the problem of entering a table of marks for two pupils in three subjects.

The top-level structure diagram is as shown in Figure 6.18; 'Read marks for a pupil' and 'Read subject marks' are shown as structure diagrams in Figures 6.19 and 6.20 respectively. The Pascal program is shown as Program 6–6. The action of this program can be followed in the trace table shown as Table 6.6, which uses the sample data of Table 6.5.

URE 6.18

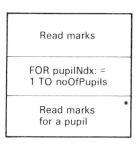

JRE 6.19

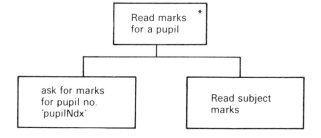

JRE 6.20

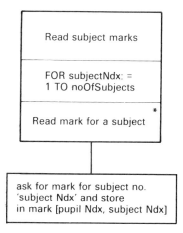

Table 6.5

	Subject 1	Subject 2	Subject 3
Pupil 1	30	40	50
Pupil 2	60	70	80

Table 6.6

Step	Procedure	pupilNdx	subjectNdx	mark [1,1]	mark [1,2]	mark [1,3]	mark [2,1]	mark [2,2]	mar [2,3
1	Read marks	1							
2		1							
3	. . . for a pupil		1						
4			1						
5				30					
6			2						
7			2						
8					40				
9			3						
10			3						
11						50			
12			undefined						
13	Read marks	2							
14		2							
15	. . . for a pupil		1						
16			1						
17							60		
18			2						
19			2						
20								70	
21			3						
22			3						
23									8
24			undefined						

PROGRAM 6–6

```
PROGRAM Ch6P6(input,output);

{Set up an array of pupil marks}

CONST
   noOfPupils = 2;
   noOfSubjects = 3;

TYPE
   PupilIndexes = 1..noOfPupils;
   SubjectIndexes = 1..noOfSubjects;
   Marks = ARRAY[PupilIndexes,
      SubjectIndexes]OF INTEGER;

VAR
   mark: Marks;
```

```
    pupilNdx: PupilIndexes;

  PROCEDURE ReadSubjectMarks;
  VAR
    subjectNdx: SubjectIndexes;
  BEGIN
    FOR
      subjectNdx:= 1 TO noOfSubjects
    DO
      BEGIN     {Read mark for a subject}
        WriteLn('Enter this pupil''s ',
          'mark in subject ', subjectNdx);
        ReadLn(mark[pupilNdx, subjectNdx])
      END       {Read mark for a subject}
    {ENDFOR}
  END;

  PROCEDURE ReadMarksForAPupil;
  BEGIN
    WriteLn('Now enter marks for pupil ',
      pupilNdx);
    ReadSubjectMarks
  END;

  BEGIN     {Read marks}

    FOR
      pupilNdx:= 1 TO noOfPupils
    DO
      BEGIN
        ReadMarksForAPupil
      END
    {ENDFOR}

  END.      {Read marks}
```

It will be seen that, once 'subjectNdx' becomes undefined at step 12, the inner FOR loop – steps 3 to 12 – is completed, and the program continues with the outer FOR loop, which moves 'pupilNdx' to its next value.

Operations on the elements of a row or of a column of such a table can be very conveniently handled using FOR loops. For instance, if we wish to find the average mark of each subject all we need is the design shown in Figure 6.21.

Note that it is possible, in Pascal, to declare an array of strings. Technically, this is a two-dimensional array, or table, and must be specified as such. In practice, however, it is likely that we will wish to

FIGURE 6.21

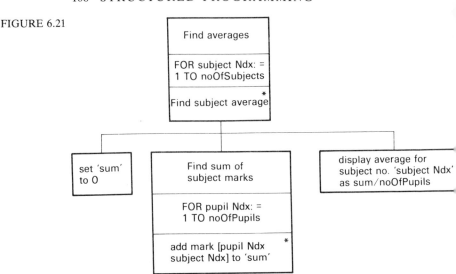

treat each string as a single element, so that, for example, we can sc
list of names into alphabetical order. Our declarations might look

```
CONST
  noOfNames = 10;
  stringLength = 24;

TYPE
  NameNdxs = 1..noOfNames;
  StrNdxs = 1..stringLength;
  String = PACKED ARRAY[StrNdxs]OF CHAR;
  NameTabs = ARRAY[NameNdxs] OF String;

VAR
  nameTable: NameTabs;
  nameNdx: NameNdxs;
  strNdx: StrNdxs;
```

and we should expect to find statements such as

```
IF
  nameTable[nameNdx]
    > nameTable[nameNdx + 1]
```

and

```
WriteLn(nameTable[nameNdx])
```

while setting up the table contents would still have to be done the
way:

```
FOR        {Create table}
  nameNdx:= 1 TO noOfNames
DO
  BEGIN      {Create single table entry}
    FOR
      strNdx:= 1 TO stringLength
    DO
      BEGIN
        Read(nameTable[nameNdx,strNdx])
      END;
    {ENDFOR}
    ReadLn
  END        {Create single table entry}
{ENDFOR} {Create table}
```

After studying this chapter, you should be able to:

1 explain the meaning of the term 'array';
2 declare arrays in Pascal;
3 use 'for' loops to operate upon the elements of arrays;
4 position the lowest valued element at the start of an array;
5 count the frequency of occurrence of various elements of an array;
6 represent a table as a one dimensional array, and access particular elements;
7 represent stacks and queues as arrays, and manipulate them;
8 understand the concept of a pointer;
9 represent a table as a two dimensional array, and perform simple operations on the data represented by the rows and columns of the table;
10 handle strings and arrays of strings in Pascal.

ses

6.5 A grocery wholesaler holds a list of prices of cases of biscuits from a certain manufacturer in an array. If the prices of all cases costing below £10 are to be increased by 10%, and the prices of the others by 7%, write and test a program to list the new prices. You will have to construct and enter a suitable list of original prices.

6.6 Write and test a program to store an array and to print the element with the highest value in the array.

6.7 Modify your solution to Exercise 6.6 to print the position (that is, the element number or index) of the highest element.

6.8 Write and test a program to put the largest element of an array at the end of the array.

6.9 Write and test a program to store an array of characters, and then to move the one which comes first in alphabetical order to the first position in the array.

6.10 Votes cast in an election are coded as 51 for Candidate 1, 52 fo
Candidate 2, and so on up to 55 for Candidate 5. A series of code
votes are supplied as input data, terminated by −1.

Write and test a program to accept the data and print the votes fo
each candidate (with the identity of the candidate), the total votes cast
and the reference of the candidate with the highest number of votes
assuming that there are no ties.

6.11 If a string of characters, finished by an asterick, is entered an
stored as an array of single characters, write and test a program whic
will:

(a) print the length of the string, and the characters from position N
onwards (where N is to be input as data), followed by the origina
string;

(b) print characters from position M to N inclusive, where M and N
are input data, and M is less than or equal to N.

6.12 Two pupils sit a series of 3 exams each. Write and test a progra
to store their marks in a one-dimensional array, and to print the mar
of pupil I in subject J when requested to do so. Print the array at th
end of the program, with the results for each pupil on one line.

6.13 Repeat Exercise 6.12, using a two-dimensional array.

6.14 Write and test a program to enter a two-dimensional array int
store, and then to print the highest element of each row.

6.15 Write and test a program to enter a square array into store, an
then to print it out with rows and columns interchanged.

6.16 Modify your solution to Exercise 6.15 so that it works for
rectangular array.

7 More about Pascal

This chapter contains a minimal discussion of those features of Pascal not touched on elsewhere in this book that are necessary for us to understand the remaining Pascal examples used to illustrate good structured program design.

7.1 The truth about semicolons

It is important to remember that, in Pascal, *semicolons separate statements*; they do not, as may at first appear, terminate them. If we remember that a Pascal statement may be either a simple statement such as

$$total:= 0$$

or a compound statement bracketed between a BEGIN and an END, containing any number of simple statements and possibly further compound statements, such as

```
BEGIN
  WriteLn('Enter your name');
  FOR
    nameIndex:= 1 TO nameLength
  DO
    BEGIN
      Read(name[nameIndex])
    END
  {ENDFOR}
END
```

then we can deduce certain rules for the use of semicolons:
1 a semicolon is never *needed* immediately before the keyword END (in all these rules, remember that comments in Pascal programs should be treated as though they are invisible);

2 a semicolon is *never used* immediately before the keyword THEN
an IF statement;
3 a semicolon is *never used* immediately before the keyword ELSE
an IF statement;
4 a semicolon is *never used* immediately before the keyword DO in
WHILE or FOR statement.

We must take care not to let our indentation delude us into misuse
semicolons. If we write

```
IF
   age >= pensionable
THEN
   AwardPension;
   GetSeniorCitizensRailcard
{ENDIF}
```

we shall be disappointed. The semicolon separates the IF stateme
from the next statement — the call to GetSeniorCitizensRailcard
and so only the call to AwardPension depends on the test for 'ag
GetSeniorCitizensRailcard will *always* be executed. The same cave
applies to the WHILE . . . DO . . . construction:

```
WHILE
   age <= schoolLeavingAge
DO
   SupplySchoolMilk;
   ExamineByMedicalService
{ENDWHILE}
```

contains a similar error. For this reason, we recommend that a BEC
. . . END pair is generally used to enclose the contents of a THEN
ELSE branch, a DO loop, or the actions of a CASE statement.

This is the method we have used in most of the programs in
book. It is true that it may appear unwieldy when there is only
simple Pascal statement in these situations, where a compo
statement enclosed by a BEGIN . . . END pair is not really necess
but who is to say that we may not want to amend the program at s
later date, when it will be very easy to fall into the traps illustra
above?

<hr>

Exercise   7.1   Examine Program 7–1 and state
(a) which semicolons are illegal;
(b) which semicolons are redundant.

PROGRAM 7–1

```
PROGRAM Ch7Pl(input,output);

{Semicolon test;}

CONST
  semicolon = ´;´;
  sentinel = ´.´;
  stopCount = 10;

VAR
  symbol: CHAR;
  count: INTEGER;

BEGIN

  {Initialise}
  BEGIN
    count:= 0;
    Read(symbol);
  END;

  WHILE      {Count semicolons}
    (symbol <> sentinel)
    AND
    (count < stopCount);
  DO
    BEGIN
      IF
        symbol = semicolon
      THEN
        BEGIN
          count:= count + 1;
        END
      {ENDIF};
      Read(symbol);
    END
  {ENDWHILE};{Count semicolons}

  {Display count}
  WriteLn(´There are ´;count;
          ´semicolons´);

END.
```

7.2 More about TYPEs

A Pascal system provides us with four ready-made types: INTEGER REAL, CHAR and BOOLEAN. We have already seen how we ca declare further types of our own. Sometimes, we may require a type which is a *subset* or *subrange* of an available type. We may declare type

$$Ages = 18..65;$$

which indicates that any variable given this type can contain *onl* integer numbers in this range — a useful check, provided that we ar not dealing with unvalidated data (for which, see Chapter 10). We ca improve the style by declaring the range boundaries as constants wit appropriate names:

```
CONST
  lowWorkingAge = 18;
  highWorkingAge = 65;

TYPE
  Ages = lowWorkingAge..highWorkingAge;
```

This technique is particularly useful when declaring the type of a array index (see Chapter 6). It can be used with other types beside integers:

```
ValidInitialLetters = ´I´..´N´;
```

We can also declare our own *enumeration types*. By giving a typ definition such as

```
LecturerGrades = (lecturerI,lecturerII,
  seniorLecturer,principalLecturer);
```

and then declaring a variable 'staffMember' of this type, we are able perform not only such tests as

```
IF
  staffMember = lecturerII
```

but also such tests as

```
IF
  staffMember > lecturerII
```

(which would be *true* if StaffMember had the value 'seniorLecturer' (

'principalLecturer'). Note that there are no quotation marks in the Pascal — we are not dealing with character strings, but with concepts. This means, of course, that we cannot read one of these values directly into 'staffMember' from the input stream, or display such a value directly on the screen or printer; some sort of conversion (generally with a CASE statement) will have to occur.

Pascal provides us with two standard functions to manipulate such values — Succ and Pred (for 'successor' and 'predecessor'). If 'staffMember' has the value 'lecturerII' then

$$\text{Succ(staffMember)}$$

will return a value of 'seniorLecturer', and

$$\text{Pred(staffMember)}$$

a value of 'lecturerI'. An attempt to find the predecessor of a 'staffMember' with value 'lecturerI', or the successor of one with value 'principalLecturer', will fail.

We should also note in passing that it is possible to convert real numbers to integers using the standard functions Trunc and Round. If 'anyOldNumber' is a real number with a value of 18.75, then

$$\text{Trunc(anyOldNumber)}$$

will return a value of 18, and

$$\text{Round(anyOldNumber)}$$

a value of 19.

7.3 More about output

Left to itself, a Pascal program will produce output in response to WriteLn statements in a form convenient to itself but not generally convenient to us. Extra facilities are, therefore, provided to enable us to format the output. We can insert extra blank lines into our output by using extra WriteLn statements, without parameters, thus:

```
WriteLn;
WriteLn
```

Provided that the previous output statement was a WriteLn and not a Write, this will produce two blank lines.

In addition, we can use *format effectors* on the items we are printing, thus:

```
WriteLn('Average age at marriage':25,
        Round(averageAge):4)
```

This indicates that the text shown is to be displayed *right-justified* in field 25 characters wide (that is, with extra spaces inserted on the left of the text to make the length up to 25 characters), and the integer number obtained by rounding the real value in 'averageAge' right justified in a field 4 characters wide. (The numbers 25 and 4, and indeed the text string, can all be declared as constants if we want to keep our program free of stray numbers.) Real numbers are generall printed in 'scientific' notation. We can make them look normal by th construction

```
WriteLn('Average age at marriage':25,
        averageAge:7:2)
```

This indicates that 'averageAge' is to be displayed right-justified in field 7 characters wide; the rightmost three characters will contain th decimal point and the first two decimal places.

The standard function Page will move to the top of the next pag before displaying any more output. It takes no parameters if it is bein applied to the standard Pascal output stream — the file 'output'. Th form of all the examples of the use of 'Write' and 'WriteLn' that w have given so also indicate that the standard file 'output' is bein written. If any other file is being written, the name of the file must b given explicitly as the first parameter of 'Write', 'WriteLn' or 'Page thus:

```
Page(editedText);
WriteLn(editedText, 'Page ':40,
        pageNumber:3)
```

This will display some such item as Page 26 at the top of the next pag of the file 'editedText'. Similarly, we can read data from files othe than the standard file 'input' by giving 'Read' and 'ReadLn' the nam of an input file as their first parameter.

7.4 Records and files

A file is made up of a number of records, which may or may not all hav the same structure. Note that, in Pascal, records can exi independently of files. The records in a file have some attribute common which gives us the reason for grouping them together — the all relate to the customers of one branch of a bank, for example, or th prices of the goods manufactured by one division of a company. Eac record is a unit of information that is conveniently kept togethe though it may be made up of items of several different types. These items are known as fields. The 'employee data' of Example 5.2 would have been held more appropriately in a file.

JRE 7.1

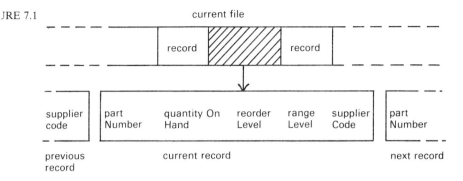

Figure 7.1 shows a file used in a stockholding system. Each item of stock has its own record, showing part number, quantity on hand, reorder level, danger level, and supplier code. We could define such a file in Pascal as follows:

```
TYPE
  Stocks = RECORD
    partNumber: INTEGER;
    quantityOnHand: INTEGER;
    reorderLevel: INTEGER;
    dangerLevel: INTEGER;
    supplierCode: CHAR
            END;   {RECORD}
  StocFiles = FILE OF Stocks;

VAR
  stockFile: StocFiles;
  stockRecord: Stocks;
```

Before we can use this file in our Pascal program, we have to make it available as a resource (sometimes called 'opening' the file). If the file is an input file — we want only to *read* data from it — then we can say

```
Reset(stockFile)
```

while if the file is an output file — we wish to *write* to it — we say

```
Rewrite(stockFile)
```

This is no need to 'close' the file, since the file is a resource which will be freed when we reach the end of the block in which it was allocated — generally, the program.

Suppose we are dealing with an input file.

```
Read(stockFile,stockRecord)
```

will make the next record from 'stockFile' available to us. We c
address the individual fields by linking them with the name of t
record:

```
IF
  stockRecord.quantityOnHand
  < stockRecord.reorderLevel
THEN
  BEGIN
    WriteLn('Reorder part no. ',
            stockRecord.partNumber,
            ' from supplier ',
            stockRecord.supplierCode)
  END
{ENDIF}
```

Clearly, since we have to write out 'stockRecord' four times in o
simple IF statement, this is a long-winded way of going about thing
A short-cut is provided for us — the WITH statement. We can repla
the above fragment of code by

```
WITH
  stockRecord
DO
  BEGIN
    IF
      quantityOnHand < reorderLevel
    THEN
      BEGIN
        WriteLn('Reorder part no. ',
                partNumber,
                ' from supplier ',
                supplierCode)
      END
    {ENDIF}
  END
{ENDWITH}
```

which means exactly the same.

With an array, we can look at the type declarations and find t
array's *lower* and *upper bounds*, that is, the lowest and high
subscripts used to index it; and so we know the size of the array

advance. With an input file, we cannot know the size of the file in advance, since the actual data is held outside the program area. How, then, do we know when we have come to the end of the data? Pascal provides us with the function EOF for this purpose.

```
EOF(stockFile)
```

returns the value *true* as soon as we have consumed all the data in the file. This may be as soon as we 'Reset' the file, if the file is empty. 'EOF' used by itself without parameters is taken to refer to the standard input file.

7.2   Re-attempt Exercise 5.2, this time using a file of input data called 'employeeData'.

7.5 More about subprograms

Pascal is a block-structured language. Resources required in a particular block can be requisitioned at the start of a block. They will be automatically released at the end of a block. In this way, resources required by the program can be minimised. Any *block* in Pascal consists of a 'declarative part' (which may be empty) followed by a 'statement part'. The statement part must consist of a compound statement (see Section 7.1). The declarative part may contain a LABEL section (see Section 10.4), a CONST section, a TYPE section, a VAR section, function declarations and procedure declarations. Any of these items, declared in the declarative part of a block, has no existence outside that block; they will be 'lost' when we exit from the procedure.

We have already seen one compulsory use of a *local* declaration of this type — the counter variable used in a FOR statement (Section 4.8). This means that, if we required another counter variable for a similar FOR loop — addressing the same array, say — then we could give the variable the same name; the compiler would regard the two items as separate variables. In fact, although all the other variables, constants and types we have used so far have been *global* — declared at the start of the program, and so available throughout any block that the program block contains — it is far better practice to make all declarations local as far as possible. In this way, each procedure or function becomes as self-contained as possible, and it cannot affect other parts of the program except in ways that we can closely control. In addition, once we are confident that we have a good working procedure, we can re-use the definition in other programs without having to change any of the code.

Of course, there must be some communication between procedures, since in any one program there will probably be data items which are to

be accessed (read from or written into) by more than one procedure. I
addition, a procedure which is being re-used in a different program wi
almost certainly be operating on a different set of data items. Similarl
we may want to execute a similar section of code within one progra
three times, but each time operating upon different items of data. W
can achieve all these objectives by the use of *parameters*.

When a subprogram is declared, we declare the *pattern* or *form* th
the code is to take. In place of the different global variables that are
be acted upon, we use *formal parameters*. These names have n
independent existence. When the procedure or function is to be ex
cuted, the names are replaced by the *actual parameters* given in th
procedure call or *function call*. A simple example will suffice. Suppo
that we define a procedure.

```
PROCEDURE MakeGap(linesReqd:INTEGER);
  VAR
    lineCounter: INTEGER;
  BEGIN
    FOR
      lineCounter:= 1 TO linesReqd
    DO
      BEGIN
        WriteLn
      END
    {ENDFOR}
  END
```

Here 'lineCounter' is a local variable — the counter for the FC
loop; but 'linesReqd' is a formal parameter. We specify it in the li
containing the procedure name, and we indicate what type of item is
be expected.

When 'MakeGap' is called, an integer must be supplied.

```
MakeGap(3)
```

will produce three blank lines, and

```
Read(howMany);
MakeGap(howMany)
```

will produce as many blank lines as the number that has just been re
The constant '3' and the integer variable 'howMany' are the *act*
parameters in these procedure calls.

When we pass a parameter to a subprogram, it may be that we
interested in the value we are passing rather than in the name of
variable which contained that value. Indeed, the value may have be
specified as a constant, as we have just seen, so that no variable na

need be involved. 'linesReqd' in the last example, as well as being a formal parameter, is also described as a *value parameter*. Only the integer value is passed to the procedure MakeGap; the source of this integer value, whether constant or variable, is ignored — so that the FOR statement is interpreted as (say)

```
FOR
    lineCounter:= 1 TO 3
```

But what happens if we want the subprogram to be aware of the variable representing the actual parameter — for instance, so that the subprogram can place a value in the variable which will be left there after the subprogram has been executed, so that the value can be used in the main program or calling routine? To do this, we need to supply a *variable parameter* (which clearly cannot be a constant). Another example will illustrate this.

```
PROCEDURE ConvertToHMS
    (inMinutes: INTEGER;
     VAR outMinutes,
         outHours,
         outDays: INTEGER);
    VAR
        remainder: INTEGER;
    BEGIN
        outDays:= inMinutes DIV (24 * 60);
        remainder:= inMinutes MOD (24 * 60);
        outHours:= remainder DIV 60;
        outMinutes:= remainder MOD 60
    END
```

Here, 'inMinutes' is a formal parameter and a value parameter; 'out-Minutes', 'outHours' and 'outDays' are formal, variable parameters; and 'remainder' is a local variable. We might invoke 'ConvertToHMS' with a procedure call such as

```
ConvertToHMS(clockFinish - clockStart,
    otimeMins, otimeHours, otimeDays)
```

where all five names in the call are variables; the contents of the last three will be altered by the procedure.

Let us further illustrate the sensible use of procedures with parameters by reconsidering the Weight Loss program we looked at in Chapter 2 (Program 2–1). For ease of reference, this program, using procedures, is reproduced as Program 7–2a.

PROGRAM 7–2a

```
PROGRAM Ch7P2a(input,output);

{Calculates the weight loss of a
substance over a week, and displays this
in imperial and metric measure - may be
 amended for other periods of time}

CONST
  ouncesPerPound = 16;
  ozToGrammes = 28.35;
  firstPeriodQuery= 'Weight last week?';
  secondPeriodQuery =
                    'Weight this week?';

VAR
  lastPounds,
  lastOunces,
  thisPounds,
  thisOunces,
  weightLossInOz: INTEGER;

BEGIN

  PROCEDURE EnterOldAndNewWeights;
    BEGIN
      WriteLn(firstPeriodQuery);
      ReadLn(lastPounds, lastOunces);
      WriteLn(secondPeriodQuery);
      ReadLn(thisPounds, thisOunces);
    END;

  PROCEDURE CalculateWeightChange;
    BEGIIN
      weightLossInOz:=
        (lastPounds * ouncesPerPound
                    + lastOunces) -
        (thisPounds * ouncesPerPound
                    + thisOunces);
    END;

  PROCEDURE DisplayWeightChange;
    BEGIN
      WriteLn('Weight loss');
      WriteLn('Imperial: ',
      weightLossInOz DIV ouncesPerPound,
            ' pounds ',
```

```
          weightLossInOz MOD ouncesPerPound,
              ' ounces');
          WriteLn('Metric: ',
            weightLossInOz * ozToGrammes,
            ' grammes')
      END;

BEGIN    {Check weight loss}

    EnterOldAndNewWeights;
    CalculateWeightChange;
    DisplayWeightChange

END.
```

This program served as an introduction to the basic use of procedures, but we cannot claim that, in its present form, it represents a professional approach to Pascal programming. Let us consider the three procedures involved, starting with 'EnterOldAndNewWeights'. This procedure asks the user two questions, and sets up values in four variables according to the user's response. These values are then used by subsequent procedures. Hence we require a procedure which will
— display constant messages;
— place values into data items and ensure they remain available after this procedure has terminated.

The second requirement clearly indicates to us that all the parameters must be variable parameters, indicated by VAR in the procedure heading (the statement starting PROCEDURE). The first requirement reminds us that the constant messages are not required outside this procedure, and so can be declared locally. Both requirements show that the actual units being referred to (pounds, ounces, grammes) are immaterial to the structure of the code, and so we could produce a general procedure that would work with any similar set of units. Taking all this into account, we arrive at the following procedure declaration:

```
          PROCEDURE EnterOldAndNewValues
            (VAR lastUnits, lastSubUnits,
              thisUnits, thisSubUnits: INTEGER);
            CONST
              firstPeriodQuery =
                'Values last week?';
              secondPeriodQuery =
                'Values this week?';
```

```
BEGIN
  WriteLn(firstPeriodQuery);
  ReadLn(lastUnits, lastSubUnits);
  WriteLn(secondPeriodQuery);
  ReadLn(thisUnits, thisSubUnits)
END;
```

Notice that we have amended the name of the procedure to reflect i⧸ more general nature.

Taking the second procedure, 'CalculateWeightChange', we not⧸ that it will access four values that have been set up before it is invoke⧸ but will not change them: these can, therefore, be implemented ⧸ value parameters. The question now arises, What should these form⧸ parameters be called? Should we use the same names as we have ju⧸ used in 'EnterOldAndNewValues'? Our decision must depend on ho⧸ far confusion is likely to arise. Suppose the invocation, or call, ⧸ 'EnterOldAndNewValues' in the main body of the program is to loc⧸ like

```
EnterOldAndNewValues
  (lastPounds, lastOunces,
   thisPounds, thisOunces);
```

Here the actual parameters are lastPounds, lastOunces, thisPoun⧸ and thisOunces.

When the procedure is invoked, then actual names will be used ⧸ place of the formal names lastUnits, lastSubUnits, thisUnits a⧸ thisSubUnits respectively. The actual parameter names will have be⧸ declared in a VAR section. We could, in fact, have used the sa⧸ names for the formal parameters, but then we would have had ⧸ realise that, on execution, the formal parameter name 'lastPoun⧸ (say) was being replaced by the actual parameter name 'lastPound⧸ Using different names avoids confusion. On the other hand, re-use ⧸ formal parameter name in another procedure is less likely to confu⧸ though we must remember that 'lastUnits' as the first formal pa⧸ meter to our revised procedure 'CalculateWeightChange' sim⧸ *represents* the first actual parameter in the procedure invocation, ⧸ has no *logical* connexion with the word 'lastUnits' in the proced⧸ "EnterOldAndNewValues'. We could just as easily use 'formerUn⧸ in 'CalculateWeightChange'.

'CalculateWeightChange' will also set up a value in one variable ⧸ we'll need at least one variable parameter. Conventionally, va⧸ parameters are declared first in the procedure heading, and varia⧸ parameters last. Finally, we appear to require a const⧸ ('ouncesPerPound' or its equivalent). This could be declared as a l⧸ constant, but then it would conflict with our aim of making the ⧸

cedure more general. Further, it is required again in the next procedure. Use of a global constant, however, would equally conflict with our aim of generality. We want our procedure to be able to use whatever constant it is supplied with; and we can do this easily by supplying the constant as a value parameter. Constants, of course, can only be supplied as value parameters, since making them variable parameters would imply that they are variable, which is a contradiction in terms.

Making an appropriate adjustment to the procedure name, we arrive at:

```
PROCEDURE CalculateValueChange
  (lastUnits, lastSubUnits,
   thisUnits, thisSubUnits,
   subUnitsPerUnit: INTEGER;
   VAR lossInSubUnits: INTEGER);

BEGIN
  lossInSubUnits:=
    (lastUnits * subUnitsPerUnit
                  + lastSubUnits) -
    (thisUnits * subUnitsPerUnit
                  + thisSubUnits)
END;
```

Finally, we improve on the procedure 'DisplayWeightChange' by supplying it with value parameters, including two constants, and also by adding format effectors to remove superfluous spaces. The complete program then becomes as shown in Program 7–2b.

PROGRAM 7–2b

```
PROGRAM Ch7P2b(input,output);

{Calculates the weight loss of a
substance over a week, and displays this
in imperial and metric measure}

CONST
  ouncesPerPound = 16;
  ozToGrammes = 28.35;

VAR
  lastPounds,
  lastOunces,
  thisPounds,
  thisOunces,
  weightLossInOz: INTEGER;
```

```
BEGIN

  PROCEDURE EnterOldAndNewValues
    (VAR lastUnits, lastSubUnits,
      thisUnits, thisSubUnits: INTEGER);
    CONST
      firstPeriodQuery =
        'Values last week?';
      secondPeriodQuery =
        'Values this week?';

    BEGIN
      WriteLn(firstPeriodQuery);
      ReadLn(lastUnits, lastSubUnits);
      WriteLn(secondPeriodQuery);
      ReadLn(thisUnits, thisSubUnits)
    END;

  PROCEDURE CalculateValueChange
    (lastUnits, lastSubUnits,
      thisUnits, thisSubUnits,
      subUnitsPerUnit: INTEGER;
      VAR lossInSubUnits: INTEGER);

    BEGIN
      lossInSubUnits:=
        (lastUnits * subUnitsPerUnit
                + lastSubUnits) -
        (thisUnits * subUnitsPerUnit
                + thisSubUnits)
    END;

  PROCEDURE DisplayValueChange
    (lossInSubUnits, subUnitsPerUnit:
      INTEGER; imperialToMetric: REAL);

    BEGIN
      WriteLn('Loss');
      WriteLn('Imperial: ',

        lossInSubUnits DIV
        subUnitsPerUnit:1, ' units ',
        lossInSubUnits MOD
        subUnitsPerUnit:1, ' sub-units');
      WriteLn('Metric: ',
        lossInSubUnits *
        imperialToMetric:1:3,
        ' metric units')
    END;
```

```
BEGIN     {Check weight loss}

    EnterOldAndNewValues
      (lastPounds, lastOunces,
       thisPounds, thisOunces);
    CalculateValueChange
      (lastPounds, lastOunces,
       thisPounds, thisOunces,
       ouncesPerPound, weightLossInOz);
    DisplayValueChange
      (weightLossInOz, ouncesPerPound,
       ozToGrammes)

END.
```

Note that we have kept our original global variable declarations, but these are never referred to by name within the procedures; they merely generate instances of data on which our generalised procedures can now operate; the procedures would operate equally well if we were dealing with, say, feet, inches and metres.

7.3 Amend Program 7–2b to convert feet and inches to metres (1 inch = 2.54 cm; 1 cm = 0.3937 inches).

7.4 In converting Program 7–2a to Program 7–2b, we lost something in user-friendliness, since the text displayed to the user now refers only to 'units', 'sub-units' and 'metric units'. Further, an assumption is made that we are always converting from 'Imperial' to 'Metric'. Amend Program 7–2b to remove these disadvantages. (Hint: further parameterisation will be necessary.)

7.5 Code the solution to Exercise 4.8 using procedures with parameters.

7.6 Arrays as parameters

The actual parameter must, as we would expect, have the same type as the formal parameter. This usually presents no problems. The one exception is where we are dealing with arrays. We will sometimes want to carry out the same set of operations on a number of arrays, particularly strings. If the arrays are of different sizes, then they violate the parameter rules by being of different types. This annoying restriction is overcome in ISO-Pascal by the introduction of *conformant array parameters*. This forbidding name simply means that we specify *within the PROCEDURE statement itself*

(a) whether the array is packed;

(b) the range of values for the index variable to be used to access the array (or for index variables to access each element of a multi-dimensional array);

(c) and the type applicable to each array element.
  Consider the following procedure declaration.

```
PROCEDURE CalcTotal(VAR anyArray:
  ARRAY[lowerBound..upperBound:INTEGER]
  OF INTEGER;
  VAR anyTotal: INTEGER);

VAR
  anyIndex: INTEGER;
BEGIN
  anyTotal:= 0;
  FOR
    anyIndex:=lowerBound TO upperBound
  DO
    BEGIN
      anyTotal:= anyTotal +
        anyArray[anyIndex]
    END
  {ENDFOR}
END
```

This procedure will add together the contents of an array of intege
of any length. Examples of its use are

```
CONST
  salesReturns = 10;
TYPE
  SalesLists = ARRAY[1..salesReturns]
              OF INTEGER;
VAR
  sales: SalesLists;
  salesTotal: INTEGER;

{....
  ....
  ....}


CalcTotal(sales,salesTotal)
```

and

```
CONST
  firstStudentIdent = 3274;
  lastStudentIdent = 3692;
```

```
TYPE
  MarksLists = ARRAY[firstStudentIdent,
    lastStudentIdent] OF INTEGER;
VAR
  marks: MarksLists;
  marksTotal: INTEGER;

{....
 ....
 ....}
```

```
CalcTotal(marks,markksTotal)
```

se 7.6 Write a procedure 'DisplayString' that will display any string and add its length to 'outputLineLength'.

7.7 Qualities of a good subprogram

Finally, we should consider what makes a good subprogram — whether procedure or function.

'Good' means much the same as it did when applied to complete programs in general: good subprograms are those which

1 give correct results;
2 are easy to understand;
3 are easy to correct;
4 are easy to alter;
5 deal sensibly with unusual data.

In order to achieve these ends, they should have the following qualities:

1 *High cohesion*. This means that subprograms should contain only closely related activities. For instance, the procedure 'SetUpStringA' in Example 6.6 has high cohesion since it deals with all the data entry for the program. The programmer can identify the part of the program dealing with data entry so that it can be programmed, corrected or amended more effectively.

2 *Low coupling*. This is often closely related to cohesion, in that high cohesion often occurs naturally alongside low coupling, which is what we want. Coupling is an indication of the complexity of the connexions between subprograms. In Pascal, this means minimising the number of parameters passed, and maximising the number of local variables. We discussed these aspects of Pascal in Section 7.5.

3 *Subprograms of a suitable size*. Professional programmers often aim to have about 40 to 60 lines of code in a 'module'. Each module is then small enough to be easily understood, and the total number of

subprograms is not large enough to obscure the design of the program. As we are learning the craft, about 10 to 20 lines in a procedure would be reasonable.

4 *Disciplined use of standard subprograms.* As discussed in Section 7.5, a subprogram can be used in several programs, but a change to adapt its use to a new environment may cause an unexpected failure elsewhere in the subprogram. This is true for subprograms generally. The programmer must be able to think of a standard subprogram as a *reliable* addition to the language. It is only reliable if it is not interfered with. The programmer should not alter it for specific situations, as it is then better to produce more than one version, and use the one which is best adapted.

5 *Delay decisions.* If decisions are put off for as long as possible when designing a program, there will be less to alter if the decision was incorrect. Further, the longer it is put off, the easier it will be to make the correct decision later, as the programmer may by then have reached a better understanding of the problem.

These comments are 'good advice' and should be followed as best one can. They do *not* guarantee a program which can be easily modified when the data changes. A more powerful method of these is given in Chapter 8.

After studying this chapter, you should be able to
1 use semicolons sensibly in a Pascal program;
2 declare subrange and enumeration types;
3 produce neatly formatted output from Pascal programs;
4 use records and files;
5 distinguish between local and global declarations, formal and actual parameters, and value and variable parameters;
6 use conformant array parameters;
7 appreciate the significance of cohesion, coupling, subprogram size, subprogram standardisation, and delayed decisions in program design.

Exercises

7.7 Read in the ages of 50 people and display under suitable headings the total number of people under 10, aged 10–19, in their twenties, their thirties and so on up to the nineties (assume no-one lives to 100).

7.8 Rewrite your solution to Exercise 7.7 as a procedure, which takes two parameters indicating the youngest age-group to be reported, and the oldest (for example, thirties to eighties only).

7.9 Design and write a program which counts how many times each of the ten digits occur in a stream of single-digit numbers, and which displays the frequency of each digit as a percentage of the total number of digits read. Display your answers with suitable headings, four figures to a line.

7.10 Modify your solution to Exercise 7.9 to produce a procedure which takes a parameter indicating the number of figures to appear across a line.

7.11 Input records contain a student's reference number, age and marks in three subjects. Read in ten such records and store them in an array. Later you discover an error in the input data: the tenth record should have been ignored, and a new record is supplied, to be inserted between the fifth and sixth records. Design a routine to do this. Then repeat the process without using an array — that is, using input and output files only.

8 Introduction to Jackson Structured Programming

8.1 Rationale

Although the top-down stepwise-refinement method of designing program is powerful, it gives no real guidance on how to break th problem down into suitable components for making into modules o subprograms. An incorrect choice of major modules at the beginnin of the design process will lead to a difficult or even impossible design Unfortunately, it is at the beginning that we are most uncertain as t what the modules should be. If we choose the wrong size of module, w may have too many small ones which can be confusing and slow dow the running of the program too much, while too few modules mean that each is large and difficult to understand. Further, there is n reason why the resulting design should be easy to amend if the form c the data changes as it often does in practice, since there is no planned coherent link between the characteristics of the data and the charac teristics of the program. Such programs often do not meet ou definition of a 'good' program discussed in the first chapter (page 3).

In many cases the information which is supplied to a program a input data, or received from a program as output data, can b described using the same constructs as we use in designing programs – sequences, selections and repetitions.

Jackson comments that data is only 'real', in the sense that it can b seen and used by people when it is outside, or external to, th computer. Hence it is quite possible to manipulate it any way we lik when it is inside the computer as long as the instructions of ou language allow us to do so. However, he argues that it is only if w respect the external structure of the data in our program that we will b able to cope easily if this changes. Michael Jackson's metho overcomes the problem of knowing what the top-level design shoul be, and indeed provides a self-checking skeleton of the whole design –

on to which the details can be added. This may sound rather vague but it is generally comparatively straightforward to carry out, since all we have to do is to draw a structure diagram for our data, and then to develop our *basic program structure* from this. We have been implicitly using JSP (Jackson Structured Programming) for the design of all the Pascal programs and fragments in the preceding chapters; in this chapter, we formalise our approach.

8.2 Data structures

Let us consider some common data structures. One such structure is a file, which, it will be recalled, is a list, or sequence, of items of data all of the same type. For instance

5	7	3	5	4

could be a file of children's ages. This could be represented in a structure diagram as shown in Figure 8.1.

URE 8.1

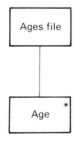

The details of how many ages there are, are omitted here as we are concerned only about the structure, or shape, of our diagram.

Another example of a data structure, which we have already met, is a sequence of electricity meter-readings, where the first reading in each pair represents a present reading and the second the corresponding previous reading. Since a pair of readings refer to the same meter, they form a record, each with a present meter-reading field and a previous meter-reading field. We could describe the data as having the physical form

5213	4631	1413	1204	7689	6301

and as having the logical form of Figure 8.2.

FIGURE 8.2

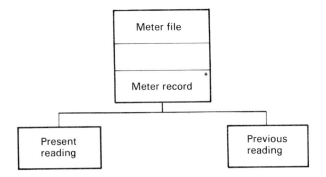

There are other structure diagrams we could draw for the same data
depending on how we wish to use the data. For instance, suppose we
want to check to see if any readings, Present or Previous, exceed 9000.
Then we are no longer interested in records, or whether the readings
we are looking at are Present or Previous. The logical data structure
then that shown in Figure 8.3.

FIGURE 8.3

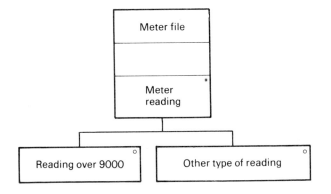

This implies that when we draw data structures, we draw the one
that describes the way in which we wish to think of the data on this
occasion. This will lead to the appropriate structure for the program.

FIGURE 8.4

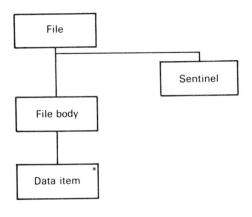

As another example of a data structure, consider how we often indicate the end of some data using a dummy sentinel record. This could be drawn as in Figure 8.4. A dummy sentinel record was used in the Porkers example of Chapter 5.

Example 8.1 Apply Jackson Structured Programming to Example 5.1 in order to derive the basic program structure diagram.

In that problem, each group of weights was terminated by a sentinel of -1, whilst the number of groups was given as an initial number. The sample data we used was

3					
10	11	12	13	14	-1
9	10	11	-1		
15	-1				

This could be described in a structure diagram as in Figure 8.5

FIGURE 8.5

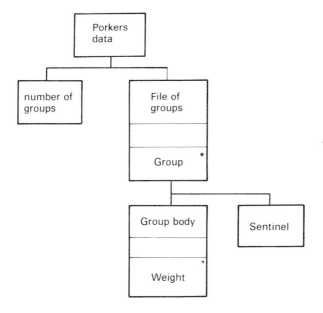

We can obtain the basic program structure diagram from this by making small changes to the contents of the boxes so as to describe what we wish to do to the data. In this case we obtain the design of Figure 8.6. It is a good principle to change the *nouns* of the data structure into *verbs*, such as Process, for the program structure.

We can now add boxes to this diagram so as to develop our design. We often need to insert them between such components as Process Group and Process Group Body to ensure that we avoid having incorrect program components, such as those shown in Figure 4.10.

This basic program structure diagram can be compared with the parts of our final design extracted from Figure 5.9 as obtained using the

FIGURE 8.6

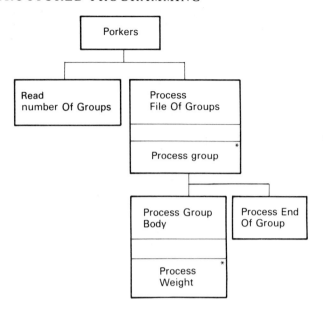

top-down stepwise refinement method in Chapter 5 and reproduced i
Figure 8.7.

FIGURE 8.7

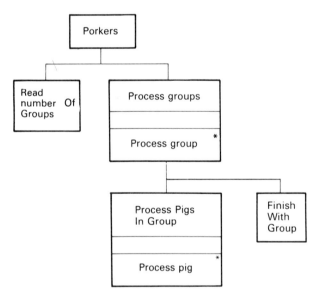

The similarity is obvious, but the difference in the methods (
obtaining these parts of the structure diagram is that the simple to
down stepwise-refinement method of Chapter 5 may, *or may not*, lea
to a good, easily amended design in appropriate modules, whilst th
data structure method of this chapter *will* do so.

8.3 Operations lists

The next example illustrates the use of an operations list in construct-
ing structure diagrams. It is of vital importance and must be followed
through very carefully.

ple   8.2 Candidates for a certain qualification have to reach a satisfactory
standard (defined as 50%) in any two of three in-course
assessments, and also in any two of the three final examinations.
   The data for each candidate is to be entered in the following
order:

Name
In-course   percentage in subject 1
Examination   percentage in subject 1
In-course   percentage in subject 2
Examination   percentage in subject 2
In-course   percentage in subject 3
Examination   percentage in subject 3

The data for the final candidate is followed by a sentinel consisting of a dummy record with a name of ****. Write a program
which will print, for each candidate, the name, the number of
in-course assessments passed, the number of examinations
passed, and the overall result of Pass or Fail under suitable
headings.

   Typical input data would be records of the following form:

Fred   60   50   70   40   80   49

which should give the following output:

Name	In-course passes	Exam passes	Result
Fred	3	1	Fail

The structure diagram for the input data is shown as Figure 8.8, and the
basic program structure diagram is shown in Figure 8.9.

FIGURE 8.8

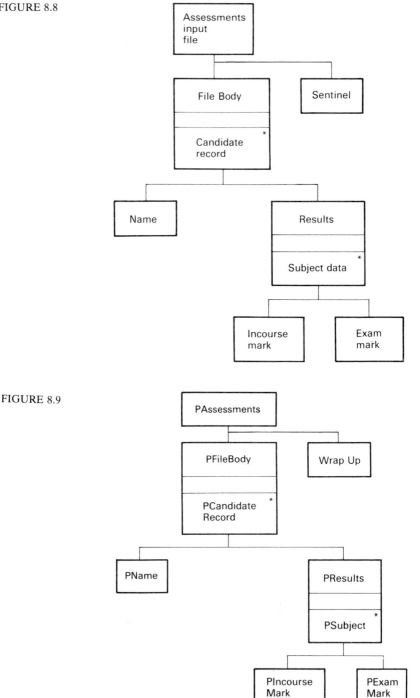

FIGURE 8.9

Before going further, we make a numbered list of the operations wh
we think might be useful in developing this. We do *not* include

details of selections or iterations at this stage. It is often useful to start with the display operations, and then to work back asking 'What did we need to do to be able to do this?

Our list in this case is:

1 Display headings
2 Display record
3 Add 1 to in-course passes count
4 Add 1 to exam passes count
5 Set in-course passes count to zero
6 Set exam passes count to zero
7 Read record

This may not be complete, and some of the operations such as 'Print record' may be too complex to be considered as elementary operations, but it provides a means of moving forwards. In the next stage, we can add the numbers of the operations (or their descriptions) to our data structure diagrams in a systematic manner.

This is done by asking the following questions:

(a) 'Is a sentinel being used?' If so, use the read-ahead technique by adding on the Read operations in the general pattern of Figure 8.10. The exact position for the initial Read statement will become evident at a later stage.

FIGURE 8.10

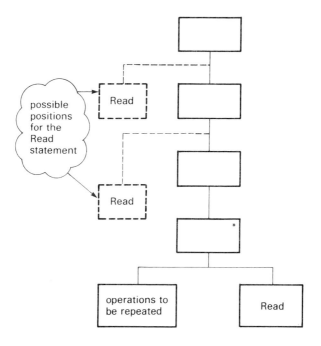

(b) 'How many times could this operation be carried out?'

This tells us which 'parent' box the operation should come under.

(c) 'Should the operation be done at the beginning, in the middle or at the end of the operation of which it is a part?'

This tells us where the operation should be attached to its parent.

If there is any serious difficulty in answering these questions, suggests that there is an error in our basic program structure design and therefore in our original data structures, and that these should b checked. This checking means that serious errors can be detecte before a significant commitment to the design is made and is a ver valuable feature of JSP.

Using these operations on our program gives:

(a) 'Read-ahead?' This leads to the design shown in Figure 8.1

FIGURE 8.11

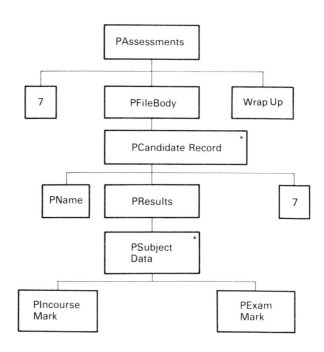

Note that the numbers used in this and future diagrams relate to t appropriate operations list. In Figure 8.11 box 7 represents 're record'.

(b) 'How many times?'

operation	frequency
1 (Display headings)	Once per record
2 (Display record)	Once per record
3 (Add 1 to incourse passes count)	Once per incourse
4 (Add 1 to exam passes count)	Once per exam
5 (Set incourse passes count to zero)	Once per record
6 (Set exam passes count to zero)	Once per record

This suggests that operations 1, 2, 5 and 6 should be details PCandidate Record. 3 and 4 belong to PSubject.

(c) 'Beginning, middle or end?'

Operation	parent	position
1	PCandidate Record	Towards the end
2	PCandidate Record	End
3	PIncourseMark	Middle
4	PExamMark	Middle
5	PCandidate Record	Beginning
6	PCandidate Record	Beginning

In this example, the order of operations 3 and 4 is not important so far as obtaining the correct results is concerned. But in general it is advisable to keep operations in the same order as in the corresponding data structures, so that if this changes, we can make corresponding changes to the program.

The same goes for operations 5 and 6. This leads us to the program structure shown in Figure 8.12.

FIGURE 8.12

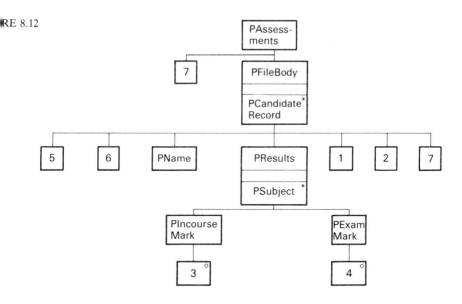

Operations 3, 4, 5, 6 and 7 are simple enough to be considered as *elementary operations*. That is, they can be coded in our programming language very easily. We can now concentrate on developing the other operations using the same techniques.

If it turned out that we had overlooked something at this stage, it would be easy enough to build it in due to the tree structure of the diagrams.

Display Headings has an operations list of:

1.   Display Headings
1.1 Display 'Name', 'In-course passes', 'Exam passes', 'Result'

This leads to the design shown in Figure 8.13.

FIGURE 8.13

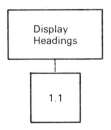

Display Record can be developed as a procedure by applying the sa
technique as we used with the outline structure diagram. The ope
tions list is:

2.   Display   Record
2.1 Display   name
2.2 Display   number of in-course passes
2.3 Display   number of examination passes
2.4 Display   'PASS'
2.5 Display   'FAIL'

Each of 2.1 to 2.5 can be carried out up to once per 'Display reco
Adding in the selection conditions leads to the design of Figure 8.

FIGURE 8.14

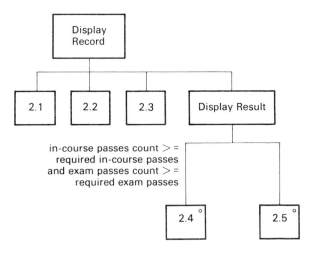

Read Record has an operations list of:

7.   Read Record
7.1 Read name
7.2 Read in-course percentage
7.3 Read examination percentage

These operations *must* follow the form of the data structure, as they are so closely related to it, and so we obtain the design of Figure 8.15.

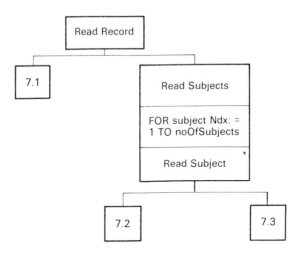

All that remains to be done is to fill in details of any remaining iterations and any missing or misplaced selections. A list of iteration controls and selection conditions can be helpful here. In this case we need to specify how many times we wish to carry out PCandidate Record.

As usual with read-ahead we need a 'while not sentinel' construct, expressed here in Figure 8.16.

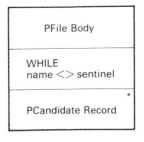

It sometimes happens that the initial read operation in the read-ahead construct has to be relocated up the structure from the position suggested in Figure 8.10. If this is so, it always becomes evident when the details of the iteration controls are being specified.

As there are three subjects, we express the PResults iteration as shown in Figure 8.17. This completes the design in as much as all the boxes have been developed into elementary operations, and all the details of iterations, controls and selections have now been written in.

FIGURE 8.17

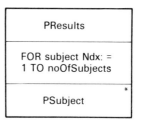

We have also developed the basis of a convenient documentation our program if we bring it together. Further, it will be easy to modif our structure diagrams by making appropriate insertions and deletion when the need arises.

For a demonstration, the major diagrams developed above will t brought together in Figures 8.18, 8.19 and 8.20 to show the form suc documentation might take.

FIGURE 8.18

PROGRAM NAME: ASSESSMENTS   PAGE 1
VERSION: 0.0   AUTHOR: R. G. JONES
DATE: 20-8-87

DOCUMENT: INPUT DATA STRUCTURE

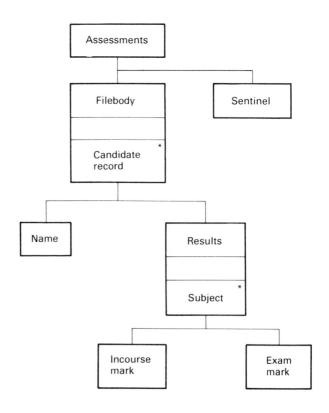

PROGRAM NAME: ASSESSMENTS PAGE 2
VERSION: 0.0 AUTHOR: R. G. JONES
DATE: 20-8-87

DOCUMENT: BASIC PROGRAM STRUCTURE

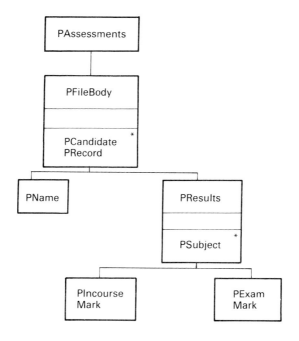

FIGURE 8.20
PROGRAM NAME: ASSESSMENTS
VERSION: 0.0
DATE: 20-8-87

PAGE 3
AUTHOR: R. G. JON

DOCUMENT: PROGRAM STRUCTURE

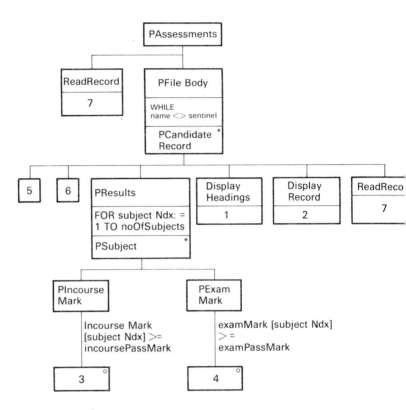

Operations list:

1. Display headings
2. Display record
3. Add 1 to incourse passes count

4. Add 1 to exam passes count
5. Set incourse passes count to zero
6. Set exam passes count to zero
7. Read record

Note: PName does not appear, since there is no processing (other than reading and writ
performed on the name, and these operations are incorporated into ReadRecord and Displa
cord.
Detailed structure diagrams for ReadRecord, DisplayHeadings, DisplayRecord should be dr
but they are not repeated here.

There is a great deal that one must sometimes include in doc
mentation, such as a written description of any unusually tricky par
testing requirements etc. However, asking for excessive doc
mentation may be self-defeating, since people may well not be p
pared to make the necessary amendments to keep such a system up
date.

The Jackson method used here provides documentation as part

the design process in an easily amendable form, and in any case, well designed programs should not need very much documentation. The Jackson method demonstrates a flexible way of describing the design of the program. As this is a simple example, separate pages have been given to quite small operations, in order to demonstrate how to use a method which is suitable for large programs.

Let us now consider what happens to the PAssessments design if the input data is reorganised so that the 3 in-course marks for a student are given together, before the 3 exam marks. The sample input record becomes

Name	In-course marks	Exam marks
Fred	60 70 80	50 40 49

and the input data structure diagram is shown in Figure 8.21.

The operations required are the same as before — it is the program structure which must change. The revised program design is easily obtained from Figure 8.21, and is given in Figure 8.23. ReadRecord is now as in Figure 8.22.

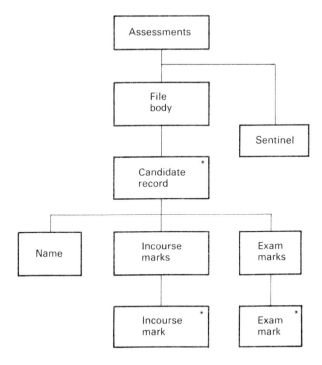

FIGURE 8.22

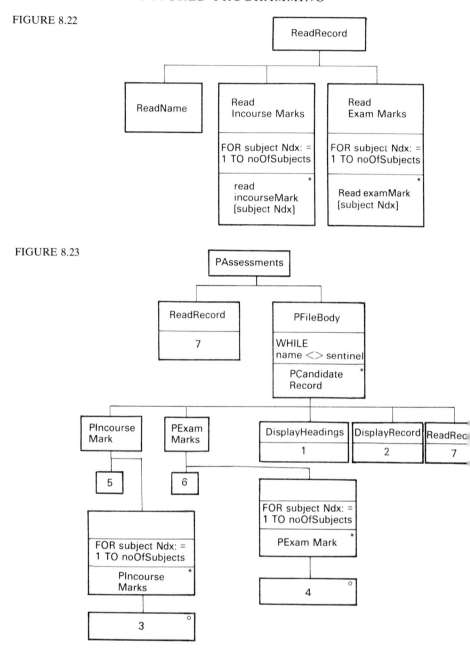

FIGURE 8.23

It would have been a mistake to change *only* the ReadReco
section. Since the user is now apparently thinking of the data in ter
of in-course Marks, followed by exam Marks, and not in terms
subjects as before, the program should reflect this, so that the futu
alterations can be incorporated as easily as this one. Of course, t
means that the person designing the data must do so correctly in
first place — but that is another story.

8.4 Program design examples

The following example illustrates the use of Jackson's method on a problem which is not as simple as it seems, due to the number of possible variations in the input data.

Example 8.3 In a stock-recording system a file of records is used to update the stock levels. The records are of two types: 'R' for replenishing stock, and 'U' for stock utilisation. The records are added to the file as they occur giving an unsorted file. In a study of the efficiency of the stores, it is necessary to find the following:

1 the number of R-type records,
2 the number of U-type records,
3 the length of the largest batch of U-type records.

A record consists of a type field, followed by other data which is to be ignored here. The file is terminated by an X-type sentinel record.

Sample data: input (Stock Movements File):

R   R   U   U   R   U   R   R   R   U   R   U   U   X

        output:

number of replenishments   7
number of utilisations   6
largest batch of utilisations 2

FIGURE 8.24

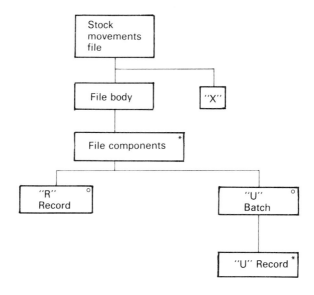

FIGURE 8.25

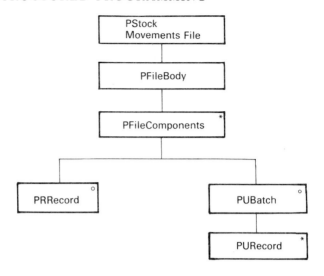

This suggests that the data structure should include references
individual replenishments, individual utilisation records, and
batches of utilisation records. These can all fit the general descriptic
of 'file components', and so this leads us to the design of Figure 8.2
and to a basic program structure as in Figure 8.25. Whilst this appea
to be very similar to Figure 8.24, it must be remembered that it
describing something very different. It is in fact describing the actio
of a program, instead of a way of looking at data. The operations list

operation	description
1	Write report
2	Increment rCount
3	Increment uCount
4	Increment uBatch Count
5	Reset longest Batch
6	Initialise Longest Batch
7	Initialise rCount
8	Initialise uCount
9	Initialise uBatch Count
10	Read record

Making our usual request we obtain:
(a) 'Read-ahead?'

Since we are using read-ahead we need an initial read and another
the end of PFileComponents. Since PUBatch needs read-ahead to fi
the end of the batch, we will have to provide it with a Read of its own
do this. PRRrecord will then also have to have one of its own. Thus
obtain Figure 8.26.

JRE 8.26

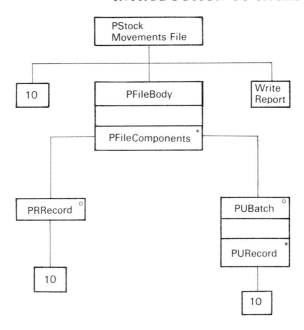

(b) 'How many times?', and (c) 'Beginning, middle or end?' give

operation	frequency	parent	position
1	Once/program	PStock Movements File	End
2	Once/PRRecord	PRRecord	Beginning
3	Once/PURecord	PURecord	Beginning
4	Once/PURecord	PURecord	Middle
5	Once/PUBatch	PUBatch	End
6	Once/program	PStock Movements File	Beginning
7	Once/program	PStock Movements File	Beginning
8	Once/program	PStock Movements File	Beginning
9	Once/batch	PUBatch	Beginning

Adding in the iteration controls and selection conditions gives the design of Figure 8.27.

FIGURE 8.27

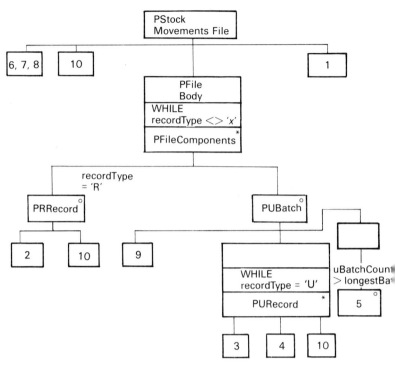

This design should now be tested for various file configuratio
including

X
U   U   X
R   X
R   R   X

While the consideration of such test data must take place, wi
Jackson's method there is no need to cater for it explicitly in our ba
program structure. As long as we ensure that the data structure
draw allows a particular data set, the design of the program will co
with that data correctly. For instance, the data structure described
Figure 8.24 allows each of the above, but will not allow such data s
as

R   X   R   R
U   4   R   X
R   U   U   R   X   U.

This type of problem is common and illustrates the power of t
approach. Even though the problem is very simple, it would not
obvious how to develop a program to cope with files of the abo
configurations if Jackson's methodology were not used.

It may be thought that the basic program structure diagram shot
always be based on the structure of the input data, but this is not alwa

the case. If, for example, the input data is a simple list, it may be preferable to base the design on the output data structure. This is illustrated by the following example.

Example 8.4 Construct a basic program structure diagram for a program to read in a file of records, where each record consists of a pair of meter readings. These are to be printed in numbered groups, where each group (except possibly the last) contains four records.

The output file is to start with a heading of 'Readings'. The input file is terminated with a sentinel of −1, −1.

Sample data: input:

	Record 1	1057	1011
	Record 2	956	023
	Record 3	881	706
and so on until . .			
	Record 10	1905	1805
	Sentinel	−1	−1

output: Readings

Group 1

1057	1011
956	023
881	706
432	401

Group 2

1321	918
1195	1066
1945	1940
1918	1914

Group 3

1895	1892
1905	1805

The input data structure is given in Figure 8.28, and the output data structure is given in Figure 8.29.

FIGURE 8.28

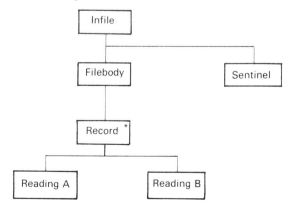

Figure 8.29 shows the way in which we must think of the data, and is easily turned into a basic program structure diagram by the insertio of suitable verbs.

FIGURE 8.29

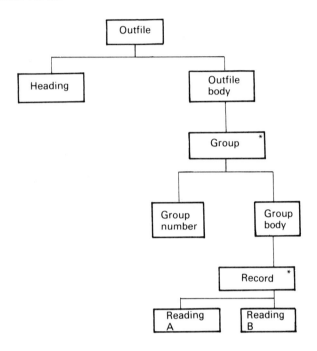

8.5 Limitations of JSP

Before leaving this section, it should be noted that it is not alwa possible to show relationships between successive data items usi structure diagrams. For instance, both sorted and unsorted files can represented as in Figure 8.30.

FIGURE 8.30

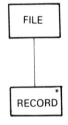

This means that Jackson's method of obtaining a basic program str ture cannot then be used. However, the techniques of drawing up operations list and asking our unusual questions:

Read-ahead?

How many times?

Beginning, middle or end?

What does this consist of?
can still be of considerable help.

We considered the use of simple top-down stepwise-refinement to obtain a top-level design in Chapter 5 and the use of subprograms in Chapter 7. Chapter 7 also demonstrated how a library of sub-programs is useful in building up programs. It should be pointed out that since yet further techniques exist, this suggests that there is no universal technique which will give a good design for all types of problems. However the above methods, combined as required, give the programmer powerful tools to deal with the problems of designing programs of many different types.

In conclusion we can summarise Jackson's fundamental procedure for program design as being:
1 draw the relevant data structure diagrams:
2 develop the most suitable of these into a basic program structure diagram;
3 use an operations list to develop the basic program structure diagram into a complete design where all the leaves are elementary operations or suitable sub-programs.

After studying this chapter, you should be able to
1 construct structure diagrams for data;
2 explain the need to relate the program structure to the data structure(s), and compare this approach with the simple top-down stepwise-refinement technique;
3 construct basic program structure diagrams based on one data structure diagram;
4 use operations lists to develop a basic program structure diagram into a full program structure diagram;
5 recognise the importance of the design of appropriate data formats by those specifying problems;
6 recognise that methods of relating basic program structure diagrams to clashing data structures are available elsewhere;
7 summarise some different techniques of program design.

8.1 Convert the design for Example 8.2 given in this chapter into a working program which should be thoroughly tested.
8.2 Amend the program developed in Exercise 8.1 to process input records having the structure shown in Figure 8.21. (Refer to Figure 8.22.)
8.3 In an election, there are 100 constituencies, each with an unknown number of candidates. The votes cast per candidate in a constituency are presented in constituency order in the form of candidate name, party name, total votes received by that candidate, and this is repeated for each candidate in the constituency. Construct a data structure diagram for this, with a view to printing for each constituency the

winning candidate, assuming there are no ties. You may add sentinels
as you think necessary.

8.4 Design and write a program to perform the requirements of
Exercise 8.3 above.

8.5 Repeat Exercise 5.5, but using the methods of this chapter.

8.6 Example 8.2 is to be amended from its original form so that a
candidate has to pass both the examination and the in-course work in
the first subject (as well as to meet the other conditions). Amend the
Assessments input file structure diagram (Figure 8.8) to incorporate
this change.

8.7 Write and test a program for the design arrived at in Exercise 8.6.

8.8 Code and test the design of Figure 8.27 for Example 8.3.

8.9 Develop Figure 8.29 into a working program for Example 8.4 and
test your solution.

8.10 In the stock-recording problem of Example 8.3, it has been
decided that changes have to be incorporated. The file is guaranteed to
contain at least one U-type record and to finish with an X-type record
but records which are not type U or R may be present. The required
additions to the report are:

   (a) all records preceding the first type U record are to be counted
and the result printed;

   (b) all records which are not of type U, R or X, and which follow the
first U-type record, are to be ignored.

Amend the data structure and design given, and code and test your
revised solution. You may assume that each record consists of a single
character.

8.11 Develop a program to read up to 10 sets of 3 strings, where each
set represents a name, the first line of an address, and the second line of
an address. These are to be printed side by side in the following format:

Name   Name
Address Line   Address Line
Address Line   Address Line

Do this

   (a) by reading in *all* the input data and storing it in arrays;

   (b) by using another approach.

Which method is the simpler?

These requirements lead to a clash between the structures of the input
data and the output data.

9 Further manipulation of sequential data

If we have an amount of data to process, we face the question: can all this data be held in the computer's store simultaneously? If the answer is 'No', then we have no option but to use files on backing storage. If the answer is 'Yes', then we may be able to hold all the data in an array. We must, however, take care; if there is only a small amount of data *now*, but it may grow into a larger amount as time goes by, then we must not be misled into using an array where the use of a file would be more appropriate.

For example, suppose we are keeping a store of goods and each record in our file consists of a part number which is the key field, and the stock level, this being the number left in our stores.

RE 9.1

Record 1	Record 2	Record 3	Record 4	Record 5
023 | 20	789 | 16	367 | 35	934 | 11	245 | 30

This file can be represented in its *abstract* state, independently of the computer, as shown in Figure 9.1, where the fields in each record are part number and quantity in stores, in that order. Such a record type could be defined in Pascal as

```
TYPE
   Goods = RECORD
              partNumber: INTEGER;
              quantity: INTEGER
           END{RECORD}
```

Records of this type could be held in an array, with some such definition as

```
TYPE
   Stocks = ARRAY[1..maxCapacity]
            OF Goods;

VAR
   stock: Stocks;
```

or we could hold them in a file, and use

```
TYPE
   Stocks = FILE OF Goods;

VAR
   stock: Stocks;
```

In the case of stocks, we would normally be dealing with a lar number, and the use of a file would be more appropriate. On the ot hand, if we were dealing with records with two similar integer fiel but whose fields indicated branch code and staff levels, it would feasible to use an array, since the number of branches would increase excessively. In this chapter, we shall be using both metho

9.1 Searching

If we want to write a *suite* (or *set*) of programs to help us administering our retail operations, it is likely that we would want to able to answer such questions as 'How many staff has branch num 789?'

The method of answering this is easy — we scan along the array u we reach a record whose *key* field (that is, the branch code) is 789; staff level field of this record will tell us that there are 16 staff at branch. (We could have achieved the same result by reading throug file of records, but, if the file had been held on backing store, would not have been feasible for more than one enquiry, since would have to start reading from the beginning of the file each tin

To be able to perform operations like this, it is necessary to be a to search arrays to locate the position of particular elements, ca *targets*.

Before we do so, however, we need to bear in mind that our sea must give a sensible result, even if the item we are looking for is no our list.

Using top-down stepwise refinement to develop our program obtain the top-level design as shown in Figure 9.2. We scan the list u we find the branch code or target we want, or until we reach the en the list. Taking suitable care over how we initialise and add 'branchIndex', so that the coding is kept as simple as possible, obtain Figure 9.3. Note that if we are going to set 'found' to TRUE when we find the target of our search, we need to set it to FALSE in the first instance.

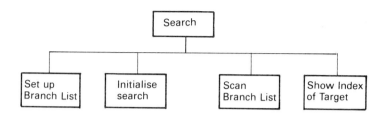

The design of Figure 9.2 can be converted to Pascal as shown in Program 9–1. In this program, the actual areas of store that we are manipulating are called 'listOfBranches', 'indexToBranches', 'requiredTarget' and 'FoundMarker'. However, what we call them is immaterial to the four procedures we have defined. The four procedures 'SetUpBranchList', 'InitialiseSearch', 'ScanBranchList' and 'ShowIndexOfTarget' make use of *parameters*, as described in Section 7.5. The *call* to the procedure 'InitialiseSearch' in the main body of the program (the part following the procedure declarations) shows that we wish to access 'foundMarker', 'indexToBranches' and 'requiredTarget'. The *definition* of the procedure 'InitialiseSearch' shows that 'found' will be taken as referring to 'foundMarker', 'branchNdx' as referring to 'indexToBranches' and 'target' as referring to 'requiredTarget'. The VAR indicates that these are variable parameters — in other words, the reference is directly to the variables themselves, whose contents may be altered by the procedure. Compare this with the formal parameter 'target' in the definition of 'ScanBranchList'.

The call in the main body of the program shows that the actual parameter 'requiredTarget' is supplied in the position corresponding to 'target', but here the procedure is only interested in the value of the actual parameter on entry; the contents of 'requiredTarget' itself are not to be changed.

PROGRAM 9–1

```
PROGRAM Ch9P1(input,output);

{Searches an array containing a list of
branches for a target}

CONST
    noOfBranches = 5;

TYPE
    Branches = RECORD
```

```
        branchCode: INTEGER;
        staffLevel: INTEGER
                END{RECORD};
    ListNdxs = 1..noOfBranches;
    Lists = ARRAY[ListNdxs]OF Branches;
    ExtendedListNdxs = 0..noOfBranches;

VAR
    listOfBranches: Lists;
    foundMarker: BOOLEAN;
    indexToBranches: ExtendedListNdxs;
    requiredTarget: INTEGER;

PROCEDURE SetUpBranchList
    (VAR branchList: Lists);
    VAR
      branchNdx: ListNdxs;
    BEGIN
      FOR
        branchNdx:= 1 TO noOfBranches
      DO
        BEGIN
          Read(branchList[branchNdx].
                branchCode,
                branchList[branchNdx].
                staffLevel)
        END
      {ENDFOR}
    END;

PROCEDURE InitialiseSearch
    (VAR found: BOOLEAN; VAR branchIndex:
     ExtendedListNdxs; VAR target:
     INTEGER);
    BEGIN
      found:= FALSE;
      branchIndex:= 0;
      WriteLn('Enter target');
      ReadLn(target)
    END;



PROCEDURE ScanBranchList
    (target: INTEGER; VAR branchList:Lists;
     VAR found: BOOLEAN; VAR branchIndex:
     ExtendedListNdxs);
```

```
      BEGIN
        WHILE
          (branchIndex < noOfBranches)
          AND
          (NOT found)
        DO
          BEGIN {Examine a branch}
            branchIndex:= branchIndex + 1;
            IF
              branchList[branchIndex].
                branchCode = target
            THEN
              BEGIN
                found:= TRUE
              END
            {ENDIF}
          END    {Examine a branch}
        {ENDWHILE}
      END;

  PROCEDURE ShowIndexOfTarget
    (found: BOOLEAN; branchIndex:
     ExtendedListNdxs; target: INTEGER);
    BEGIN
      IF
        found
      THEN
        BEGIN
          WriteLn('Branch ', target:3,
            ' found at element ',
            branchIndex:2)
        END
      ELSE
        BEGIN
          WriteLn('Branch ', target:3,
            ' not found')
        END
      {ENDIF}
    END;

BEGIN {Search}

  SetUpBranchList (listOfBranches);
  InitialiseSearch
    (foundMarker, indexToBranches,
     requiredTarget);
```

```
ScanBranchList
   (requiredTarget, listOfBranches,
    foundMarker, indexToBranches);
ShowIndexOfTarget
   (foundMarker, indexToBranches,
    requiredTarget)

END.   {Search}
```

FIGURE 9.3

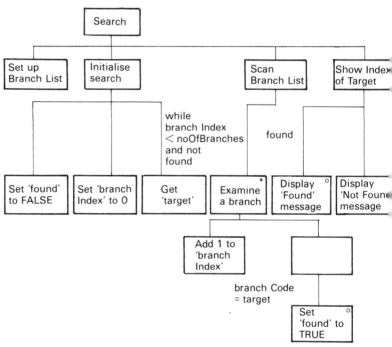

9.2 Linear search

If there are *n* elements in our list, it is reasonable to assume that we need, on average, to go half way along before we come to the item we are looking for. That means we have to do about *n*/2 comparisons. This type of search is called a *linear search*.

A slight improvement on this can be made if the keys are in order, since we can give up our search if the key is not present in the list at the point where we expect to find it.

Continuing in the context of retailing, if we use an ordered array of five branch codes as our test data, our array could be as shown in Figure 9.4. If our target is 367, we search until we reach it and display the contents of this record. If our target is 030, which is not in this list, then we search until we find the first item greater than it (that is, 245) or the end of the list, and then give up.

URE 9.4

index	1	2	3	4	5
branchList	023 20	245 30	367 35	789 16	934 11

ole   9.1   Design a subprogram 'LinearSearch' to search an ordered array of records called 'branchList' containing 'noOfBranches' elements to find the index of a target branch code, 'target'. If the target is missing, then the main program must be able to detect this and 'index' should be left pointing at the next record in the table, whose value is (or would be) greater than the target.

First we must decide on the type of subprogram to use. If we only wanted to find the position of the target we could use a function (returning the position as its value), but, since we also need to show whether the target is missing, we need to return a Boolean variable also. We shall, therefore, use a procedure.

The formal parameters will then be 'target' and 'noOfItems' as value parameters, and 'found' and 'index' as variable parameters. We will assume that the array itself is declared in the main program block. Sample data (using the data shown in Figure 9.4) is given in Figure 9.5. To cater for the case when the target is beyond the last element in the array (target = 1000), we need to set 'index' to one more than the length of the array ('noOfItems') when this occurs.

JRE 9.5

target	found	index
367	TRUE	3
250	FALSE	3
1000	FALSE	6
010	FALSE	1

The design for 'LinearSearch' is given in Figure 9.6. We shall trace this routine using a new form of trace-table, where we cross-reference the alterations in the value of the variables to the numbered elementary operations in the design diagram. Tables 9.1 and 9.2 show traces for 'target' values of 367 and 250 respectively. The cases where 'target' has the values 1000 and 010 are left as an exercise for the reader.

Table 9.1

elementary operation	target	noOf Items	past It	found	counter	index	branch Code 1	2	3	4	5
1	367	5	FALSE	FALSE	0		023	245	367	789	934
2					1						
2					2						
2					3						
3				TRUE							
5						3					

Table 9.2

elementary operation	target	noOf Items	past It	found	counter	index	branch Code 1	2	3	4	5
1		250	FALSE	FALSE	0		023	457	367	789	934
2					1						
2					2						
2					3						
3			TRUE								
5						3					

FIGURE 9.6

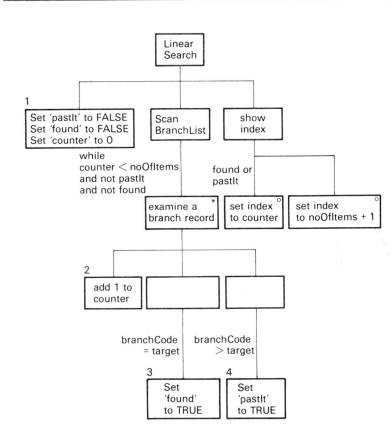

Note that had we been using an ordered serial file instead of ordered array, the same basic design would be correct. Minor chang would be the inclusion of a RESET operation in 'Initialise search' a a read operation in 'Examine a branch record', and the alteration the first test in 'Scan branchList' to check for eof. It would n however, be appropriate to return an integer value in 'index'; rath the record itself should be returned. (This could, of course, also done with an array of records.)

Exercise   9.1 Write a program to test the procedure in Figure 9.6.

Write and trace the elementary operations of a procedure to insert an element called 'newPart' into an array called 'part', which is a one-dimensional array of integers representing part numbers.

The array contains 'noOfParts' data items initially, but has been defined as containing more than 'noOfParts' elements. If 'newPart' is already in 'part', we are only required to display an error message.

  We can use the procedure 'LinearSearch' that we developed in Example 9.1, Figure 9.6, in our solution. We shall use a formal parameter called 'presentLength' to indicate the length of the section of 'part' which is used at present, and 'thisPart' will be the formal parameter corresponding to 'newPart' as far as the procedure is concerned.

Sample data:
(a)   newPart: 250
        part (initial state):

index	1	2	3	4	5	6	7
part	023	245	367	789	934	—	—

        part (final state):

index	1	2	3	4	5	6	7
part	023	245	250	367	789	934	—

(b)   newPart: 245
        display: Part number 245 is already present.
The design of 'insert' is given in Figure 9.7.

  Remember that subprograms which have been thoroughly tested can be regarded as extensions of the language, that is, as if they were elementary operations. This will apply to 'LinearSearch'. Table 9.3 shows the trace table for the first set of sample data given above; we have noted the values of some parameters and variables on entry to and return from 'LinearSearch'.

Table 9.3

elementary operation	newPart/ this Part	noOfParts/ present Length	counter	index	found	part 1	2	3	4	5	6	7
	250	5				023	245	367	789	934	–	–
1 (entry)	250	5										
1 (return)				3	FALSE							
3			5			023	245	367	789	934	934	
3			4			023	245	367	789	789	934	
3			3			023	245	367	387	789	934	
4						023	245	250	387	789	934	

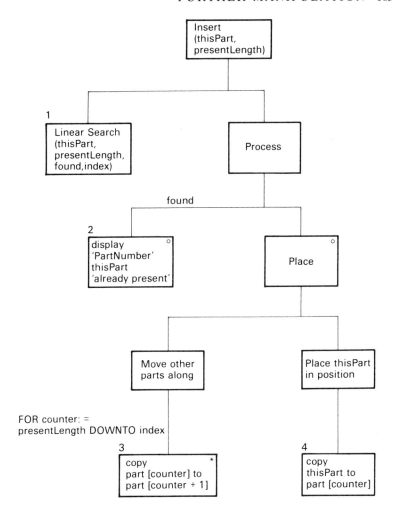

Write a program to read elements already in order into an array, and then use a procedure to insert an additional element into the correct position. Ensure your solution works when the additional element is
(a) to be the first in the array;
(b) to be the last in the array;
(c) already present — in which case, a suitable message is to be printed.

Write a program to delete an element from 'part'. Design and use a procedure called 'Delete' in your solution.

9.3 Binary search

There is a far better method of searching an ordered list of a reasonable length than using a linear search. It is called a *binary search*, and it is based on the idea of finding which side of the middle of a list the target value is on.

In developing a method of performing such a search, we shall need to find the middle of the list. This is simple if the list has an odd number of elements since the basic formula for finding the middle is

$$mid = \frac{index\ of\ first\ element + index\ of\ last\ element}{2}$$

For example, if our list is held as

Index	1	2	3	4	5
part	023	234	367	789	934

then mid $= \dfrac{1+5}{2} = 3$

However if the number of elements is uneven, we will need to round the value of 'mid' either up or down to fix on an approximately central element. Let us agree to round down. We can use the standard Pascal function 'Trunc'.

If there are N elements in our array then the top-level structure diagram is as shown in Figure 9.8 and 'Basic Binary Search' is given in Figure 9.9.

FIGURE 9.8

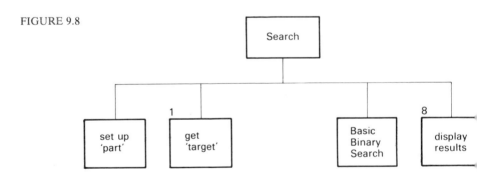

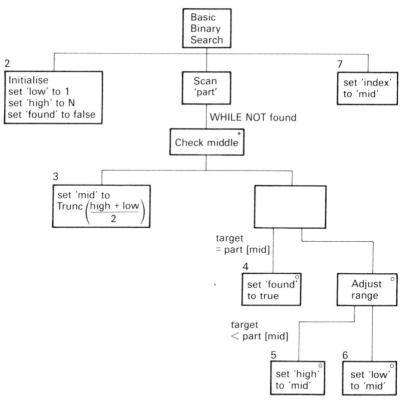

Tracing this to find the position of 234 in the list given above, and using the reference numbers written above the boxes in Figure 9.9 we have:

List

Index	1	2	3	4	5
part	023	234	367	789	934

The targetKey is 234, and N = 5. Table 9.4 shows the trace-table for this data.

Table 9.4

elementary operation	box	target	low	high	mid	index	found	comment
1	1	234						
2	2		1	5			false	
3					3			234=part [3]
5				3				
3				2				
4							true	234=part [2]
7						2		
8						2		

The number of comparisons made is representative of the efficien
of this search. The number of elements we are interested in is appro>
mately halved at each comparison, and we continue until the list is ju
one item — that is, the one we are looking for.

Let us think of this process in the reverse order. We finish with a l
of 1 item. At the previous stage, we had a list of double that length, th
is, 2. At the stage before that, the list length was double again, that is
= 4, and so on. If we double it M times in all, representing
comparisons we finish up with a list of length 2^M. If there are N items
our final list then

$$2^M = N$$

Taking logarithms to the base 10 gives

$$M \log 2 = \log N$$

$$M = \frac{\log N}{\log 2} = \frac{\log N}{0.3010} \simeq 3 \log N$$

Therefore we can say that if we have a list of N items, the bin;
search will find the position of our target in approximately

$3 \log_{10} N$

comparisons.

For example, if N is 1000, then we will only need about

$X = 3 \log 1000 = 3.3 = 9$

comparisons, which is a great improvement on the 500 needed by
linear search method.

Unfortunately, there are problems. Confirm this by performin
trace on the design of Figure 9.8 to find each of the following p
numbers:

020 , 235 , 934 , 936

Before examining the methods of overcoming these weaknes
you may wish to try to find them yourself.

Let us consider why these part numbers caused our design to fa:
1 020 and 936 were out of the range (outOfRange) of values of our
2 235 was within the range of values in the list, but was missing
other words it was not equal to part [mid] when the difference betw
'high' and 'low' is 1 at the end.
3 934 was missed since it is the last element. Suppose our list is redu
to two elements, where 'low' is 4 and 'high' is 5. Then

$$\text{mid} = \text{Trunc} \left(\frac{(\text{high} + \text{low})}{2} \right) \text{ gives Trunc} \left(\frac{(4-5)}{2} \right)$$

gives Trunc (4.5) gives 4

So we set 'low' to 4 and so on indefinitely. There are many ways of tidying up our solution. In keeping with our aim of designing simple programs we shall deal with the problems by performing initial checks on the range of values and on the last element in the array, and admitting that targetKey is missing from the array when

high −low = 1

Example 9.3 Develop a procedure, 'Binary Search', which will perform a binary search to find a target T, in an array, 'part', of length N. The procedure should return a Boolean, 'found', and a variable 'index', being either the position of the target in the array if it is present, or the position of the next element if it is not.

We can base our design on that given in Figure 9.9, with the additional checks indicated above. This leads to the design given in Figure 9.10.

FIGURE 9.10

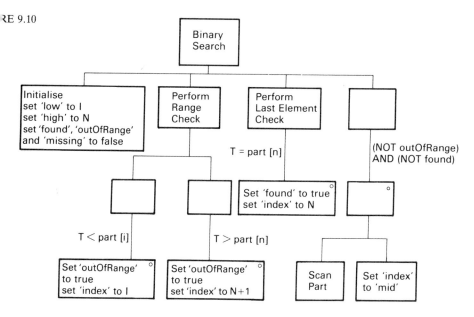

Noting that 'mid' must have a value to pass to 'index' when 'missing' or 'found' becomes true, we develop 'ScanPart' as shown in Figure 9.11.

Whilst this design has no claim to elegance, it is at least straightforward. This is just as well, since binary searches are notoriously difficult to design and code correctly.

FIGURE 9.11

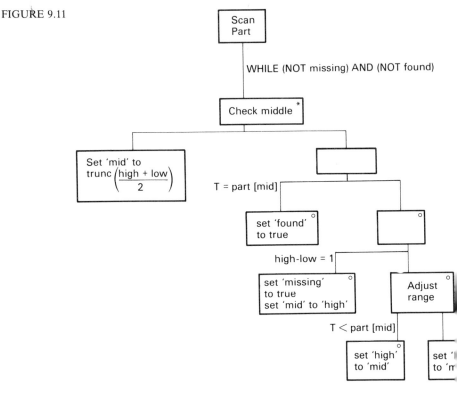

<u>Exercise 9.4</u> Code 'BinarySearch' and test it as a substitute for 'LinearSearch' your solution to Exercise 9.1. If it performs satisfactorily, you can it wherever 'LinearSearch' has been used, as the actual metho search used will be 'hidden' from the calling program.

9.4 Sorting

There are other situations in which it is necessary to keep our rec in key number order. For example, it is only efficient to search for amend a large proportion of the records in a large file if the file order.

The drawback is that it is so troublesome to sort records into or the first place that sorting can use a significant proportion o running time of a commercial computer. Consequently, a great d research into sorting methods has taken place, and standard prog for sorting can be purchased. We shall limit ourselves to two ty sort which can be used when the complete list can be held in an ar store. One is very simple, but slow. The second is more diffic understand, but it is generally a little faster. Neither method wou fast enough to be used satisfactorily with large files.

9.5 Selection sort

First let us consider a *selection* sort.

It will be recalled that in Example 6.4 we developed a fragment of code which moved the lowest element of an array to the front position. Suppose we make this into a routine called GetLowestToFront.

Repeated use of this will eventually sort an array as follows. Suppose our list is

5	4	6	2	3

Applying GetLowestToFront gives

2	5	6	4	3

the position of the last four elements being immaterial.

Applying our routine to these four elements only, gives

2	3	6	5	4

Applying it next to the last three elements gives

2	3	4	6	5

Applying it to the last two elements gives us the sorted list

2	3	4	5	6

In a structure diagram, this can be described as shown in Figure 9.12.

JRE 9.12

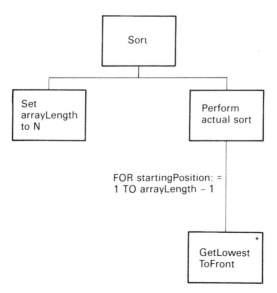

Exercise 9.5 Trace Figure 9.12 with suitable test data of your choice.

To consider how efficient a sort is we generally need to calculate how many comparisons and exchanges of data items the sort requires. These calculations are sometimes very involved, but if we make suitable approximations, a useful estimate can sometimes be achieved without great difficulty.

In this case, if the unsorted part of the array is N elements long, we will need $N - 1$ comparisons.

Then to sort a list whose total length is N, the number of comparisons is

$C =$ (comparisons needed when unsorted list has length N)
    +(comparisons needed when unsorted list has length $N - 1$) . .
    +1
$C = (N - 1) + (N - 2) + (N - 3) \ldots + 1.$
This forms an arithmetic progression whose sum is given by

$$C = \frac{(N - 1)}{2} (N - 1 + 1) = \frac{1}{2} (N^2 - N), \text{ or}$$

$$\doteq \frac{N^2}{2} \text{ if N is large.}$$

The number of interchanges required on average is not easily found but is approximately
$M = N \ln N$

(where ln stands for log to the base 'e'), if N is large.

If N is 10, C is 40 and M is about 23.
If N is 20, C is 190 and M is about 60.
If N is 100, C is about 5000 and M is about 460.

This method is called an N^2 method, since C is proportional to N^2 when N is large enough. N^2 methods are obviously poor if N is large.

9.6 Insertion sort

The *insertion sort* is also an N^2 method, but is generally an improvement on the selection sort method. It consists of inserting new elements taken one by one from an unsorted array, A, into a sorted array using a procedure based on Example 9.2 which places a new element in its correct position in an array. For convenience, let us refer to the sorted array as 'part' and assume that the number of parts given by 'numberOfParts'.

'sortLength' is the current length of 'part' at any stage. 'InsertionSort' is as shown in Figure 9.13.

FIGURE 9.13

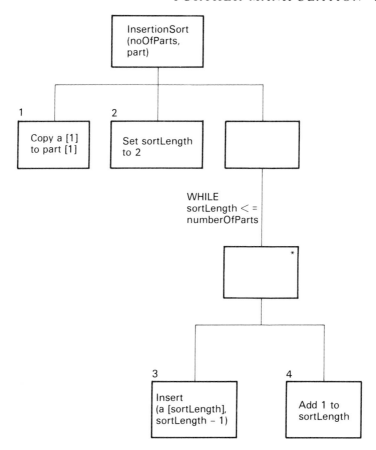

Table 9.5

element operation	sortLength	a [sortLength]	noOfParts	part [1]	[2]	[3]	[4]	[5]
			5					
1				307				
2	2							
3 (entry)	2	934		307				
3 (return)				307	934			
4	3							
3 (entry)	3	245						
3 (return)				245	307	934		
4	3							
3 (entry)	4	023						
3 (return)				023	245	307	934	
4	5							
3 (entry)	5	789						
3 (return)				023	245	307	789	934
4	6							

Example 9.4 Construct a trace-table to demonstrate the operation of th insertion sort.

Sample data:

input: Index

Index	1	2	3	4	5
a	307	934	245	023	789

output: part

part	023	245	307	789	934

Refer to Table 9.5 for the trace-table.

Exercise 9.6 Write and test a procedure to perform an insertion sort. Is there ar reason for array 'a' to be a different concrete array from the arra called 'part'?

On average, the new element will be inserted half way along the sorte array, 'part'. When 'part' has length N, the number of comparison needed is approximately $(N-1)/2$ and so to sort an array of length N we will need approximately a number of comparisons given by

$$C = 1 + \frac{2}{2} + \frac{3}{2} \cdots \frac{N-1}{2}$$

$$= \frac{(N-1)}{2} \cdot \left(1 + \frac{N-1}{2}\right) \simeq \frac{N^2}{4} \text{ if N is large.}$$

For example, if N is 100, $C \simeq 2500$.

The number of data movements in moving elements up to make roo for the new item is also close to the number of comparisons, $N-1/2$, that the total number of movements, M, is also approximately $N^2/4$

9.7 Comparison of N^2 and N log N sorts

Thus for data in random order the insertion sort only needs about ha as many comparisons as our simple selection sort. If the data is alrea in order, and we wish only to insert one more item into the array, the the insertion sort is much more efficient.

In theory, we can improve on this by using a binary search instead a linear search to find where to insert the new item. If the sorted arr has length N, then we have seen that it will take about 3 $\log_{10}$ comparisons to place the new item.

If there are N + 1 items altogether, then we shall need

$$C = 3 \log (N) + 3 \log (N-1) \ldots 3 \log (1)$$

This is obviously not going to be greater than N. 3 log (N) as there a only N terms and so we shall use this as an approximation for C. This serves to classify the insertion sort using a binary search as an 'N log (N)' method, since the number of comparisons is proportional to N log N.

If N is 20, C is approximately 20.3.1.3 = 78.
If N is 100, C is approximately 100.3.2 = 600.

This appears to be a significant improvement on the 2500 of the straight insertion method. Unfortunately, this improvement is not often worth the complexity it brings, since it leaves the number of data movements unchanged. As the time taken to make a data movement is usually longer than the time taken to make a comparison, this tends to swamp the improvement gained.

Further information on sorting can be found in 'Algorithms + Data Structures = Programs' by Wirth (see Appendix 3).

One way of reducing the time spent sorting is to choose a more efficient sort such as an 'N log N' method instead of an 'N²' method. Figure 9.14 compares values of N² and N log N for values of N up to 50. Unfortunately, these sorts are often obscure in their operation and are difficult to code. However, if we can hold all our records in *working store* in the computer's memory, without using magnetic tapes or discs, then we can sometimes improve matters if we are sorting large records by simply leaving them in whatever order they come in, and keeping a note of the required order in an array called an *access vector*. This saves the time which would have been spent moving the records about in store during a sort.

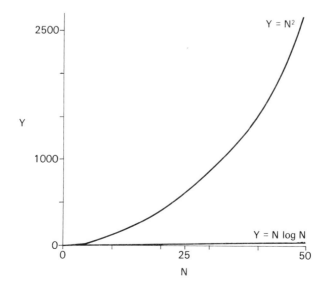

9.8 Access vectors

Let us suppose that our stock-control records have a large number of fields, making them slow to manipulate into order.

We will use the 'part' field as the key field in the following explanation of an access vector. Although the remainder of each record is large, it is irrelevant to the understanding of an access vector and will be ignored in the following explanation.

FIGURE 9.15

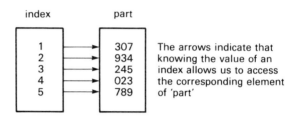

The arrows indicate that knowing the value of an index allows us to access the corresponding element of 'part'

Suppose we have stored our unsorted data in an array, as shown in Figure 9.15. We can print these in the order in which they are stored using the method of Figure 9.16. We now add an access vector 'vector' as shown in Figure 9.17.

FIGURE 9.16

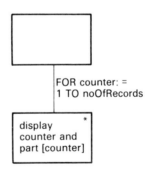

FIGURE 9.17

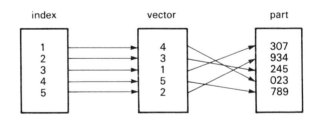

Now, the first element of the access vector is the index for the first record in alphabetic order — that part [4] which is 023. The second access vector element is 3, which points us to part [3] which is 245.

In programming terms, we can express this latter value as

part[vector[2]]

This is easily interpreted by starting at the innermost brackets. Here we have

vector[2]

which is 3, leading us to

part[3]

which is 245.
    We can now print the records in order using the method of Figure 9.18.

FIGURE 9.18

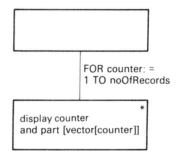

Example   9.5   Trace the operation of Figure 9.18, using the sample data of Figure 9.17.

Table 9.6

counter	vector [counter]	name printed part [vector [counter]]
1	4	023
2	3	245
3	1	307
4	5	789
5	2	934

Table 9.6 shows that the part numbers are printed in the required order. It leaves us with the problem of setting up the access vector in the right order. This is not difficult, as all we have to do when using an access vector is to
(a) use the *actual* keys in *comparisons* — for example,

```
IF
   part[vector[counter]]
        < part[vector[counter + 1]]
   THEN
        {....}
```

(b) move the access vector elements in the array, not the actual key
or records — for example,

```
vector[counter]:= vector[counter + 1]
```

 Example 9.6 Design a structure diagram for a program to read in a sequence of
5 records where each record has fields as follows:

branchCode	town	staffLevel

These records are to be stored in an array, 'branches', and an
access vector 'vector' provided to allow access to the records in
branchCode order.

The initial design 'SetUp' is given in Figure 9.19.

FIGURE 9.19

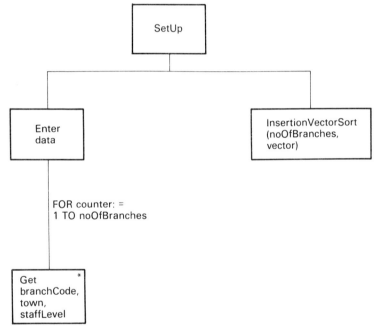

'InsertionVectorSort' (Figure 9.20) is similar to 'InsertionSort'
(Figure 9.13), but refers to the array 'vector' rather than 'part', and
uses 'InsertVector' instead of 'Insert'.

'InsertVector' (Figure 9.21) is similar to 'Insert' (Figure 9.7), but
this also refers to 'vector' rather than 'part', and also uses
'LinearVectorSearch' instead of 'LinearSearch'. We also insert the
position of the new element (presentLength + 1) into 'vector' rather
than the value of the element itself.

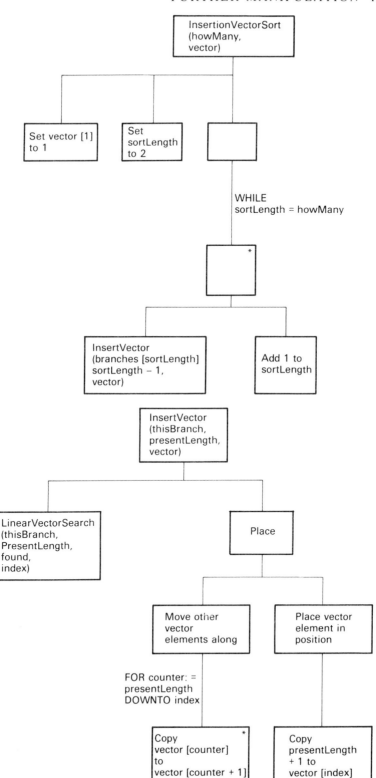

InsertionVectorSort
(howMany,
vector)

Set vector [1]
to 1

Set
sortLength
to 2

WHILE
sortLength = howMany

*

InsertVector
(branches [sortLength]
sortLength – 1,
vector)

Add 1 to
sortLength

InsertVector
(thisBranch,
presentLength,
vector)

LinearVectorSearch
(thisBranch,
PresentLength,
found,
index)

Place

Move other
vector
elements along

Place vector
element in
position

FOR counter: =
presentLength
DOWNTO index

Copy   *
vector [counter]
to
vector [counter + 1]

Copy
presentLength
+ 1 to
vector [index]

'LinearVectorSearch' (Figure 9.22) is similar to 'LinearSear
(Figure 9.6), except that we use branches [vector [counter]] in
comparisons rather than branchList [counter].

FIGURE 9.22

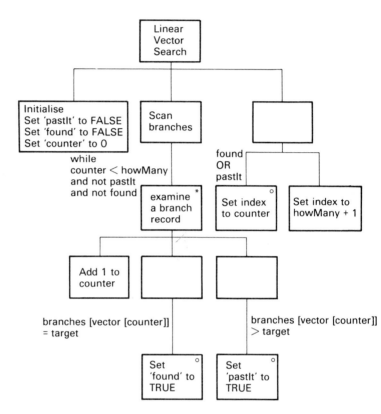

<u>Example   9.7</u> Code the design of Example 9.6.

The program is shown as Program 9–2. Once an array and an ac
vector have been set up as in Example 9.6, it is straightforward to u
procedure based on 'LinearVectorSearch' to find the position
record with a particular branch code in the array, and then to disp
information derived from this record, or to alter a field contair
information such as the staff level.

PROGRAM 9–2

```
PROGRAM Ch9P2(input,output);

{Searches an array containing a list of
branches for a target}

CONST
  noOfItems = 5;
  limit = 6;
```

```
TYPE
  Branches = RECORD
     branchCode: INTEGER;
     staffLevel: INTEGER
              END{RECORD};
  ListNdxs = 1..noOfItems;
  Lists = ARRAY[ListNdxs]OF Branches;
  ExtendedListNdxs = 0..noOfItems;
  ListExtended = 1..limit;

VAR
  listOfBranches: Lists;
  foundMarker,
  pastItMarker: BOOLEAN;
  branchCounter: ExtendedListNdxs;
  targetBranch: INTEGER;
  branchIndex: ListExtended;

{... SetUpBranchList defined here ...}

PROCEDURE InitialiseSearch
  (VAR pastIt, found: BOOLEAN;
   VAR counter: ExtendedListNdxs;
   VAR target: INTEGER);
  BEGIN
    pastIt:= FALSE;
    found:= FALSE;
    counter:= 0;
    WriteLn('Enter target');
    ReadLn(target)
  END;



PROCEDURE ScanBranchList
 (target: INTEGER; VAR branchList:Lists;
  VAR pastIt, found: BOOLEAN;
  VAR counter: ExtendedListNdxs);
  BEGIN
    WHILE
      (counter < noOfItems)
      AND
      (NOT pastIt)
      AND
      (NOT found)
    DO
      BEGIN {Examine a branch}
        counter:= counter + 1;
```

```
                  IF
                    branchList[counter].
                       branchCode = target
                  THEN
                    BEGIN
                      found:= TRUE
                    END;
                  {ENDIF}
                  IF
                    branchList[counter].
                       branchCode > target
                  THEN
                    BEGIN
                      pastIt:= TRUE
                    END
                  {ENDIF}
                END   {Examine a branch}
              {ENDWHILE}
          END;

    PROCEDURE ShowIndex
      (found, pastIt: BOOLEAN;
       counter: ExtendedListNdxs;
       index: ListExtended);
      BEGIN
        IF
          found OR pastIt
        THEN
          BEGIN
            index:= counter
          END
        ELSE
          BEGIN
            index:= noOfItems + 1
          END
        {ENDIF}
      END;




      BEGIN {Linear search}

        SetUpBranchList (listOfBranches);
        InitialiseSearch
          (pastItMarker, foundMarker,
           branchCounter, targetBranch);
```

```
ScanBranchList
  (targetBranch, listOfBranches,
  pastItMarker, foundMarker,
  branchCounter);
ShowIndex
  (foundMarker, pastItMarker,
  branchCounter, branchIndex)

END.   {Linear search}
```

9.9 Serial file update

In general, there will not be enough working storage space for us to hold the complete set of records concerning a related collection of items at any one time. We are constrained to hold such a collection of records as a *file* on backing storage. To alter such data, we need to be able to read in a record from an input file holding the original data, and then to amend it, if necessary, before writing it to an output file. By dealing with one record at a time, we can update very large files without running out of storage on the computer.

This technique is known as a *serial file update* and clearly requires at least two files to be available, or *open*, at the same time. Since the required changes, or *transactions*, are commonly held on a file also, then we need three files open. This precludes us from using cassette tapes with an ordinary microcomputer, but presents no problems if we are using one or more floppy discs, or if we are using a larger computer. The records on all three files need to be sorted into the same order using a *key* field, so that they are all *serial-sequential* files.

There are three operations that we will consider carrying out:
1 inserting a new record;
2 deleting an existing record;
3 altering an existing record.

Let us suppose that we have a sequential file, 'telephone1', containing telephone directory information. The required changes are held in the same order in a file called 'phoneUpdate'. By having both files in the same order, we can make our changes as we go along, without having to refer back to an earlier record in the file — which is not practical anyway. The updated information will be placed in a file called 'telephone2'.

We shall find it convenient to refer to the files 'telephone1', 'phoneUpdate' and 'telephone2' as 'oldMaster', 'transactions' and 'newMaster' respectively, since files being processed are often given names similar to these.

The serial file update is rather a difficult program to write, partly because we need to read-ahead in 'oldMaster' when processing insertions, but do not need to read-ahead to find the end of the file itself since we could use the 'EOF' function. The simplest way of dealing with this is not to use 'EOF', but to provide a sentinel on each file by guaranteeing a dummy record with the highest or last key possible, say 'zzzz' for an alphabetic field using the ASCII code. This key must be reserved for this purpose.

If we look at both files at any time, and note which one is presenting the record with the lower key to us, we can make some useful deductions. In particular, if the 'oldMaster' file has the record with the lower key and the keys are different, then there is no matching 'transactions' file record, and all we have to do is to transfer the 'oldMaster' record to the 'newMaster' file. Otherwise, if it is the 'transactions' file record that has the lower key and the keys are different, it means that the 'transactions' file key is not on the 'oldMaster' file, and so we must insert the 'transactions' file record in the 'newMaster' file. (This assumes, of course, that the transaction data is correct.)

If the next key on both files is the same, and is not the sentinel 'zzzz' we will need to decide whether we wish to delete or to amend the 'oldMaster' record.

If it is to be deleted, we merely decline to write it to the 'newMaster' file, and carry on. If it is to be amended, we carry the amendment from the 'transactions' file record to the 'newMaster' file. Notice how the value of the next lower key we come to has been used in all our major decisions. If the next lower key we find is the sentinel, we have reached the end of the file with the lower key.

We can choose between the options available if we have used a *tag field* in each 'transactions' record. The layout of the fields following the tag field in a record depends on the current value of the tag field. Our 'transactions' record could have been declared with the following TYPE:

```
TransactionRecs =
  RECORD
    surname: String;
    CASE transType: CHAR OF
      'D':();
      'X':(
            {.... remaining fields ....}
          )
  END{RECORD}
```

where *String* has been previously defined. This indicates that a record may consist simply of the surname-string followed by a code of 'D' for 'delete': since the surname is the key field, the remainder of the information is redundant in a deletion transaction. Alternatively, the record may consist of the surname, followed by a code of 'X', followed by the remaining fields as described.

In the sample data in Figures 9.23 and 9.24, only the relevant fields of the records are shown, as the other data does not affect the design of the program. The input files are shown as Figure 9.23 and we form the updated output file by making the changes specified by 'PhoneUpdate' to 'telephone1'.

For instance, we insert 'Croston', delete 'Headon' and alter 'Jones'. The resulting output file is shown as Figure 9.24.

FIGURE 9.23

telephone1 (oldMaster)		phoneUpdate (transactions)

surname		surname	transtype
Headon		Croston	X
Jackson		Headon	D
Jones		Jones	X
Mayoh		Scott	X
Zealand		zzzz	
zzzz			

FIGURE 9.24

telephone2 (newMaster)

surname
Croston
Jackson
Jones (amended)
Mayoh
Scott
Zealand
zzzz

We can draw the 'oldMaster' and 'newMaster' file structures as in Figure 9.25 and 9.26, and the 'transactions' file structure is as in Figure 9.27.

FIGURE 9.25

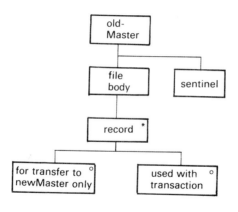

FIGURE 9.26

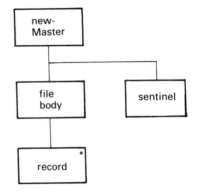

FIGURE 9.27

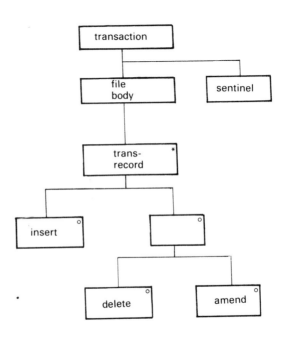

The 'newMaster' file structure is simple in that all we have to do is
ensure that the output file consists of records, and is terminated with
sentinel. This will be easily incorporated into an outline structu
diagram based on the two more complicated data structures. We no
that the data item called 'oldRecord' in the 'oldMaster' data structu
must interact with the one called 'transRecord' in the 'transaction
data structure. The components can then be combined quite natural
to form 'PNextItem' as shown in Figure 9.28. (We use 'P . . .' as a
abbreviation for 'Process . . .'.)

RE 9.28

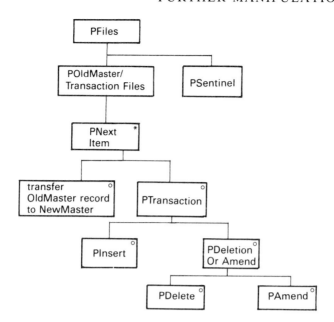

We can now draw up the following operations list:

1 RESET input files
2 REWRITE output file
3 Read oldRecord from oldMaster file
4 Read transRecord from transactions file
5 Write oldRecord to newMaster file
6 Write transRecord to newMaster file
7 Set nextSurname to lower-value surname from those in oldMaster and transactions files; if they are equal, take it from oldMaster file
8 Write sentinel record to newMaster.

9.7 Write and run a program to set up the file 'transactions'.

9.8 Allocate operations 1, 2, 5, 6 to the outline structure diagram of Figure 9.28.

Operation 7 (setting 'nextSurname') is used in determining when the end of the input files are reached, and in all the major decisions, and so should be set up in the usual read-ahead positions. Whenever a process (such as 'PInsert') is carried out, we deal with at least one of 'oldRecord' and 'transRecord', and these have to be replaced before 'nextSurname' can be identified again. The exact replacement needed depends on the processing to be carried out, and must therefore be done in the relevant process. This is done in Example 9.7, but the reader should try the problem before examining the solution in Figure 9.29.

FIGURE 9.29

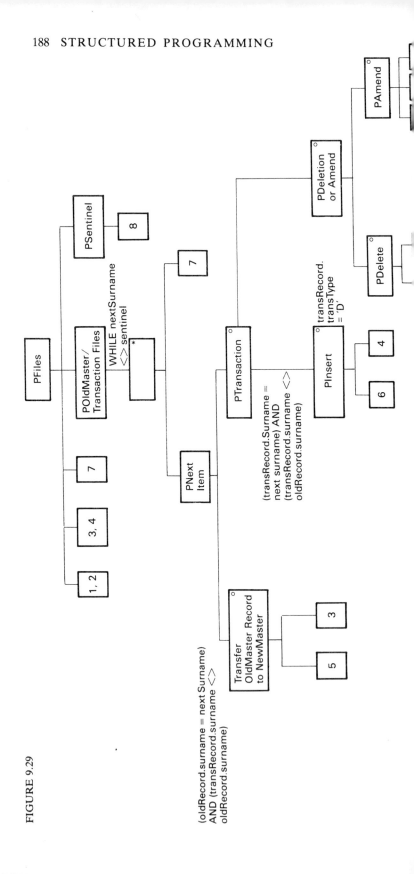

9.8 Complete the design of Figure 9.28, including all conditions.

The complete design is given in Figure 9.29.

Note that it is not necessary to test for end-of-file at any stage, because the sentinel records are guaranteed to be present.

9.9 Trace Figure 9.29 with the test data provided, and with data of your own choice.

We have assumed throughout the above examples that there are no errors or inconsistencies in the files and data we are using. We shall discuss ways of making our program more robust against these dangers in Chapter 10. Nor have we dealt with files where there are several transactions with a particular key, but the above techniques provide a firm foundation for future developments.

After studying this chapter, you should be able to

1 perform linear and binary searches on arrays;
2 use procedures as elementary operations;
3 compare the efficiency of linear and binary searches;
4 sort arrays using two methods;
5 discuss the efficiency of the sorting methods described;
6 explain the need for an access vector;
7 use an access vector in maintaining an array of data;
8 update (that is, make insertions to, make deletions from, and amend) a serial-sequential file, using a transaction file in the same order.

9.10 It is claimed that the design of Figure 9.30 performs a binary search to find a target in an array x which has n elements. Test the claim and code and run the design.

If 'set low to 1' is replaced by 'set low to 2', what happens?

9.11 Design and test a routine to insert a record into a file held as a concrete array with an access vector. You should use a binary search and provide a suitable error message if the target is already present in the array.

9.12 Design and test routines to
(a) locate,
(b) amend,
(c) insert,
(d) delete,
(e) list in order
records from a set of data held in store as an array with an access vector.

FIGURE 9.30

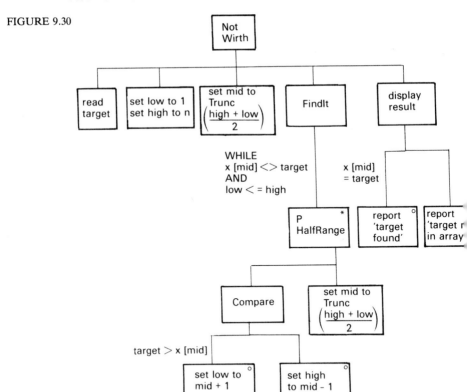

10 Data vetting and backtracking

Data vetting or *validation* is concerned with checking the quality of the data presented to a computer for processing. If the data read in is in some way faulty, then the program will often need to inform the user of this instead of processing it in the usual way. As was stated at the beginning of this book, a good program should cope with incorrect data in an appropriate way, and its ability to do this is often a good indication of the program's quality. The importance of having an effective routine to vet the data in a program is often such that it becomes a major part of the program.

If a suite of programs is used in a data-processing system, then all the data entering the system should be vetted, so that the data-vet routines form a fence around the system to prevent its corruption by faulty data.

10.1 Data classification

We can consider a set of data as consisting entirely of three subsets.

Good data	which will be processed normally,
Error data	which will be detected and reported or otherwise dealt with in an acceptable way,
Invalid data	which will have unpredictable or unacceptable consequences.

The first two sets constitute the set of *valid data*, and the aim of the programmer should be to increase the size of this set to be as large as is practically possible.

The data can be represented in a structure diagram as shown in Figure 10.1.

When error data is easily detected, it is convenient to base the data structure for the data which our program will process appropriately on the design of Figure 10.2. This often leads to a basic program structure diagram using a routine such as CheckData, and has the form shown in Figure 10.3.

FIGURE 10.1

FIGURE 10.2

FIGURE 10.3

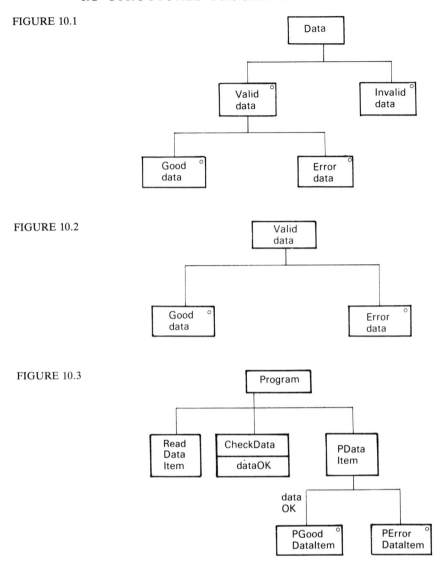

Exercise 10.1 Develop Figure 10.3 to deal with the case where dataItems are recin a file which is terminated by a sentinel. Attempt to identify
invalid data item with respect to your solution.

In the less general case where we wish to process a file of data ite
terminated by a sentinel, and merely to report or to ignore the e
items, we can use a routine similar to GetGoodData, as in Figure 1
to acquire good data items for processing.

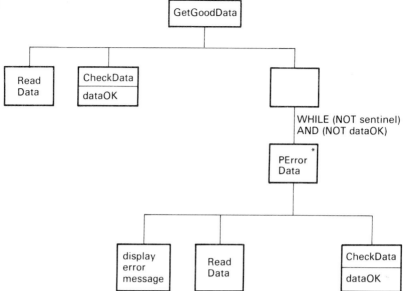

The types of check that can be built into CheckData are illustrated by the following examples.

10.2 Data validation techniques

Range validity
Suppose that a number representing a percentage mark in an examination is to be processed. The program should include a construct which will test the range validity such as that shown in Figure 10.5. We could code this as in Pascal Fragment 10–1,

PASCAL FRAGMENT 10–1

```
IF
  (mark >= minMark)
  AND
  (mark <= maxMark)
{....}
```

but we could also code it in what some might consider a more elegant form by using a set constructor, as in Pascal Fragment 10–2.

PASCAL FRAGMENT 10–2

```
IF
  mark IN [minMark..maxMark]
{....}
```

FIGURE 10.5

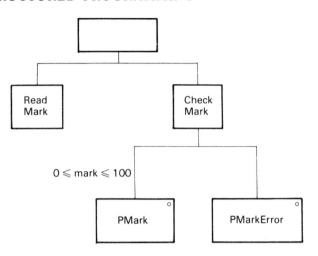

Incorrect field lengths and incorrect numeric fields
The former occurs when (say) the data contains a seven-digit num
which is meant to be stored in a six-digit data field, or when the d
contains a five-digit number in the same circumstances, follow
immediately by a non-numeric character.

An incorrect numeric field contains characters which do not fo
part of a number — perhaps 4I for 41 or 6OO for 600. These overlap
course: a program looking for a six-digit date followed by a six-let
name which finds 18065DAVIES may take the date as 18065D —
incorrect numeric field; however, if we are using a language l
Pascal, which will stop at the first non-numeric character, it may t
the date as 18065 — an incorrect field length.

There is only one foolproof way of trapping these types of erro
numeric data, and that is to treat it in three stages:

assume that the data is in character form, and read it one character
time;
examine each character and check that it is numeric;
convert the set of characters to a number.

Pascal Fragment 10–3 will perform these operations for us. It conv
a character string held in 'cSource' to a positive integer hel
'iDestination'. If any non-numeric characters are found, the Bool
variable 'valid' is set *false* and the loop terminates. The struc
diagram is shown in Figure 10.6.

FIGURE 10.6

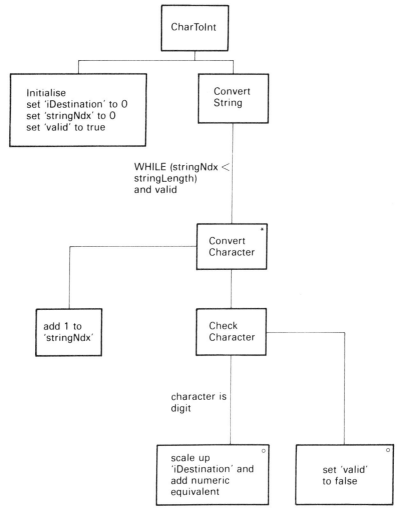

PASCAL FRAGMENT 10–3

```
PROCEDURE CharToInt(stringLength:
  INTEGER; valid:BOOLEAN;
  VAR cSource: String; VAR iDestination:
  INTEGER);

{CharToInt routine
 Converts character string of length
 stringLength in array cSource to a
 positive integer in iDestination}

VAR
  stringNdx: INTEGER;
```

```
BEGIN
  iDestination:= 0;
  stringNdx:= 0;
  valid:= TRUE;

  WHILE
    (stringNdx < stringLength) AND valid
  DO
    BEGIN
      stringNdx:= stringNdx + 1;
      IF
        cSource[stringNdx] IN ['0'..'9']
      THEN
        BEGIN
          iDestination:=
            iDestination * 10 +
          Ord(cSource[stringNdx])-Ord('0')
        END
      ELSE
        BEGIN
          valid:= FALSE
        END
      {ENDIF}
    END
  {ENDWHILE}
END
```

The expression

$$Ord(cSource[stringNdx])-Ord('0')$$

may require some explanation. The function 'Ord', when used with a character, gives that character's numerical value in the character set being used. Suppose cSource [stringNdx] contains '2' and we are using the ASCII character set. Consulting Appendix 2, we see that the ASCII code for '2' has a value of 32 in hexadecimal or 50 in decimal, and the ASCII code for '0' has a value of 30 in hexadecimal or 48 in decimal. Hence

$$Ord(cSource[stringNdx])-Ord('0')$$

equals 50–48 which equals 2 in decimal.

Character validity
Suppose that a field representing a part-reference in a stock control system is meant to contain only capital letters, digits, and possibly a hyphen. The presence of any other character means that the part-

reference is incorrect. A character validity check is required to pick out incorrect characters.

We can easily do this in Pascal by using a set constructor within a loop. In fact, we used just this technique above, when we were testing for digits only. See Pascal Fragment 10–4.

PASCAL FRAGMENT 10–4

```
FOR
  partRefNdx:= 1 TO partRefLength
DO
  BEGIN
    IF
    (partRef[partRefNdx] IN ['A'..'Z'])
    OR
    (partRef[partRefNdx] IN ['0'..'9'])
    OR
    (partRef[partRefNdx] = '-')
{....}
```

cise 10.2 Write a fragment of Pascal that accepts only spaces and 0 to 9 as valid characters.

Illogical data

It is possible for each field in a record to be correct in itself, but to be obviously incorrect when taken in conjunction with another field. This is described as illogical data.

For example, a pupil's record may contain a 'date of birth' field, and a 'date of joining school' field. The following is obviously incorrect.

Date of birth   Date of joining school

| 08 | 01 | 66 | | 12 | 09 | 62 |

Suitable checks have to be recognised and implemented by the program designer.

Invalid dates

Dates are often held as a string of six characters. For instance, 030179 represents 3rd January 1979. A program reading in dates in this format needs to check that dates such as 310479 or 290286 or 290200, which are invalid, are not accepted as good data. (Years ending in 00 are not all leap years.)

If the date is held in a six-character string, we first need to convert it to an integer. We can do this using the 'CharToInt' routine described above. If we ignore leap years, the code to check the integer might look something like Pascal Fragment 10–5.

PASCAL FRAGMENT 10–5

```
valid:= FALSE;
day:= date DIV 10000;
month:= (date DIV 100) MOD 100;
valid:= (month IN [1..12])AND (day > 0);
IF
  valid
THEN
  BEGIN
    CASE
      month
    OF
      1,3,5,7,8,10,12:
        BEGIN
          valid:= day <= 31
        END;
      2:BEGIN
          valid:= day <= 28
        END;
      4,6,9,11:
        BEGIN
          valid:= day <= 30
        END
    END{CASE}
  END
{ENDIF}
```

Exercise 10.3 Modify fragment 10–5 to cope with leap years, assuming that the year is given as 4 digits. (Leap years are those which are exactly divisible by 4, but not by 100, except when they are exactly divisible by 400.)

Before leaving dates, it should be noted that the normal American format for dates is month, day, year — which can sometimes cause confusion when using American software. European dates can be compared if the day and year parts are interchanged, so that 120583 representing 12th May, 1983 becomes 830512. This is then greater than the representation for 20th April 1982, which is 820420, and so we can easily decide which is the earlier date of the two.

Check digits

Errors in keying in data are inevitable, and can have serious consequences. For instance, a sum of money could be paid into an account with reference number 43175 instead of the one whose reference number is 41375, due to the operator transposing the second and third digits. The use of *check digits* makes this sort of error nearly impossible.

Let us consider how this system works when applied to the International Standard Book Number (ISBN) which publishers and others use to identify books.

340   26899   9

is a typical ISBN. The final digit is the check digit. To find this, the first digit is multiplied by 9, the second by 8 and so on for the first 8 digits. The resulting numbers are added together giving

$$(3 \times 9) + (4 \times 8) + (0 \times 7) + (2 \times 6) + (6 \times 5) + (8 \times 4) + (9 \times 3) + (9 \times 2) = 178$$

The next step is to add on the final digit — the check digit — to this to give a result which is exactly divisible by 11. The required digit is 9 in this case since

$$178 + 9 = 187$$

and $11 \times 17 = 187$

Now suppose a mistake results in

340   26899   9

being entered as

340   26889   9

We check this by performing multiplications and additions as above, and seeing if the result is exactly divisible by 11.

$$(3 \times 9) + (4 \times 8) + (0 \times 7) + (2 \times 6) + (6 \times 5) + (8 \times 4) + (8 \times 3) + (9 \times 2) + 9 = 184$$

As this is not exactly divisible by 11, the error can be detected. This example shows how the 'modulus 11' check-digit system works. It is not absolutely foolproof, but it will detect all cases where adjacent digits are switched, and all cases where digits are accidentally repeated. About nine out of ten random errors will be found.

   It should be noted that a check digit of X merely represents 10 — the Roman numeral being preferred to its hexadecimal equivalent of A.

―――――
e   10.4 Are the following ISBNs valid?
   (a) 86238 011 1
   (b) 905433 25 7
   (c) 340 36448 3

Incorrect quantity of data
We have already encountered the problem of incorrect quantity of data in Exercise 4.14.

In that question, the supposed sum of the data items entered is cal a *checksum* and is derived elsewhere — probably by an independ person. This is checked against the actual sum of the items entered guard against additional items being inserted into the data, or exist items being removed from the data, either mistakenly or dishones Further, although 5 data items were expected, this was not rel upon, and the actual number entered was also checked.

The problem of checking for missing or extra items of data difficult one, particularly where interactive programs are be designed. The use of *files* of fixed-format *records* can alleviate problem in batch mode. The techniques described above can be u to check data as it is entered on an interactive system. If the dat suspect, the program can interrogate the keyboard user about it either case, if read-ahead is being used, it is difficult to cope sensib a recognisable sentinel is not supplied. Some of these problems addressed in Sections 10.5 and 10.6

A set of procedures based on the above techniques should be par every serious programmer's tool kit, so that the standard of e individual's programming can be raised from amateur to professio

Complications arise when the correctness of the data is not ea ascertained, as in the following example.

Example 10.1 *Develop a program to input a record consisting of three numbe x, y and z. Print their squares if y and z are valid. For y to be val must be less than a certain limit which depends on the value and is calculated by a complicated function YLimit(x), wh takes half an hour to execute. Similarly, z must be less than a li given by an equally lengthy function ZLimit(y).*

An error message is to be printed if y or z exceed their limit

Obviously we will wish to abandon the processing the moment detect an error. We could draw the data structure as shown in Fig 10.7. This diagram is strictly structured but it is rather complex for s a simple problem, and it will lead to an over complicated basic prog structure diagram.

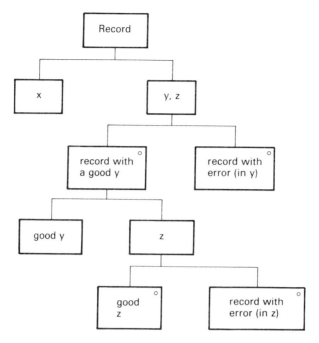

10.3 Backtracking: posit/quit/admit

Jackson's *backtracking* technique avoids the complexities which Figure 10.7 leads to. It uses an instruction which does not conform to our structured programming components and has not appeared in any of our designs. This is the *unconditional branch*, or GOTO statement.

Some authorities point out, quite correctly, that all programs can be designed without a single GOTO, which leads to a program which can be read through from start to finish with no jumping about and which is therefore relatively easy to understand.

Some go so far as to insist that GOTO is never used in the design of a program, and that it should not even be provided in a language which has the components necessary for structured programming. Others, such as Professor Dijkstra, who is one of the originators of structured programming, do not go as far as this and merely say that GOTO is undesirable. Michael Jackson maintains that one of the fundamental aims of good programming is to produce programs which are easily understood, and that there are circumstances where GOTO if properly used is a help, not a hindrance.

The way in which GOTOs are used in backtracking is strictly controlled, and hence all GOTOs in a program will be used in a standard manner which will be readily recognised by all programmers using the technique. Their very appearance in a program will set a programmer on guard, and this helps to ensure that GOTOs are used only with the greatest care.

Backtracking may be used in all cases where a process may
abandoned before it runs its full course. It consists of three sim
steps. The steps must be done one at a time, and not mixed togeth

step 1 Assume you can tell from the start which of two processes (
example, PGoodData, PErrorData) your program carries out, a
design the program fully.

step 2 Accept that you cannot really choose correctly beforeh
which process you need, and build in the required checks so you
abandon one and go on to the other if required.

step 3 Examine the side effects of abandoning a process, and deal w
the unacceptable ones.

The second step is usually described more formally using th
technical terms:

posit   to propose the hypothesis that a particular process is the
          required.

quit   to abandon a process, (such as, for example, the posited p
          cess).

admit to enter a process on quitting a posited process.

We shall now apply backtracking to our x, y, z problem of Exam
10.1.

step 1 We assume that we can identify good and error records from
start. The input data structure is now drawn — much more simply t
in Figure 10.7 — as shown in Figure 10.8.

FIGURE 10.8

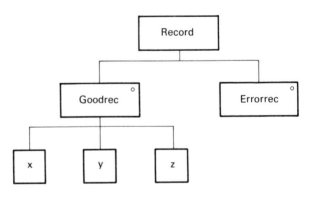

Note that we do not define every possible type of errorRec. Al
have to do is to define a goodRec. We do not have to specify y and
being 'good' in this diagram. If they were not, they would no
components of goodRec. Records which are not goodRecs are
automatically errorRecs. As the processing of goodRec is very (

we can go straight on and produce the following program structure diagram. (In larger examples, we will need to draw a basic program structure diagram and an operations list, and then to allocate the operations in the usual way.)

Our basic program structure is shown in Figure 10.9.

ЗURE 10.9

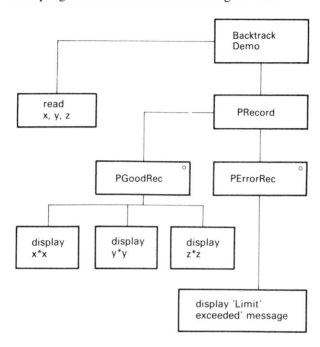

It will be seen that we are assuming that we can choose between the process of PGoodRec and PErrorRec.

step 2 Remove the selection between the two main processes and 'Posit goodRec'; build in the *checks* and *quits*, and be prepared to 'Admit errorRec'.

This leads to the design of Figure 10.10.

Notice that when we have successfully carried out 'Posit goodRec', we do not need to 'Admit errorRec', and hence we *quit* the PRecord operation completely.

step 3 This is the actual 'backtracking' part where we go back over what we have done to deal with the side effects of introducing the *quits*.

Side effects are the consequences of the parts of 'Posit goodRec' that we will have carried out before we have to *quit* it due to failing a check. Some side effects can be useful, or neutral, but some are unacceptable. In this example, we are going to display the squares of x, y and z only if all are valid, and so we have to reposition the operations to display the squares so that they can only be carried out if all the checks are successfully completed. It is important that we should not be concerned with side effects during step 2, so as to avoid undue complication.

The final structure diagram is shown in Figure 10.11.

FIGURE 10.10

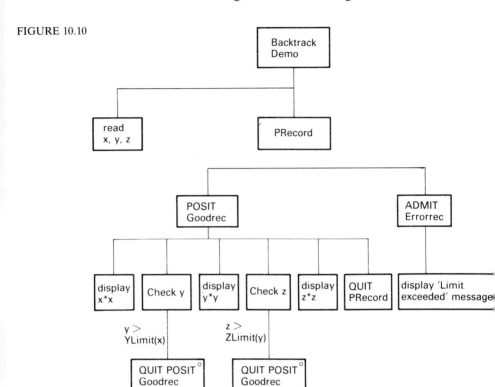

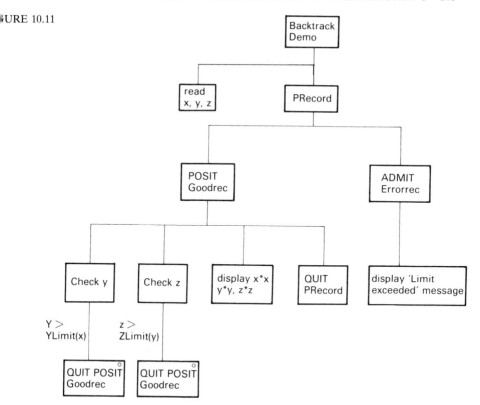

Before we can convert this design into Pascal (using dummy functions for YLimit and ZLimit), we need to examine how *quit* can be implemented using the Pascal GOTO construction.

10.4 GOTO in Pascal

A jump in Pascal is achieved by a statement such as

GOTO 100

The number following the keyword GOTO, which must be an unsigned integer, is called a *label*. Like any label, it has no inherent significance; it is used simply as a marker. The above statement jumps, or transfers control, to the statement labelled

100:

Labels, like constants, types, and variables, must be declared before they can be used. Since they have no inherent value, only their form need be specified. This is done in a section headed LABEL, which must precede other types of declaration.

We can now construct Program 10–1. Notice how, using this method

of backtracking, at least two labels will always be required. Notice als
that an END statement can be labelled.

It may seem in this case that backtracking is rather a complicate
way of dealing with a simple problem. It must be emphasised that
works equally easily with problems which could otherwise be ver
complex, and that it is the *only* technique we have covered whic
allows a GOTO (or *quit*) to appear in the structured design. Henc
quit must *not* be used except in backtracking.

Notice also that it is inadvisable to make 'Posit goodRec' and 'Adm
errorRec' into separate procedures. If we are obliged to use GOT
statements, then we should produce code where their effect can easi
be judged.

It should also be recalled that we should *never* quit a FOR-typ
iteration, since the effect of doing this is undefined. In any cas
FOR-type iterations should be used only when we know how mar
times we are to carry out an operation. If there is *any* chance of quittir
an iteration, then we do *not* know how many times the operation is
be executed.

PROGRAM 10–1

```
PROGRAM Ch10P1(input, output);

LABEL
  200,
  300;

VAR
  x,
  y,
  z: INTEGER;

FUNCTION YLimit(a: INTEGER): INTEGER;
  BEGIN
    YLimit:= 0
    { dummy statement in place of
      some complicated code to check
      the given parameter }
  END;

FUNCTION ZLimit(b: INTEGER): INTEGER;
  BEGIN
    ZLimit:= 0
    { dummy statement in place of
      some complicated code to check
      the given parameter }
  END;
```

```
BEGIN {Backtrack Demo}

   Read(x, y, z);

   { PRecord }

   { Posit goodRec }
   IF      {Check Y}
     y > YLimit(x)
   THEN
     BEGIN
       GOTO 200 {Quit Posit goodRec}
     END;
   {ENDIF} {Check Y}

   IF      {Check Z}
     z > ZLimit(x)
   THEN
     BEGIN
       GOTO 200 {Quit Posit goodRec}
     END;
   {ENDIF} {Check Z}

   WriteLn(x * X:15, y * y:15, z * z:15);
   GOTO 300;     {Quit PRecord}

200: {Admit errorRec}
   WriteLn('Limit exceeded')

300:
END.   {Backtrack Demo}
```

Another example of where we could abandon one process in favour of another was encountered in the search of Figures 9.2 and 9.3, where we gave up our linear search of an unordered array, 'branchList' when we had found our target. We achieved this by setting a Boolean variable, 'found', to true when appropriate, and using an iteration control statement of

```
WHILE
   (branchIndex < noOfBranches)
   AND
   (NOT found)
```

le 10.2 This example uses backtracking to develop a procedure to perform a linear search on an unsorted array, 'part', for the 'position' of a 'target'. The variable names correspond to those in 'LinearSearch' (Figure 9.6).

Solution

step 1 Assume that we can tell from the start if the target is present or not.

The data structure is as shown in Figure 10.12. This is more helpful than it seems, and using this with suitable operations leads us to the design of Figure 10.13.

FIGURE 10.12

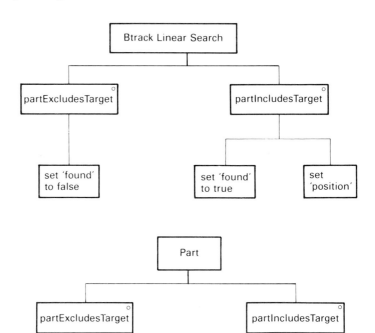

FIGURE 10.13

step 2 Remove the selection between the two main operations and

Posit partExcludesTarget

write in the Checks and Quits and be prepared to

Admit partIncludesTarget

This leads to the design of Figure 10.14.

step 3 Deal with side effects of abandoning Posit partExcludesTarget In this example there is a beneficial side effect in that the value of 'partNdx' when the target is found can be used to set 'position' to its appropriate value.

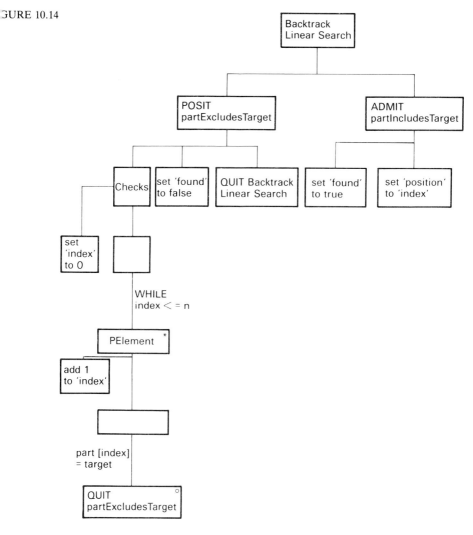

Exercise 10.5   Write a program to test the design of Figure 10.14.

Exercise 10.6   A file of records concerning pupils' performance is to be keyed into a computer, and printed one record per line. The record layout is

Record Type, Name, Exam percentage

The Record Type should always be a '1', whilst the Exam percentage should be between 000 and 100 inclusive.

Unfortunately there are errors in the data, with some records having incorrect fields, although there are none with missing or extra fields. In the case of an erroneous record the message, 'ERROR'. followed by the name field as keyed in, is to be printed.

The file is terminated by a sentinel record.

Use backtracking to develop a program to perform this operation.

FIGURE 10.15

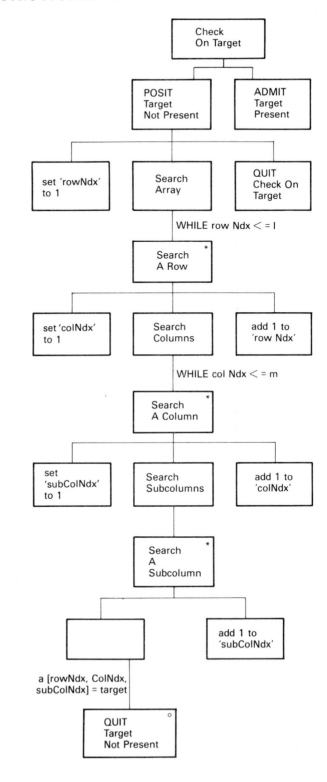

If backtracking is not used then large and clumsy Boolean expressions can arise in iteration control statements when we wish to abandon a set of nested loops on encountering a particular condition in the innermost loop. This could occur in searching a multidimensional array to find the indexes of first occurrence of a particular element, as in the following exercise.

<table>
<tr><td>e 10.3</td><td>'a' is a 3-dimensional array, where there are l rows and m columns, and each column contains n subcolumns. Develop a procedure to give the row, column and subcolumn for the first occurrence of an element which is equal to a target.</td></tr>
</table>

The completed design is shown in Figure 10.15.

10.5 Multiple read-ahead

It is sometimes necessary to examine a whole group of records or transactions before the necessary type of processing can be selected. A similar situation could arise during a dialogue between a keyboard operator and a program. The use of some procedure such as 'ReadGroup' appears attractive, but would lead to difficulties with groups of incorrect size, and the unexpected appearance of sentinel records. A simple solution, which can be used in conjunction with backtracking, is to hold a group of records in a buffer so that they can be examined prior to processing. There must be enough room in the buffer to hold $n+1$ records, where the nominal group size is n. The first record in a group is normally the first in the buffer, while the record at the end of the buffer is normally the first record of the next group or the sentinel record. This is illustrated in Figure 10.16, where we are dealing with groups containing 3 records. If we designate the records in one group A1, A2, A3, and the records in the next group B1, B2, B3 then Figure 10.17 illustrates how the contents of the buffer are built up.

E 10.16

headRec	First record of a 3-record group A
	Second record of 3-record group A
	Third record of 3-record group A
tailRec	First record of 3-record group B

We read ahead several records to the 'group sentinel' — that is, the first record of the new group *or* the end-of-file sentinel — while

FIGURE 10.17

	first Read	second Read	third Read	fourth Read
headRec				A1
			A1	A2
		A1	A2	A3
tailRec	A1	A2	A3	B1

retaining the preceding records in the group in store, ready for ⸱cessing. We can interpret 'ReadRecord' as 'Copy the records ⸱position along the buffer, from tailRec towards headRec, replacing⸱last record with a new record if there is one available'. The struct⸱diagram for this is shown as Figure 10.18, and for the comp⸱program as Figure 10.19.

FIGURE 10.18

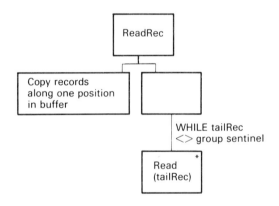

The buffer could be more efficiently implemented using the t⸱niques for handling *queues*, as described in Section 6.6.

10.6 Reconciliation errors

The approach to serial file updating outlined in Section 9.9 is fin⸱long as there is no error data for the program to process. We ⸱assume that the data-vet routines will be used on all input data to ⸱error data, but we may still be left with *reconciliation errors*. Thes⸱errors caused by discrepancies between the 'oldMaster' and 'tra⸱tions' files, and for which 'transactions' will be responsible, ⸱'oldMaster' will have been built up correctly, stage by stage.

For instance, we may try to insert a record in 'oldMaster' wh⸱already contains a record with that key. Or we may try to dele amend a record which is not present in 'oldMaster'. The design of Figure 9.29 can be developed to do this without great difficulty, whereas many approaches to serial file updating cannot.

RE 10.19

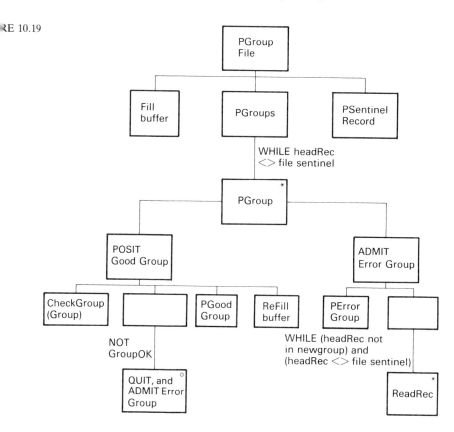

Instead of deducing that we have to insert a record from the values of keys, we now need to state this explicitly by placing an 'I' in the 'transType' field by the transaction record. If we wish to be able to guard against incorrect transaction types, we will also need to place an 'A' for amend in the 'transType' field of amendment transactions, so that the data-vet routine can detect transaction records without an 'A', 'D' or 'I' in this field. The sentinel record on the transaction file should be said to be an amendment, and this must always be present.

The next question is deciding what to do about the reconciliation errors we discover. The usual technique is to *spool* or write the error transactions to a file, 'transErrors', which can be examined later.

We now introduce an extra operation into the operations list of Figure 9.29:

9 Write transRecord to transErrors.

Operation 2 must be expanded to cater for 'transErrors'.

If we use backtracking to abandon an error, we obtain the design of

Figure 10.20. Applying backtracking to 'PDeletionOrAmend' giv
the design of Figure 10.21.

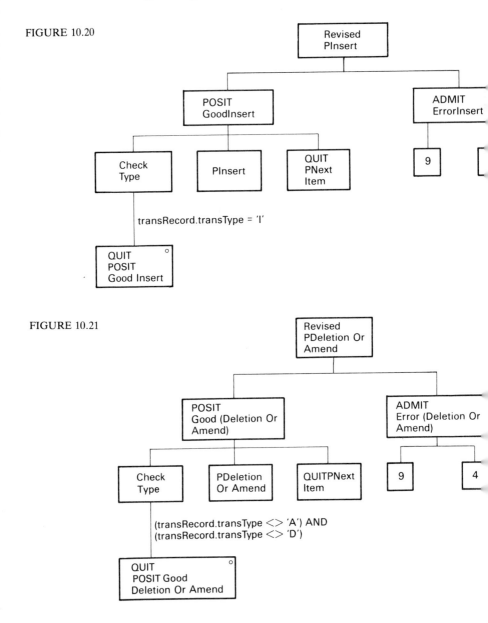

FIGURE 10.20

FIGURE 10.21

Exercise 10.7 Make up suitable test data for the design of Figure 9.29, as amende
Figures 10.20–21 and trace the amended design.

Exercise 10.8 Code and test the design of Figure 9.29 amended as above.

The design of Figure 9.29 dealt with

1 a particular key occurring on both files,
2 a particular key occurring on 'oldMaster' only,
3 a particular key occurring on 'transactions' only.

This means that updating the design is one of a general class of processes called *collating*, that is, comparing one file with another and producing a third. *Merging* is another form of collating, in which the transactions file contains only insertions.

10.9 Use backtracking to write a program to merge two serial files.

After studying this chapter, you should be able to:
1 recognise the importance of vetting data;
2 design programs based on straightforward recognition of error data;
3 design and code procedures to perform checks for
  range of data
  field length and validity
  illogical data
  invalid dates
  invalid numeric keys using check digits
  incorrect quantity of data;
4 describe and use Jackson's backtracking technique;
5 use GOTO to implement backtracking in Pascal;
6 use backtracking to abandon an iteration, both as part of a data-vet and otherwise;
7 use multiple read-ahead to deal with data in groups;
8 use backtracking to deal with reconciliation errors in file handling.

10.10 Write a program to test the design of Example 10.3.

10.11 Write a program to carry out the problem of Example 10.3 *without* using backtracking.

10.12 In an engineering problem, four readings (A, B, C, D) are supplied as data. These have to be checked by calculations which are assumed to take a long time to execute. If all are acceptable, they are to be printed. Otherwise, the message 'Data unstable' is to be printed. Develop a program to do this using backtracking. The calculations and conditions are as follows:
(a) 5*A must exceed B
(b) B*A must be less than C
(c) B*A + C must not equal D

10.13 Use backtracking to develop a procedure to meet the specification for 'LinearSearch' in Example 9.1. It may be useful to posit partIncludesTarget and to admit partExcludesTarget.

10.14 Develop a procedure using backtracking to perform a binary search.

10.15 The records of a customer file have the format of

Record Type	'D'	(deposit)
	'R'	(repayment)
Customer		
account number	Integer	
Amount	Real	

The records are in customer order, with each pair of consecuti
records forming a customer report. The first record in the report is
type 'D', and the second of type 'R'.

Design and write a program to produce a list of validated custom
reports on the left hand side of a display.

Reports which have too many, or too few records, or which do n
have a 'D' type record followed by an 'R' type record, or which ha
the amount on the 'D' type record as being less than the amount on t
'R' type record, are to have the customer account number shown
the right hand side of the display, under a suitable heading.

11 Program inversion

11.1 One-to-one data correspondences

In Chapter 8, it was suggested that program designs should be based on the more complex of the input and output data structures. This works with many simple problems since there is usually a *one-to-one correspondence* between the data structures. For this to occur, the number of potential occurrences or *instances* of data items represented in both structure diagrams must be the same in each diagram. For example, if an input data structure diagram represents a certain number of instances of a certain data item (say 20 instances of a record), then so, potentially, must the output data structure diagram. Furthermore, the instances of these data items must be in the same order with respect to both each other and to other data items in each structure. That is, no data item overtakes another whilst it is in working store. When this happens, the data structures can be combined to form the basic program structure as in the following example.

> 11.1 An input file consists of a number of records. A paged report is to be printed, showing the key field of each record on a separate line if the key is of a type we will call HiKeys, as opposed to being of type LoKeys. A final summary giving the total number of records in the input file is also needed. Derive a basic program structure diagram for doing this.
> The input and output data structure are shown in Figure 11.1.

These data structures can now be verified as having one-to-one correspondences and then combined to give the basic program structure.

First, confirm that there is a one-to-one correspondence (frequency and order) between each box in one structure, and any related box in the other structure. These are shown by the arrows linking the structures in Figure 11.2, the text having been omitted from the unrelated

boxes. We now use these corresponding boxes to combine the origin
data structures, giving the basic program structure of Figure 11.3. Th
includes within it both the original data structures.

The use of hyphenated text (or similar) in the combined boxes
helpful.

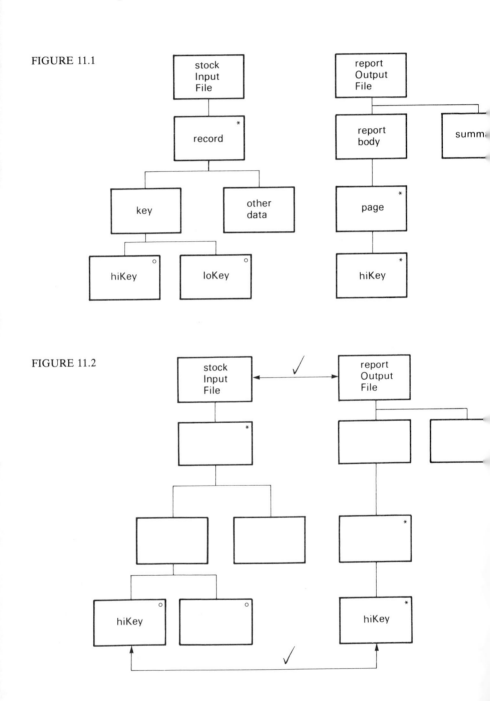

FIGURE 11.1

FIGURE 11.2

This technique can be extended to cases where programs have more than two data structures — such as where an error report is being produced as well as the output file derived from good data.

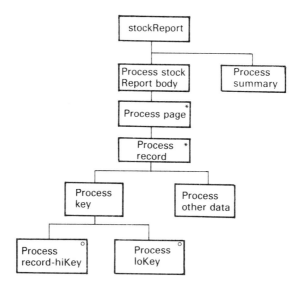

Solve the problem of Example 8.4, confirming that the data structures can in fact be combined.

11.2 Data structure clashes

These occur when we discover that the necessary one-to-one correspondences do not exist. This presents us with a dilemma if we are using the Jackson Structured Programming method as described up to now — and an even worse one if we are not using JSP at all. JSP provides a powerful inversion method of handling the problem which is standard, simple, and which provides a very robust program. It is therefore fully consistent with the aims of structured programming.

However, the method takes a little getting used to, not least because it uses GOTO statements in a manner which, initially, appears to be totally contrary to the philosophy of structured programming. But once the technique has been mastered, it is very satisfying to use. First let us consider the three types of structure clashes which can occur.

11.3 Ordering clash

This arises when the input and output data occur in different orders, as in the following example.

The input file of students' assessments as used in Example 8.2 is to be listed in a report, with all the in-course marks in a record preceding all the examination marks for that record. Design a program to do this.

The input and output data structures together with the one-to-one correspondences and clashes are shown in Figure 11.4.

FIGURE 11.4

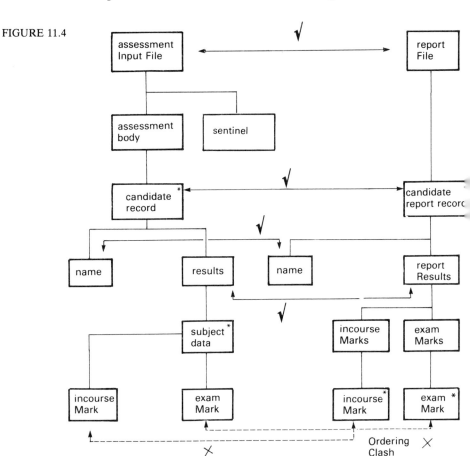

In this case, the problem of the ordering clash is easily resolved by basing the design of a section of program such as a procedure PinRec (which is used to read a record) on the input file data structure, and basing the design of procedure PoutRec (to write a record) on the output file structure. The outline program design is then as shown in Figure 11.5.

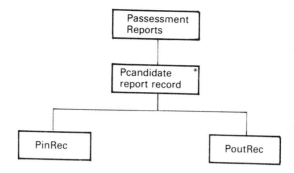

An array could then be used to store the data in the computer's working store. In this common sense approach, we have in fact introduced two techniques of fundamental importance.

These are

1 Separating the parts of the program dealing with input and output, and basing the design of each on its own data structure.

2 Using intermediate data storage (such as an array or a serial file) to hold the data between the different parts of the program.

These techniques can also be used with the following types of data clashes.

11.4 Boundary clash

This clash often occurs due to the physical characteristics of the peripherals being used. The basic problem is frequently that the programmer wishes to handle some abstract data structure such as a record to produce an output file, and therefore will need a section of program which can be called some name such as ProcessRecord. The input peripheral, on the other hand, may handle data only in an indivisible physical unit called a block, and this can only be accessed using operations such as ReadBlock and which are carried out once per ProcessBlock.

If all the boundaries of the physical and abstract data items do not coincide then a data structure clash exists between their data structures, as is shown in Figure 11.6.

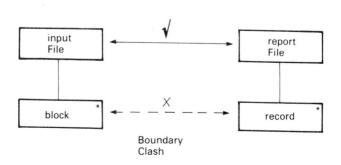

To develop the topic further, we shall consider a very simple and artificial problem, remembering that it is only a vehicle to demonstrate the development of techniques which will deal with far more formidable difficulties. For convenience we shall refer to this as the 'name listing' problem.

The Name Listing Problem

An input text file consists of lines of 80 characters, where each line consists of 2 names, each of 40 characters. The output file to be produced from this consists of lines of 120 characters, each containing 3 names. The number of names on the input file is a multiple of 6. Lines have to be read and written as a whole — operations such as ReadName being not permissible.

Example 11.3 Identify the data clashes in the above problem. These are shown in Figure 11.7.

Exercise 11.2 Spend no more than 15 minutes trying to design a program to solve the problem.

Exercise 11.3 Spend no more than 5 minutes amending your solution to Exercise 11.2 to cope with up to 5 names per line on input, printing up to names per line.

FIGURE 11.7

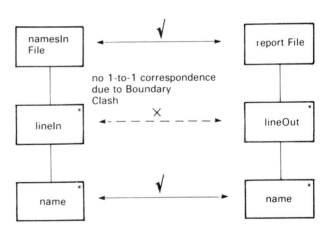

It is possible that many solutions to Exercise 11.2 will be rather complicated, and will use switches to try to synchronise the production and consumption of names. A different approach, which would be quite reasonable, would be to use a 3 by 2 array of names to hold data in working store. However, we shall not pursue this line, since our aim is not so much to solve this particular problem as to demonstrate an approach which can be used with a very wide variety of problems

Some of the many varied solutions may work, but will need extensive testing to ensure that this is so — especially when the end of the data is reached. Amending solutions to meet the conditions of Exercise 11.3 will probably not have been easy.

Difficulties in this type of problem arise out of the use of switches in the solution. They lead to complex programs, with a multitude of possible switch combinations. These make it difficult to understand, test, or amend the program. Further, a particular solution has to be developed for each type of problem where a data structure clash occurs.

The approach we shall use to produce a solution to this problem is to write one program (P1) to deal with reading in the lines of the input file and another (P2) to deal with writing the lines to the output file. We shall use an intermediate file to store data between P1 and P2.

To identify what this intermediate serial file should contain, we add more detail to the input and output file structures, as shown in Figure 11.8.

JRE 11.8

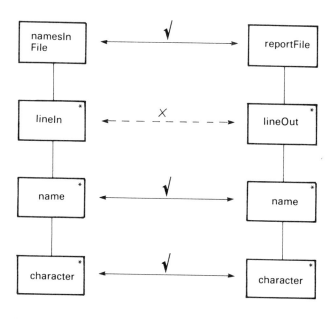

We now look for the largest data item which occurs in both structures, and which possesses one-to-one correspondences for both itself *and its components* — analogous to a 'highest common factor' in mathematics. In this case, it is 'name'.

We can now write names to the intermediate file from P1, and read these from the intermediate file into P2. P1 writes a sentinel record to the intermediate file when the end of the input file is reached. The resulting data structures are given in Figure 11.9 and these show that the data structure clashes have been removed.

FIGURE 11.9

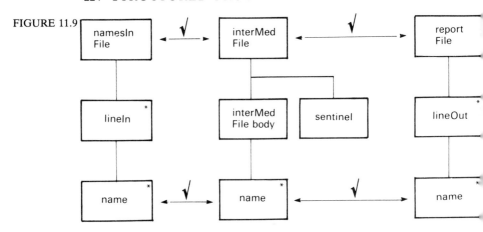

Example 11.4 It is preferable that this example be treated as an exercise before the solution given in program C11P1 and C11P2 is studied.

Using procedures with titles such as ReadNamesLine and WriteNamesLine, design and test programs P1 and P2 as described above. (You should introduce End-of-line-markers into your data structure diagrams.)

PROGRAM 11–1

```
PROGRAM C11P1(input,output,
                          interMed);
{ P1, producing the intermediate
  file of names.  The lengths of lines
  and names have  been shortened for
  convenience in this solution }

CONST
    nameLen    =4;
    sentinel   =´ZZZZ´;

TYPE
    InNamesPtrs=(firstIn,secondIn);
                {firstIn points to the
                 first name in an input
                 line, and so on.}
    NamesType   =PACKED ARRAY
                [1..nameLen] OF CHAR;
    InNamesArray =ARRAY[InNamesPtrs]
                        OF NamesType;

VAR
    inNames    :InNamesArray;
    inNamesPtr :InNamesPtrs;
    interMed   :FILE OF NamesType;
```

```pascal
PROCEDURE  ReadNamesLine;

CONST
   lineLen    =8;
TYPE
   InLineImages=PACKED ARRAY
                  [1..lineLen] OF CHAR;
VAR
   inLineImage:InLineImages;
   chCtr      :1..lineLen;
   chPtr      :INTEGER;
   inNamesPtr :InNamesPtrs;

BEGIN
   FOR chCtr:= 1 TO lineLen DO
       Read(inLineImage[chCtr]);
   ReadLn;
   chPtr:=1;
   BEGIN { Pick up names }
    FOR inNamesPtr:=firstIn TO secondIn
        DO
        FOR chCtr:=1 TO nameLen DO
          BEGIN
            inNames[inNamesPtr,chCtr]:=
                  inLineImage[chPtr];
            chPtr:=chPtr+1
          END
   END { Pick up names }
END;

BEGIN { P1 }
  ReWrite(interMed,´intrMed´);
  WriteLn(´Enter names: ´);
  WHILE NOT Eof DO
   BEGIN { Process line in }
     ReadNamesLine;
     FOR inNamesPtr:=firstIn
                     TO secondIn DO
       Write(interMed,
                  inNames[inNamesPtr]);
     WriteLn(´Enter names: ´)
   END; { Process line in }
  Write(interMed,sentinel);
  WriteLn(´Wait for finish´)
END { P1 } .
```

PROGRAM 11–2

```
PROGRAM CllP2(input,output,
                      interMed);
{ P2,  consumes the intermediate file
 of names and produces the output. }
CONST
   nameLen     =4;
   sentinel    ='ZZZZ';

TYPE
   OutNamesPtrs    =(firstOut,secondOut,
                              thirdOut);
   NamesType       =PACKED ARRAY
                   [1..nameLen] OF CHAR;
   OutNamesArray   =ARRAY[outNamesPtrs]
                           OF NamesType;

VAR
   name        :NamesType;
   outNames    :OutNamesArray;
   outNamesPtr:OutNamesPtrs;
   interMed    :FILE OF NamesType;


PROCEDURE  WriteNamesLine;
VAR
   outNamesPtr:OutNamesPtrs;
BEGIN
 FOR outNamesPtr:=firstOut TO thirdOut
   DO
     Write(outNames[outNamesPtr]:10);
 WriteLn
END;


BEGIN { P2 }
 Reset(interMed,'intrMed');
 Read(interMed,name);
 WHILE name<>sentinel DO
   BEGIN { Process line out }
     BEGIN { Fill line out }
       outNames[firstOut]:=name;
       FOR outNamesPtr:=secondOut
                   TO thirdOut DO
         BEGIN
           Read(interMed,name);
           outNames[outNamesPtr]:=name
```

```
            END;
        END; { Fill line out }
        WriteNamesLine;
        Read(interMed,name)
    END { Process line out }
END { P2 } .
```

It may be argued that this approach to resolving data structure clashes is both slow and expensive of storage. This is perfectly true, but these disadvantages will be overcome later. The important thing at the moment is to establish that using an intermediate file produces programs which are easy to develop, understand and implement. This approach also allows us to deal with the following *interleaving clash*.

11.5 Interleaving clash

This class of data structure clashes will be illustrated using the following example, drawn from a process control environment. We shall call it the 'data logging' problem, — being a more realistic version of the problem we met in Chapter 6.

The Data Logging Problem

le 11.5   A chemical plant contains a number of valves, referenced by codes 'A', 'B', 'C' etc. When a valve opens, it sends its reference code, followed by a time signal to the computer. When it closes, it again sends its code followed by a time signal to the computer. The system uses a multiplexor so that all the signals enter the computer through a single port.

The problem is to write a program to report the total time a valve spends in the open position during a specified period. All valves are assumed to be in their closed position to start with. (In reality, the computer would generate its own time signal, and the data to be processed could be far more complicated, but the above is sufficient for our purposes.)

One simple approach would be to allocate one microcomputer to each valve, and then to leave it permanently switched on. We shall dismiss this as being inappropriate at present, but it is at least straightforward as far as the individual valves are concerned.

Returning to our JSP approach, the output data structure is straightforward, being as shown in Figure 11.10.

The difficulty comes in drawing the input file data structure. The output data structure suggests that we are going to need some component such as 'Process Valve Cycle Record' in the program structure so that a valve's total open time can be found. A Valve Cycle

Record for a particular valve would contain its opening time and i
closing time, but there is no way in which the data of a Valve Cycl
Record can be represented in a single input data structure diagram.

FIGURE 11.10

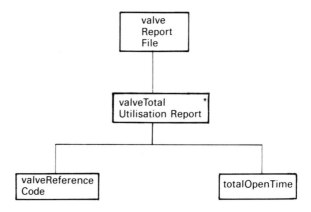

Consider the following sample data, in which time is given by
certain clock:

Valve Code	Time (secs)	Action
A	27	valve A opens
B	30	valve B opens
A	35	valve A closes
C	40	valve C opens
A	42	valve A opens
A	50	valve A closes
C	55	valve C closes
B	60	valve B closes

This shows that valves 'A', 'B' and 'C' have been open for 16, 30 and
seconds respectively.

FIGURE 11.11

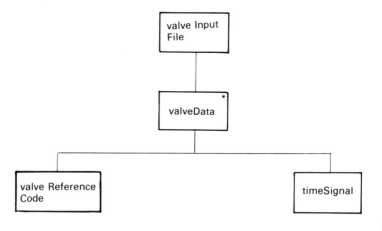

The best single data structure diagram we can draw is given in Figu
11.11, but this does not contain any 'Valve Cycle Record' componer

The way out of this difficulty is to use the same technique as before — that is, to introduce intermediate files.

For this we use not just one such file, but one for each valve. We can then use one program (P1) to produce these files, and use another program (P2) to produce the report. The contents of these files for the above sample data is

Valve 'A' InterMedFile : (VAIM) : 27 35 42 50
Valve 'B' InterMedFile : (VBIM) : 30 60
Valve 'C' InterMedFile : (VCIM) : 40 55

where a pair of readings forms a Valve Cycle Record.

The data structures are shown in Figure 11.12. We have satisfactory one-to-one correspondences as shown, and the problem is solved. Of course, there will be possibly hundreds of intermediate files if we have a moderate sized plant, and we would have difficulty answering a question such as 'For how long has valve 2 been open so far during this run?'

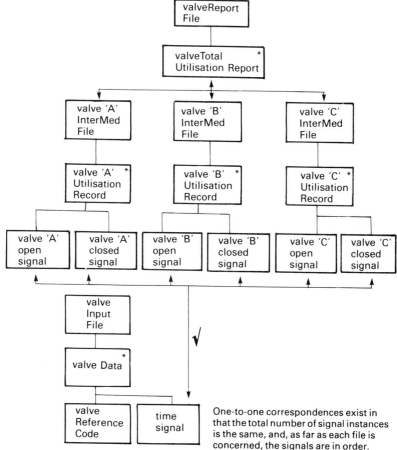

One-to-one correspondences exist in that the total number of signal instances is the same, and, as far as each file is concerned, the signals are in order.

Exercise   11.4 Make a list of examples of possible interleaving clashes drawn from real time environments.

11.6 Inversion with boundary clashes

We have seen above how to resolve structure clashes in a very simple but somewhat impractical manner. The steps taken so far can be summarised as:

1 Identify the largest data item possessing a complete one-to-one correspondence for itself and its components in the data structures. Data elements of this type will form the intermediate file.

2 Develop completely and test a program (P1) to produce this intermediate file.

3 Develop completely and test a program (P2) to read from the intermediate file and produce the required output.

We must now take this process one step further and remove the need for the intermediate file. Essentially, what we must do is to synchronise the 'write to intermediate file' operations of P1 with the 'read intermediate file' operations of P2.

The technique, which is called *inversion* by Jackson, will be illustrated using the name listing problem described in Section 11.4 on Boundary clashes. We shall, however, assume that there are exactly six records. With this assumption we can write P1 and P2 in *nest-free* form — that is as a linear program without loops. The resulting code is given in Figure 11.13. The labels (single digit in P1 and triple digit in P2) are used here for tracing purposes.

FIGURE 11.13

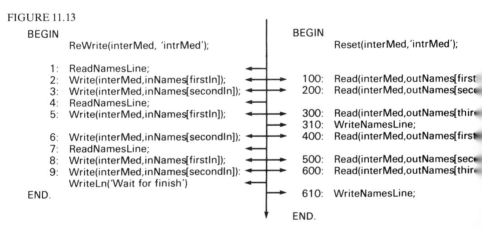

The arrows show the required flow of control if these programs are executed concurrently. A write operation is assumed to invoke automatically the corresponding read operation, and so read/write are

considered as one operation, thereby removing the need for the intermediate file. Table 11.1 illustrates the initial stages of the execution of
the programs in this desired manner, using names of one character for
the demonstration.

Sample input data: A   B
    C   D
    E   F

ise 11.5 Complete trace table 11.1

Table 11.1

Text labels	in Names [firstIn]	inNames [secondIn]	outNames [firstOut]	outNames [secondOut]	outNames [thirdOut]
1	A	B			
2–100			A		
3–200				B	
4	C	D			
5–300					C
310			<u>A</u>	<u>B</u>	<u>C</u>

To be able to implement such an approach we need a text pointer —
usually called qs — so that when we go to P2 from P1, we will be able to
carry on from where we left off. This will initially be set to 100 in P1.
We will also remove references to the intermediate file, replacing
statements in P1 such as

    Write (interMed, inNames [secondIn])

with

    Pass inNames [secondIn] to P2 (to position indicated by text
    pointer, qs)

Statements in P2 such as

    Read (interMed, outNames [secondOut])

become

    Set (the text pointer), qs
    Return (to P1 to fetch a name)
    Assign name (received from P1) to outNames [secondOut]

The only exception is the first 'read' statement, which is changed to

    Assign name (received from P1) to outNames [firstOut]

The results of doing this are shown in Figure 11.14.

    Noting the values of qs, and using these in the reference column to
show where we enter P2 from P1, the initial trace table becomes as
shown in Table 11.2.

FIGURE 11.14   *P1*   *P2*

Text label	*Operation*		*Text label*	*Operation*
0:	Set QS to 100			
1:	ReadNamesLine			
2:	Pass inNames [firstIn] to P2		100:	Assign name to outNames [firstOu
				Set qs to 200
				Return
3:	Pass inNames[secondOut] to P2		200:	Assign name to outNames [secon
				Set qs to 300
				Return
4:	ReadNamesLine			
5:	Pass inNames [firstIn] to P2		300:	Assign name to outNames [thirdO
			310:	WriteNamesLine
				Set qs to 400
				Return
6:	Pass inNames [secondOut] to P2		400:	Assign name to outNames [firstO
				Set qs to 500
				Return
7:	ReadNamesLine			
8:	Pass inNames [firstIn] to P2		500:	Assign name to outNames [secon
				Set qs to 600
				Return
9:	Pass inNames [secondIn] to P2		600:	Assign name to outNames [thirdO
			610:	WriteNamesLine

Table 11.2

Text labels	*qs, Text Pointer*	*inNames [firstIn]*	*inNames [secondIn]*	*outNames [firstOut]*	*outNames [secondOut]*	*outNames [thirdOut]*
0	100					
1		A	B			
2–100				A		
	200				B	
3–200						
	300					
4		C	D			
5–300				C		
310				A	B	C

<u>Exercise   11.6</u> Complete trace table 11.2.

The method of implementing this in a programming language may b
now be suggesting itself. What we must do is to make P2 into
procedure of P1.

   To implement a text pointer we need a set of GOTOs controlled b
qs at the start of P2, so that P2 can be restarted at the appropriat
point. The text pointer is initially set by P1. The return to P1 from P2

achieved using a GOTO to the end of P2, whilst the data, 'name', is passed to P2 using a parameter.

This has been done in Program C11P3, based on Figure 11.13. Since the local variables of P2 (now procedure processOut) will be lost when a return to P1 is carried out, the relevant types and variables have been made common or global. This practice is generally undesirable, but is unavoidable here, although a file on backing store — or better still a data base — would be preferable.

Procedures ReadNamesLine and WriteNamesLine are unchanged from Programs C11P1 and C11P2 and, apart from their first lines, are omitted from the listing of C11P3 and other programs.

PROGRAM 11–3

```
PROGRAM C11P3(input,output);
{ This progam has P1 reading the input
  file and calling P2 (procedure
  ProcessOut) as an inverted program,
  thereby removing the need for the
  intermediate file. The design of P2
  is unchanged from Fig. 11.13 but is
  implemented in a suitable way for
  Pascal. }

LABEL    0,1,2,3,4,5,6,7,8,9;

CONST
    nameLen       =4;

TYPE
    InNamesPtrs    =(firstIn,secondIn);
    NamesType      =PACKED ARRAY
                    [1..nameLen] OF CHAR;
    InNamesArray   =ARRAY[inNamesPtrs]
                        OF NamesType;
    OutNamesPtrs   =(firstOut,secondOut,
                             thirdOut);
    OutNamesArray  =ARRAY[OutNamesPtrs]
                        OF NamesType;

VAR
    inNames      :InNamesArray;
    inNamesPtr  :InNamesPtrs;
    outNames     :OutNamesArray;
    outNamesPtr:OutNamesPtrs;
    qs           :INTEGER;

{ PROCEDURE ReadNamesline; as C11P1 }
```

```
PROCEDURE ProcessOut(name:namesType);
LABEL 100,200,300,310,400,500,
                        600,610,700;

 { PROCEDURE WriteNamesline; as CllP2 }



BEGIN { P2, inverted as ProcessOut }      {BEGIN | for principal original code,
                                          {                 see Fig. 11.13
   if qs=100 then GOTO 100;
   if qs=200 then GOTO 200;
   if qs=300 then GOTO 300;
   if qs=400 then GOTO 400;
   if qs=500 then GOTO 500;
   if qs=600 then GOTO 600;


100: outNames[firstOut]:=name;            {100: Read(interMed,outNames[firstOut]
        {get next name    }
        qs:=200;  {set text pointer}
        GOTO 700; {return to Pl     }
200: outNames[secondOut]:=name;           {200: Read(interMed,outNames[secondOut
        {get next name    }
        qs:=300;  {set text pointer}
        GOTO 700; {return to Pl     }
300: outNames[thirdOut]:=name;            {300: Read(interMed,outNames[thirdOut]

310: WriteNamesLine;                      {     WriteNamesLine
        qs:=400;
        GOTO 700;

400: outNames[firstOut]:=name;            {400: Read(interMed,outNames[firstOur]
        GOTO 700;
500: outNames[secondOut]:=name;           {500: Read(interMed,outNames[secondOut
        GOTO 700;
600: outNames[thirdOut]:=name;            {600: Read(interMed,outNames[thirdOut]
610: WriteNamesLine;                      {610: WriteNamesLine;
700:END; {inverted program, P2 }         {     END.


BEGIN { Pl, Main program }
0:    qs:=100;
1:    ReadNamesLine;
2:    ProcessOut(inNames[firstIn]);
3:    ProcessOut(inNames[secondIn]);
4:    ReadNamesLine;
5:    ProcessOut(inNames[firstIn]);
6:    ProcessOut(inNames[secondIn]);
7:    ReadNamesLine;
8:    ProcessOut(inNames[firstIn]);
9:    ProcessOut(inNames[secondIn]);
END { Pl, Main program } .
```

e   11.7   Trace the coding of C11P3.

It is perhaps natural in this problem to think in terms of P1 as the main program with P2 as a secondary procedure being inverted and then called by P1. There is however no reason why P2 should not be the main program, calling P1 as the inverted program, and this will appear to be more natural in other problems.

e   11.8   Invert P1 (as given in Figure 11.13) and test your coding. Use the style of C11P3.

The benefits of inversion are

1 We have separated P1 and P2. The only variables actually used in both of them are qs and the parameters. Hence they can be developed separately and tested separately, using a real intermediate file if required. P2 can also be tested using an intermediate file derived by some means other than by using P1.

2 The equivalents of P1 and P2 are much simpler than the corresponding monolithic programs when the technique is used with programs of any realistic size.

3 The task of inverting P2 is straightforward and requires little thought. It could be automated if required. It is a good technique to just follow the rules and *not* to think too much about it when making the inversion. For instance, if a statement needs to have two labels on it, do not try to rationalise them, just use a null statement. For example

```
 50:  ;
400: END
```

4 The approach is standard which means that different programmers using the method will produce very similar programs, with obvious advantages for maintenance.

5 All structure clashes can be solved using inversion, as can a number of other problems.

11.7 Flat-coding

The ISO specification for Pascal severely restricts the usage of GO[?] statements. This means for example, that we will have trou[?] branching into a 'WHILE' loop, although some compilers will per[?] this with a warning message. The only safe way out of the problem i[?] code the inverted program in a *flat-coded* manner.

This means that structured program components such as compou[?] statements, 'FOR', 'WHILE' and 'REPEAT' iterations, 'IF .[?] THEN ... ELSE' selections etc. must be coded using (n[?] compound) statements, simple selections (IF ... THEN) a[?] 'GOTO' statements. It is also necessary for the reference to the t[?] pointer, qs, to be kept out of procedures within the inverted progra[?]

When flat coding has been used, the design of the program can [?] kept immediately apparent by including the original coding of, say, [?] alongside the implementation of the inverted P2, in the form [?] comment. The various structured program components of Pascal a[?] their flat-coded forms are given in Table 11.3. In this table, sim[?] statements are represented by 'Sn' and conditions or Boolean Expr[?] sions evaluated as TRUE are represented by 'c'. Labels are rep[?] sented by integers.

Note that with the flat-coded form of the FOR iteration, the Pas[?] function 'Succ' can be used to increment the counter-variable. If thi[?] done, it will advance the counter-variable one increment beyond [?] range of values actually used. This will cause a run time error w[?] subrange and enumeration type variables if this is not allowed fo[?] the declarations.

Table 11.3

Structured Pascal	Flat-Coding

Selections:

```
IF c THEN                    IF NOT c THEN GOTO 1;
   BEGIN (this)                 (BEGIN this)
      S1;                          S1;
      S2                           S2;
   END (this)                   (END this)
                             1: .....


IF c THEN                    IF NOT c THEN GOTO 1;
   BEGIN (this)                 (BEGIN this)
      S1;                          S1;
      S2                           S2;
   END (this)                   (END this)
ELSE                            GOTO 2;
   BEGIN (that)              1: (BEGIN that)
      S3;                          S3;
      S4                           S4;
   END (that)                   (END that)
                             2: .....
```

Iterations:

```
WHILE c DO                   2: IF NOT c THEN GOTO 1;
   BEGIN (this)                 (BEGIN this)
      S1;                          S1;
      D2                           S2;
   END (this)                   (END this)
                                GOTO 2:
                             1: .....


FOR counter:=initialValue    counter:=initialValue;
         To finalValue DO    2: If counter>finalValue THEN
BEGIN (this)                        GOTO 1;
   S1;                           (BEGIN this)
   S2                              S1;
END (this)                        S2;
                                (END this)
                                counter:=Succ(counter);
                                GOTO 2;
                             1: .....


REPEAT                          (BEGIN this)
   BEGIN (this)              1:   S1;
      S1;                          S2;
      S2                        (END this)
   END (this)                 IF NOT c THEN GOTO 1;
UNTIL c;
```

Example　11.6 Assuming there is a *multiple* of six names to be processed (henc ensuring that there are no partially full lines) invert progra C11P2 with respect to programs C11P1, forming one program.

The coding is shown in Program C11P4.

PROGRAM 11–4

```
PROGRAM C11P4(input,output);
{ In this program, P1 reads the input
  file, which has a multiple of 6 names.
  P1 calls P2 (procedure ProcessOut),
  thereby removing the need for the
  intermediate file. The designs are
  unchanged from programs C11P1 and
  C11P2. }

CONST
   nameLen    =4;
   sentinel   ='ZZZZ';

TYPE
   OutNamesPtrs =(firstOut,secondOut,
                  thirdOut,dummyOutPtr);

{ Other TYPE and VAR declarations as in
                              C11P3 }

{ PROCEDURE ReadNamesLine; as in C11P1 }

PROCEDURE  ProcessOut(name:NamesType);
LABEL 100,200,300,400,
      1000,2000,3000,4000;

  { PROCEDURE WriteNamesLine; as C11P3
```

```
BEGIN { P2, inverted as ProcessOut }
  IF qs=100 THEN GOTO 100;
  IF qs=200 THEN GOTO 200;
  IF qs=300 THEN GOTO 300;
100:;
2000: IF name= sentinel THEN GOTO 1000;
  { BEGIN Process line out    }
    { BEGIN Fill line out    }
      outNames[firstOut]:=name;
      outNamesPtr:=secondOut;
3000:   IF outNamesPtr>thirdOut THEN
                       GOTO 4000;
        qs:=200;
        GOTO 400;
  200:    outNames[outNamesPtr]:=name;
          outNamesPtr:=Succ(outNamesPtr);
        GOTO 3000;
```

```
{BEGIN P2, principal original c
{ | has been used to delimit
{comments within comments.

{  Read(interMed,name);
{  WHILE  name<>sentinel DO
{    BEGIN | Process line out
{      BEGIN | Fill line out
{        outNames[firstOut]:=na

{        FOR outNamesPtr:=secc
{                    TO thirdOu
{        BEGIN
{          Read(interMed,name
{          outNames[outNamesF
{
{            END
```

```
  { END Fill line out    }              {      END | Fill line out     |    }
000:WriteNamesLine;                     {        WriteNamesLine;            }
     qs:=300;                           {        Read(interMed,name);       }
     GOTO 400;
00:GOTO 2000;
{ END Process line out     }            {     END | Process line out    |   }
000:;                                   { END |P2 |.                        }
00:END { P2, inverted } ;

EGIN { P1, Main Program }
 qs:=100;
WriteLn('Enter names: ');
 WHILE NOT Eof DO
   BEGIN { Process line in }
   ReadNamesLine;
   FOR inNamesPtr:=firstIn TO secondIn
     DO
       ProcessOut(inNames[inNamesPtr]);
   WriteLn('Enter names: ')
   END { Process line in }
ND { P1, Main Program } .
```

We have used GOTOs to achieve executable code, but the disadvantages of doing this are cosmetic. We have produced very ugly code, forced on us by the limitations of Pascal. (Similar problems arise with most other high level languages lacking co-routines.) The important point, though, is that we have clear, intelligible program structures, derived in a simple standard, systematic manner. The ugly code is a small price to pay for this when well documented.

e 11.9 Invert Program C11P1 (assume that the number of names is still a multiple of six).

Having dealt with the principles of inversion, we can now make our example into a more realistic one by removing the constraint that the number of names is a multiple of six. Names which are space-filled in the input file are to be ignored.

Backtracking can be used in P2 to cope with the final partly filled line. The input and output file data structures are now as in Figures 11.15 and 11.16.

FIGURE 11.15

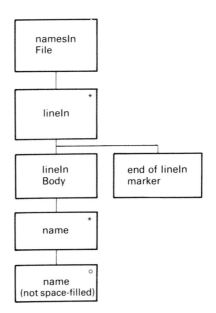

FIGURE 11.16

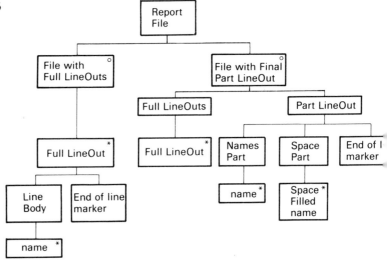

11.10 Develop, code and test programs (P1 and P2) to solve the name listing problem, using an intermediate file. There can be any number of names in the input file. The reader may wish to examine the solution before proceeding.

11.11 Solve Exercise 11.10, using the coding of the solution to Exercise 11.10 or your own, inverting P2.

11.12 Solve Exercise 11.11, using the coding of the solution to Exercise 11.10 or your own, inverting P1.

11.8 State vector separation

In Section 11.5 we saw — in the data logging problem — how an interleaving clash could be resolved by using a large number of intermediate files. We can remove the need for these files by using inversion. First, we must consider how the problem would be handled if there were only one valve. Once this straightforward problem has been solved using the usual JSP method of program design, the difficulty of having many valves becomes trivial in that following certain rules will lead to a simple, effective design.

11.7 Use inversion to solve the data logging problem, assuming that there is only one valve.

We can use data structures based on Figure 11.12 to develop the program structure diagrams of Figure 11.17, in which P1 produces the intermediate file of valve records (that is, valve reference code and time signal) and P2 consumes them to produce its report. Applying the rules for program inversion leads to the Program C11P5, where P1 signals the end of the intermediate file to P2 by passing a sentinel record to P2. P2 becomes procedure ProcessTimeSignal when it is inverted.

PROGRAM 11–5

```
PROGRAM C11P5(input,output);
{ This assumes one valve, and has P2
  inverted as procedure
  ProcessTimeSignal. The designs are
  based on Figure 11.17. }

CONST
    sentinel    =-1;
    prompt      ='Enter valve record: ';
```

```
TYPE
   Valverecs    =RECORD
                    valveRef  :CHAR;
                    eventTime :INTEGER
                END;

VAR
   eventTime     :INTEGER;
   openTime      :INTEGER;
   closeTime     :INTEGER;
   totalOpenTime:INTEGER;
   qs            :INTEGER;
   valveRec     :ValveRecs;


PROCEDURE ProcessTimeSignal
                    (eventTime:INTEGER);
LABEL    1,2,
         100,200,300,400;
```

```
BEGIN { P2, inverted }                      {BEGIN |P2, based on Figure 11.1
   IF qs=100 THEN GOTO 100;
   IF qs=200 THEN GOTO 200;
   IF qs=300 THEN GOTO 300;

100: totalOpenTime:=0;                      {  totalTime:=0;
   { BEGIN Process valve cycles }           {  BEGIN | Process  valve cycle
2: IF eventTime=sentinel THEN               {    WHILE eventTime<>sentinel D
                         GOTO 1;            {
       { BEGIN Process valve cycle }        {      BEGIN | Process valve cycl
           openTime:=eventTime;             {        openTime:=eventTime;
           qs:=200;                         {        Read(eventTime);
           GOTO 400;                        {
200:       closeTime:=eventTime;            {        closeTime:=eventTime;
           totalOpenTime:=totalOpenTime     {        totalOpenTime:=totalOpen
                          +closeTime        {                       +closeTim
                          -openTime;        {                       -openTime
           qs:=300;                         {        Read(eventTime)
           GOTO 400;                        {
300:       GOTO 2;                          {
       { END Process valve cycle }          {      END; | Process valve cycle
   {END Process valve cycles }              {  END | Process valve cycles
1: WriteLn(´Total Valve Open Time: ´:30,    {  WriteLn(totalOpenTime)
                     totalOpenTime:5);
 400: END { P2, inverted };                 {END.
```

```
BEGIN { P1, Main program }
  qs:=100;
  WriteLn(prompt);
  WHILE NOT Eof DO
    BEGIN { Process valve record }
```

```
    ReadLn(valveRec.valveRef,
         valveRec.eventTime);
    ProcessTimeSignal
            (valveRec.eventTime);
    WriteLn(prompt)
  END; { Process valve record }
  ProcessTimeSignal(sentinel);
END { P1, Main Program } .
```

RE 11.17

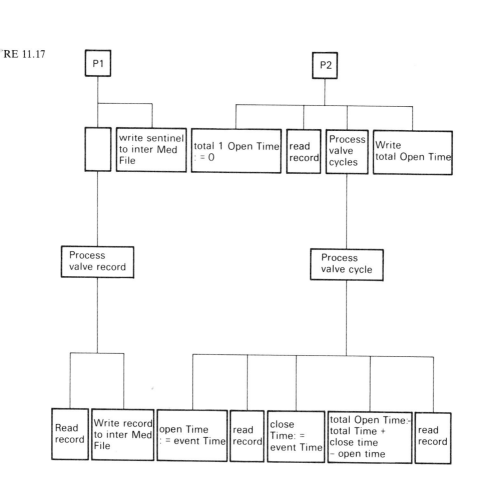

Now consider what would happen if there were two valves, with reference codes 'A' and 'B'. We could implement a design to deal with this by having two intermediate files, or two copies of the inverted P2 (called P2v), together with two sets of the variables needed to record the activities of valves 'A' and 'B', including the text pointers, qs. It will be apparent that the second copy of the P2v text is not really necessary, since the text pointer tells us all we need to know about it — that is, how far we have reached in P2v with the particular valve.

We can collect the variables and the text pointer together to form what is known as a *state vector*, and then use an array of these, one for each valve. This can, in this example, be implemented using

```
TYPE
    StatVecs            = RECORD
                            openTime        :INTEGER;
                            closeTime       :INTEGER;
                            totalOpenTime :INTEGER;
                            qs              :INTEGER
    END;
VAR
    StatVec             :ARRAY['A' . . 'B'] OF StatVecs
```

This array will have to be global so that the date is not lost when P2v is left. However, the data fields of the state vectors are not the concern of P1, and so should not be referenced by P1. It will sometimes be necessary for P1 to use the 'communications' fields of the state vector (qs in this case), but here this is limited to the initial setting of the text pointers. When we enter P2v, we will have to call the relevant state vector into use. This can be done by passing the valve reference code to P2v when it invoked, together with the other data, so that the appropriate state vector can be selected.

Example 11.8 Modify the coding of Program C11P5 to cope with 5 valves, with reference codes 'A' to 'E'.

PROGRAM 11–6

```
PROGRAM C11P6(input,output);
{ This is similar to C11P5, but has
  an array of state vectors, to allow
  several valves. The valve code is
  used by P2, inverted as
  ProcessTimeSignal, to select the
  appropriate state vector.  }

CONST
    sentinel    =-1;
    prompt      ='Enter valve record: ';

TYPE
    ValveRecs   =RECORD
                    valveRef  :CHAR;
                    eventTime :INTEGER
                END;
```

```
StatVecs        =RECORD
                    openTime   :INTEGER;
                    closeTime  :INTEGER;
                    totalOpenTime
                                :INTEGER;
                    qs          :INTEGER
                END;

VAR
   valveRec        :ValveRecs;
   ptr             :CHAR;
   statVec         :ARRAY[´A´..´E´]
                        OF StatVecs;


PROCEDURE InitialiseStatVec;
VAR
   ptr             :CHAR;
BEGIN
   FOR ptr:=´A´ TO ´E´ DO
     WITH statVec[ptr] DO
       BEGIN
          openTime       :=0;
          closeTime      :=0;
          totalOpenTime  :=0;
          qs             :=100
       END
END;



PROCEDURE ProcessTimeSignal
                  (valveRec:valveRecs);

LABEL   1,2,
        100,200,300,400;


BEGIN { P2, inverted  }
 WITH statVec[valveRec.valveRef] DO
  BEGIN { Update status vector }
   IF qs=100 THEN GOTO 100;
   IF qs=200 THEN GOTO 200;
   IF qs=300 THEN GOTO 300;

100: ; { BEGIN Process valve cycles }
2: IF valveRec.eventTime=sentinel
                  THEN GOTO 1;
```

```
              { BEGIN Process valve cycle }
                openTime:=
                         valveRec.eventTime;
                qs:=200;
                GOTO 400;
      200:     closeTime:=
                         valveRec.eventTime;
                totalOpenTime:=totalOpenTime
                               +closeTime
                               -openTime;
                qs:=300;
                GOTO 400;
      300:     GOTO 2;
            { END Process valve cycle }
      1: WriteLn('Total Valve ':15,
            valveRec.valveRef,' Open Time: '
                              totalOpenTime:5)
          { END Process valve cycles }

       END; { Update status vector }
      400: END { P2, inverted } ;

      BEGIN { P1, Main program }
        InitialiseStatVec;
        WriteLn(prompt);
        WHILE NOT Eof DO
          BEGIN { Process valve record }
            ReadLn(valveRec.valveRef,
                 valveRec.eventTime);
            ProcessTimeSignal
                      (valveRec);
            WriteLn(prompt)
          END; { Process valve record }
        BEGIN { Shut down valves }
         FOR ptr:='A' TO 'E' DO
          WITH valveRec DO
           BEGIN
             valveRef:=ptr;
             eventTime:=sentinel;
             ProcessTimeSignal(valveRec)
           END
        END { Shut down valves }
      END { P1, Main Program } .
```

The coding is given in Program C11P6. Examination will show that the basic design is unchanged from that of Program C11P5. The state vector variables have been initialised in procedure InitialiseStatVec. At the end of the input file, P1 writes a sentinel for each valve.

ise 11.13 Trace the coding of C11P6 with suitable sample data.

11.9 Long running programs

In real-time data processing it is often necessary for a program to be suspended when a physical process finishes and to be resumed at some later time when the process restarts. The data already accumulated must be recovered and the program re-entered as if it had never been left. Programs of this nature are said to be *long running*. Examples of their uses might be the logging of a customer's bank account through transactions entered from a cashpoint, and the logging of some inter-mittent industrial process where interrupt signals from equipment might signal an operating system to load, run and subsequently stand down the data logging program or routine.

In effect, we have already used a method of achieving this in that in Program C11P6 we were suspending the processing for one valve whilst we were dealing with another. The state vector carries all the information we need: the accumulated data and the text pointer. To allow the state vector to be preserved when the program is not active in the computer, all we need to do is to keep it on backing store. If this could be done using a file allowing random access, it would have the advantage of allowing any number of state vectors, of any size and complexity, to be used. Although this facility is not available in ISO Pascal, we can still use a serial file to hold the state vectors when the program is inactive, reading them into an array in memory when required. This makes for rapid processing, given that sufficient memory is available. The task of setting up the state vector file can be done by a program such as C11P7. (Although only the text pointer needs to be initialised here, initialising the other fields avoids the complications of writing and reading illegal field formats.)

PROGRAM 11–7

```
PROGRAM C11P7(input,output,sv00);
{ This initialises the state vectors
  of several valves. The essential
  part of this is the setting of the
  text pointers, qs. }
```

```
CONST
    first          = ´A´;
    last           = ´E´;

TYPE
    StatVecs       =RECORD
                        openTime    :INTEGER;
                        closeTime   :INTEGER;
                        totalOpenTime
                                    :INTEGER;
                        qs          :INTEGER;
                    END;
    ValveRefCodes=first..last;
VAR
    ptr            :valveRefcodes;
    statVec        :StatVecs;
    sv00           :FILE OF StatVecs;


BEGIN
    ReWrite(sv00);
    FOR ptr:=first TO last DO
      BEGIN
        WITH statVec DO
          BEGIN
            openTime       :=0;
            closeTime      :=0;
            totalOpenTime  :=0;
            qs             :=100;
          END;
        Write(sv00,statVec)
      END
END.
```

Example 11.9 Develop Program C11P6 into a long running program.

The coding is given in Program C11P8. It includes a facility **f** specifying generation numbers for particular state vector files, a procedures for loading and saving these. The basic design, however still that of Program C11P5, and is still apparent in the coding ev without comments. This illustrates the power of the inversion meth in implementing programs for real time systems.

```
PROGRAM CllP8(input,output,oldSvFile,
                         newSvFile);
{ The existing state vector is loaded
  from oldSvFile (with appropriate two
  digit generation number),  whilst
  the one produced is saved for further
  use in newSvFile. This allows the
  program to be suspended and restarted
  as required. }

CONST
   first        ='A';
   last         ='E';
   sentinel     =-1;
   prompt       ='Enter valve record: ';
TYPE
   ValveRecs    =RECORD
                   valveRef  :CHAR;
                   eventTime :INTEGER
                 END;
   StatVecs     =RECORD
                   openTime   :INTEGER;
                   closeTime  :INTEGER;
                   totalOpenTime
                             :INTEGER;
                   qs         :INTEGER;
                 END;
   ValveRefCodes=first..last;
   FileNames    =PACKED ARRAY[1..4]
                             OF CHAR;
VAR
   valveRec     :ValveRecs;
   ptr          :valveRefcodes;
   statVec      :ARRAY[ValveRefCodes]
                     OF StatVecs;
   newSvFile,oldSvFile
               :FILE OF StatVecs;
   newSvFileName,
   oldSvFileName:FileNames;



PROCEDURE LoadStatVec;
VAR
   ptr           :valveRefCodes;
```

```
BEGIN
  oldSvFileName:=´sv  ´;
  WriteLn(´Enter old state vector ´,
      ´file gen. number (2 digits):´);
  ReadLn(oldSvFileName[3],
               oldSvFileName[4]);
  newSvFileName:=´sv  ´;
  WriteLn(´Enter new state vector ´,
      ´file gen. number (2 digits):´);
  ReadLn(newSvFileName[3],
               newSvFileName[4]);
  ReSet(oldSvFile,oldSvFileName);
               { ReSet form is non-ISO }
  FOR ptr:=first TO last DO
    Read(oldSvFile,statvec[ptr]);
  Writeln(´Status Vector loaded.´)
END;


PROCEDURE SaveStatVec;
VAR
   ptr            :valveRefCodes;
BEGIN
  ReWrite(newSvFile,newSvFileName);
            { ReWrite form is non-ISO }
    FOR ptr:=first TO last DO
      Write(newSvFile,statvec[ptr])
END;

PROCEDURE ProcessTimeSignal
                 (valveRec:valveRecs);


LABEL    1,2,
         100,200,300,400;


BEGIN{ P2,inverted, based on Fig 11.17}
 WITH statVec[valveRec.valveRef] DO
  BEGIN { Update status vector }
    IF qs=100 THEN GOTO 100;
    IF qs=200 THEN GOTO 200;
    IF qs=300 THEN GOTO 300;

100: totalOpenTime:=0;
   { BEGIN Process valve cycles }
2: IF valveRec.eventTime=sentinel
                       THEN GOTO 1;
```

```
      { BEGIN Process valve cycle }
          openTime:=valveRec.eventTime;
          qs:=200;
          GOTO 400;
200:      closeTime:=valveRec.eventTime;
          totalOpenTime:=totalOpenTime
                          +closeTime
                          -openTime;
          qs:=300;
          GOTO 400;
300:      GOTO 2;
      { END Process valve cycle }
   {END Process valve cycles }
1: WriteLn('Total Valve ',
              valveRec.valveRef,
               ' Open Time: ',
              totalOpenTime:5)
   END; { Update status vector }
400: END { P2, inverted };

BEGIN { P1, Main program }
  LoadStatVec;
  WriteLn(prompt);
  WHILE NOT Eof DO
    BEGIN { Process valve record }
      ReadLn(valveRec.valveRef,
           valveRec.eventTime);
      ProcessTimeSignal
                (valveRec);
      WriteLn(prompt)
    END; { Process valve record }
  BEGIN { Shut down valves }
   FOR ptr:=first TO last DO
     WITH valveRec DO
       BEGIN
        valveRef:=ptr;
        eventTime:=sentinel;

        ProcessTimeSignal(valveRec)
       END
  END; { Shut down valves }
  SaveStatVec
END { P1, Main Program } .
```

11.14 Trace Program C11P8 with suitable sample data. Include a break in the
processing requirement by entering an End-of-file marker on the input
file and then restarting the program.

It could be argued that the above programs are not realistic in that the do not deal with error data such as a valve being stuck in the ope position at the end of a session. These types of problems requi careful handling, but the basic technique is to expand the 'communica tions' area of the state vector to hold other data as well as the te pointer. In order to preserve the integrity of our coding, we need keep the coupling between the main program and the inverted pr grams to a minimum. This can be done by allowing P1 to inspect th state vectors of the inverted programs to see if the input data consistent with the history recorded by the state vector, but not to alt them directly. Instead, P1 can pass communications information to th inverted program as procedure parameters, which can then be used it to alter the state vectors.

Example 11.10 Suggest alterations to Programs C11P7 and C11P8 to allow P1 report that a valve is in the open position when the end of th input file is reached.

Suggestion: We need to include a 'position' field, and an 'endFi field in the state vector.

Exercise 11.15 Use backtracking to develop program P2 of Figure 11.17 so that forms the basic design of a program to cope with faulty valve cycles, a long running program.

Example 11.11 Alter Programs C11P7 and C11P8 so that the report on a valve total open time is not given by ProcessTimeSignal until a 'sh down' signal is read on the input file for that particular val (This could be simulated by a time field of, say, −1.) When th occurs, a Boolean variable ('eF') is passed as a parameter ProcessTimeSignal. If this comes when the valve is in the op position ProcessTimeSignal should report it as having failed. should give an appropriate warning if any further data is receiv from a shut down valve—beyond that it is ignored. When the e of the input file is reached, on any occasion, P1 is to list the valv which are in the open position, and indicate which of these h failed.

The solution is given in Programs C11P9 and C11P10.

PROGRAM 11.9

```
PROGRAM C11P9(input,output,svFile);
CONST
    first      ='A';
    last       ='E';
```

```
TYPE
   Positions    =(open,closed);
   StatVecs     =RECORD
                    openTime   :INTEGER;
                    closeTime  :INTEGER;
                    totalOpenTime
                               :INTEGER;
                    qs         :INTEGER;
                    position   :Positions;
                    endFile    :BOOLEAN
                 END;
   ValveRefCodes=first..last;

VAR

   ptr          :valveRefcodes;
   statVec      :StatVecs;
   svFile       :FILE OF StatVecs;

BEGIN
  ReWrite(svFile,´sv00´);{ non ISO }
  FOR ptr:=first TO last DO
    BEGIN
      WITH statVec DO
        BEGIN
          openTime       :=0;
          closeTime      :=0;
          totalOpenTime  :=0;
          qs             :=100;
          position       :=closed;
          endFile        :=FALSE
        END;
      Write(svFile,statVec)
    END
END.
```

PROGRAM 11.10

```
PROGRAM C11P10(input,output,oldSvFile,
                            newSvFile);
{ The state vector is loaded from
oldSvFile, whilst the one produced
by this program is saved for further
use in newSvFile. This allows the
program to be suspended and restarted
as required. }
```

```
CONST
   first       = 'A';
   last        = 'E';
   sentinel    =-1;
   prompt      = 'Enter valve record';

TYPE
   Positions   =(open,closed);
   ValveRecs   =RECORD
                  valveRef  :CHAR;
                  eventTime :INTEGER;
                  eF        :BOOLEAN
                END;
   StatVecs    =RECORD
                  openTime  :INTEGER;
                  closeTime :INTEGER;
                  totalOpenTime
                            :INTEGER;
                  qs        :INTEGER;
                  position  :Positions;
                  endFile   :BOOLEAN
                END;
   ValveRefCodes=first..last;
   FileNames   =PACKED ARRAY[1..4]
                        OF CHAR;

{ VAR declarations as in CllP8 }


{ PROCEDURE LoadStatVec and Save StatVec
                         as in CllP8 }

PROCEDURE ProcessTimeSignal
              (valveRec:valveRecs);

LABEL   1,2,
        10,20,
        100,200,300,400;

BEGIN { P2, inverted. See Fig S11.17 }
 WITH statVec[valveRec.valveRef] DO
  BEGIN { Update state vector }
   IF qs=100 THEN GOTO 100;
   IF qs=200 THEN GOTO 200;
   IF qs=300 THEN GOTO 300;
```

```
100:;
    {BEGIN Process valve cycle batch }
      {BEGIN Posit good valve cycle batch}
        {BEGIN Process valve cycles }
2:  IF valveRec.eF THEN GOTO 1;
        { BEGIN Process valve cycle }
            openTime:=valveRec.eventTime;
            position:=open;
            qs:=200;
            GOTO 400;
200:        IF valveRec.eF THEN { Admit
                    error valve cycle batch }
                                GOTO 10;
            closeTime:=valveRec.eventTime;
            position:=closed;
            totalOpenTime:=totalOpenTime
                        +closeTime
                        -openTime;
            qs:=300;
            GOTO 400;
300:        GOTO 2;
        { END Process valve cycle }
      { END Process valve cycles }

1:   WriteLn('Total Valve ',
                valveRec.valveRef,
                ' Open Time: ',
                totalOpenTime:5);
        endFile:=true;
      { END Posit good valve cycle batch }
    GOTO 20;
10:{ BEGIN Admit error valve
                            cycle batch }
        Writeln('Valve ',valveRec.valveRef,
                        ' failed.');
        endFile:=true;
      { END Admit error valve cycle batch }
    { END Process valve cycle batch }
20: END; { Update state vector }
400:END { P2, inverted } ;

BEGIN { P1, Main program }
  LoadStatVec;
  WriteLn(prompt);
  WHILE NOT Eof DO
    BEGIN { Process valve record }
```

```
        ReadLn(valveRec.valveRef,
               valveRec.eventTime);
        IF valveRec.eventTime=sentinel THEN
           valveRec.eF:=true
        ELSE
           valveRec.eF:=false;
        IF statVec[valveRec.valveRef]
                            .endFile<>true

    THEN
         ProcessTimeSignal(valveRec)
    ELSE
         WriteLn(valveRec.valveRef,
            ' is shut down or failed!');
    WriteLn(prompt);
    END; { Process valve record }
BEGIN { Check for open valves }
 FOR ptr:=first TO last DO
    BEGIN
    IF statVec[ptr].position=open
                                THEN

    BEGIN
      Write('WARNING! Valve ',ptr,
                       ' still open');
      IF statvec[ptr].endFile=true
         THEN Write(' and failed!');
      WriteLn
    END

    END; { Check for open valves }
    SaveStatVec
END { Pl, Main program } .
```

Further development of the subject of communication between grams is outside the scope of this book, but can be found in Jackson

It should be pointed out that since inversion makes for min: coupling between programs, there is no reason why an inverted gram should not have other programs inverted with respect to it and so on. In fact whole networks of programs can be linked toge in this manner.

The techniques used in this section have led in a systematic wa the implementation of simple program designs which, altho straightforward, have allowed us to dispense with intermediate and also removed the need to dedicate one processor permanent each of the entities whose data we wished to process. The conce the dedicated processor is nevertheless useful in the design of syst since, as has been shown, it can be implemented without great difficulty. It is in fact used in the Jackson System Development method (JSD), which provides a rewarding approach to the design of both industrial and commercial data processing systems. The interested reader is referred to Jackson (6).

After completing the study of this chapter you should be able to

1 Identify one-to-one correspondences in simple cases,
2 Combine suitable data structures to form a basic program structure,
3 Recognise ordering, boundary and interleaving clashes,
4 Resolve structure clashes using intermediate files,
5 Carry out the steps of the inversion process,
6 Implement inversion in Pascal using flat coding, in order to resolve data structure clashes,
7 Use state vector separation to implement long-running programs,
8 Use appropriate communication methods between processes.

Having reached the end of this book, the authors hope that the reader has gained some ability in the design and implementation of good programs and is curious to learn more about the methods described here by further study, and, above all, by using them!

---

e 11.16 A bank allows its customers to update their accounts from any of a number of cash points. Hence, the central computer has to carry on a simultaneous dialogue with a number of customers at a number of terminals. If each message identifies the cash point and the customer as well as providing other data, write a program to carry out the processing of customers' accounts. You may like to approach this problem by keeping the possible dialogue at a simple level initially (withdrawal only, no mistakes by customers, no equipment malfunctions and only one cash point) and then make your solution more and more sophisticated as your skills improve, and you gain access to more sophisticated hardware.

Of course, a real system should be properly planned in the first place (possibly using JSD) and not developed like this. However, you should be pleasantly surprised at what you can achieve using the principles of structured program design as described in this book.

Appendix 1
Pascal reserved words
and pre-defined names

Reserved words:

AND	DO	FUNCTION	NIL	PROGRAM	TYPE
ARRAY	DOWNTO	GOTO	NOT	RECORD	UNTIL
BEGIN	ELSE	IF	OF	REPEAT	VAR
CASE	END	IN	OR	SET	WHILE
CONST	FILE	LABEL	PACKED	THEN	WITH
DIV	FOR	MOD	PROCEDURE	TO	

Pre-defined names:

Abs	EOF	Max Int	Put	Sin	Unpack
Arctan	EOLn	New	Read	Sqr	Write
BOOLEAN	Exp	Odd	ReadLn	Sqrt	WriteLn
CHAR	FALSE	Ord	REAL	Succ	
Chr	Get	Pack	RESET	Text	
Cos	INTEGER	Page	REWRITE	TRUE	
Dispose	Ln	Pred	Round	Trunc	

Appendix 2
ASCII character code

Table A2.1

hexadecimal code	ASCII character	hexadecimal code	ASCII character	hexadecimal code	ASCII character
20	space	40	@	60	`
21	!	41	A	61	a
22	"	42	B	62	b
23	#	43	C	63	c
24	$	44	D	64	d
25	%	45	E	65	e
26	&	46	F	66	f
27	'	47	G	67	g
28	(	48	H	68	h
29	)	49	I	69	i
2A	*	4A	J	6A	j
2B	+	4B	K	6B	k
2C	,	4C	L	6C	l
2D	−	4D	M	6D	m
2E	.	4E	N	6E	n
2F	/	4F	O	6F	o
30	0	50	P	70	p
31	1	51	Q	71	q
32	2	52	R	72	r
33	3	53	S	73	s
34	4	54	T	74	t
35	5	55	U	75	u
36	6	56	V	76	v
37	7	57	W	77	w
38	8	58	X	78	x
39	9	59	Y	79	y
3A	:	5A	Z	7A	z
3B	;	5B	[	7B	{
3C	<	5C	\	7C		
3D	=	5D	]	7D	}
3E	>	5E	^	7E	~
3F	?	5F	_		

Table A2.2 decimal, hexidecimal and binary equivalents

decimal	hexadecimal	4 bit binary
0	0	0000
1	1	0001
2	2	0010
3	3	0011
4	4	0100
5	5	0101
6	6	0110
7	7	0111
8	8	1000
9	9	1001
10	A	1010
11	B	1011
12	C	1100
13	D	1101
14	E	1110
15	F	1111

Appendix 3
Recommended further reading

1 Jackson, M. A. *Principles of Program Design*. Academic Press. (ISBN 0 12 379050 6)
The source for many of the principles used in this book, the above is essential reading for professional programmers, but is not easy reading for the inexperienced.

2 M252/PM952 *Computing and Computers: Data Structures*. Open University. (ISBN 0 335 14071 8)
This is part of a correspondence course of the Open University. It includes useful information on arrays, and will be of value to readers studying courses at 'A' level and above.

3 M252/PM951 *Computing and Computers: Files and File Processing*. Open University. (ISBN 0 335 14070 X)
This is a companion to the above and covers file organisation and processing.

4 Wirth, N. *Algorithms + Data Structures = Programs*. Prentice-Hall. (ISBN 0 13 022418 9)
This is for the experienced programmer, and contains the designs of numerous algorithms for data manipulation.

5 Cameron, J. R. *JSP and JSD, The Jackson Approach to Software Development*, IEEE Computer Society Press. (ISBN 0 8186 8516 6)
A useful overview of system and program design using Jackson's methods. This is strictly for the professional.

6 Jackson, M. A. *System Development*. Prentice-Hall. (ISBN 0 13 880328 5)
This describes the JSD systems development method. Again, strictly for the professional.

Solutions to selected exercises

The solutions given may be presented as structure diagrams or program code. In some cases, the output from test runs has been shown although the output shown is not intended to represent all the tests actually required or carried out. Additional 'WriteLn' statements have been included in some programs where they help to illustrate the action of the program.

Where solutions are expressed in Pascal, they are given the title ChxSy (standing for Chapter x, Solution to exercise y).

Chapter 2

Exercise 2.1 The 'ReadLn' statement will read four data items (from the same line) into a, b, and q: suppose they are 10, 66, 12 and 82 respectively. The innermost functions are evaluated first: Larger (a, b) returns 66, and Larger (p, q) returns 82. The 'WriteLn' statement thus becomes

$$\texttt{WriteLn(Larger(66,82))}$$

and so 82 is displayed.

Exercise 2.2 Choose declarations such as

```
VAR
  dayOfMonth: INTEGER;
  married: BOOLEAN;
  initial: CHAR;   {Be careful if you are
                    also using names such
                    as "Initialise"!}
  patientsTemperature: REAL;
```

Exercise 2.3

```
PROGRAM Ch2S3(input,output);

{Requests old and new bank balances,
and displays difference and dates.}
```

```
CONST
  qBalance1 = ´Enter old balance´;
  qBalance2 = ´Enter new balance´;
  qDate1 = ´Enter old date as dd mm yy´;
  qDate2 = ´Enter new date as dd mm yy´;
  stroke = ´/´;

VAR
  oldBalance,
  newBalance,
  difference,
  day1, month1, year1,
  day2, month2, year2: INTEGER;

BEGIN

  {Enter old and new balances}
  WriteLn(qBalance1);
  ReadLn(oldBalance);
  WriteLn(qDate1);
  ReadLn(day1, month1, year1);
  WriteLn(qBalance2);
  ReadLn(newBalance);
  WriteLn(qDate2);
  ReadLn(day2, month2, year2);

  {Calculate change in balance}
  difference:= oldBalance - newBalance;

  {Display change in balance}
  WriteLn(´In the period from ´,
    day1,stroke,month1,stroke,year1,
      ´ to ´,
    day2,stroke,month2,stroke,year2);
  WriteLn(´your balance fell by ´,
    difference)

END.
```

se   2.4

```
PROGRAM Ch2S4(input,output);

{Requests old and new bank balances,
and displays difference and dates.}

CONST
  qBalance1 = ´Enter old balance´;
```

```
      qBalance2 = ´Enter new balance´;
      qDate1 = ´Enter old date as dd mm yy´;
      qDate2 = ´Enter new date as dd mm yy´;
      stroke = ´/´;

  VAR
    oldBalance,
    newBalance,
    difference,
    day1, month1, year1,
    day2, month2, year2: INTEGER;

  PROCEDURE EnterOldAndNewBalances;
  BEGIN
    WriteLn(qBalance1);
    ReadLn(oldBalance);
    WriteLn(qDate1);
    ReadLn(day1, month1, year1);
    WriteLn(qBalance2);
    ReadLn(newBalance);
    WriteLn(qDate2);
    ReadLn(day2, month2, year2)
  END;

  PROCEDURE CalculateChangeInBalance;
  BEGIN
    difference:= oldBalance - newBalance
  END;

  PROCEDURE DisplayChangeInBalance;
  BEGIN
    WriteLn(´In the period from ´,
      day1,stroke,month1,stroke,year1,
      ´ to ´,
      day2,stroke,month2,stroke,year2);
    WriteLn(´your balance fell by ´,
      difference)
  END;

  BEGIN {Ch2S3}

    EnterOldAndNewBalances;
    CalculateChangeInBalance;
    DisplayChangeInBalance

  END.  {Ch2S3}
```

Chapter 3

cise   3.1   See Figure S3.1.

;URE S3.1

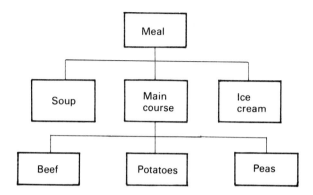

:ise   3.2   The structure diagram is shown as Figure S3.2, and the Pascal is shown as Ch3S2.

URE S3.2

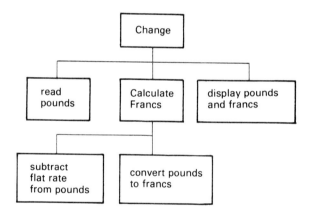

```
PROGRAM Ch3S2(input,output);

{This program performs a currency
conversion from pounds to francs,
including the charging of a commission.}

CONST
   flatRate = 1;
   rateOfExchange = 11;

VAR
   pounds,
   francs:INTEGER;

BEGIN   {Change}
```

```
WriteLn('Enter pounds');
ReadLn(pounds);

{Calculate francs}
pounds:= pounds - flatRate;
francs:= pounds * rateOfExchange;

WriteLn('After deducting commission,',
    pounds, ' pounds gives ',
    francs, ' francs')

END.    {Change}
```

Exercise   3.3   See Figure S3.3

FIGURE S3.3

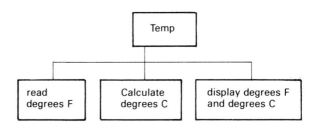

Chapter 4

Exercise   4.1

```
PROGRAM Ch4S1(input,output);

{Checks a student's grade}

CONST
    failGrade = 'F';

VAR
    referenceNumber: INTEGER;
    grade: CHAR;

BEGIN

    WriteLn('Enter reference number');
    ReadLn(referenceNumber);
    WriteLn('Enter grade');
    ReadLn(grade);

    IF    {Display result}
        grade < failGrade
```

```
        THEN
          BEGIN
            WriteLn(referenceNumber,´ Accept´)
          END
        ELSE
          BEGIN
            WriteLn(referenceNumber,´ Reject´)
          END
    {ENDIF} {Display result}

    END.
```

Exercise 4.2

```
        PROGRAM Ch4S2(input,output);

        {Checks access authorisation}

        CONST
          lowerLimit = ´G´;
          higherLimit = ´M´;

        VAR
          referenceNumber: INTEGER;
          code: CHAR;

        BEGIN

          WriteLn(´Enter reference number´);
          ReadLn(referenceNumber);
          WriteLn(´Enter code´);
          ReadLn(code);

          {Display results}
          Write(referenceNumber);
          IF      {Display access assessment}
            (code >= lowerLimit)
            AND
            (code <= higherLimit)
          THEN
            BEGIN
              WriteLn(´ Access authorised´)
            END
          ELSE
            BEGIN
              WriteLn(
                ´ Code not accepted for access´)
            END
```

```
        {ENDIF} {Display access assessment}

END.
```

See Figure S4.3.

FIGURE S4.3

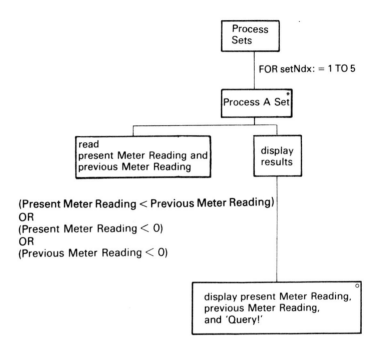

```
PROGRAM Ch4S4(input,output);

{Displays table showing cost of milk}

CONST
  maxCost = 100;
  maxNoOfPints = 6;

VAR
  noOfPints,
  pintaCost,
  cost: INTEGER;

BEGIN    {Pintas}

  BEGIN    {Initialise}
    noOfPints:= 1
  END;     {Initialise}
```

```
  WriteLn('Enter cost of pinta');
  ReadLn(pintaCost);

  BEGIN     {Display table}
    WriteLn('Pints    Price');
    REPEAT    {Calc & display lines}
      BEGIN     {Calc & display a line}
        cost:= pintaCost * noOfPints;
        WriteLn(noOfPints, cost);
        noOfPints:= noOfPints + 1
      END        {Calc & display a line}
    UNTIL
      (cost > maxCost)
      OR
      (noOfPints > maxNoOfPints)
    {ENDREPEAT} {Calc & display lines}
    END        {Display table}

END.      {Pintas}
```

Exercise 4.5 See Figure S4.5.

FIGURE S4.5

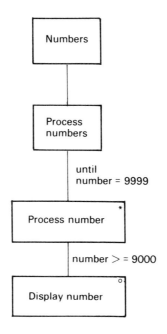

Exercise 4.6

```
PROGRAM Ch4S6(input,output);

{Displays two numbers in order}
```

```
VAR
  firstNumber,
  secondNumber: INTEGER;

BEGIN    {Order}

  WriteLn('Enter first number');
  ReadLn(firstNumber);
  WriteLn('Enter second number');
  ReadLn(secondNumber);

  IF         {Display numbers in order}
    firstNumber < secondNumber
  THEN
    BEGIN
      WriteLn(firstNumber,secondNumber)
    END
  ELSE
    BEGIN
      WriteLn(secondNumber,firstNumber)
    END
  {ENDIF}   {Display numbers in order}

END.      {Order}
```

Exercise 4.8   There are many possible solutions to this problem, all of them rather clumsy. One possible approach, which should be coded and tested, is given in Figure S4.8.

FIGURE S4.8

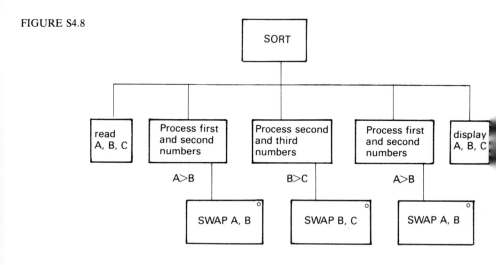

```
PROGRAM Ch4S10(input,output);

{Display a given number of hyphens or
other symbols}

CONST
  symbol = '-';

VAR
  howMany,
  counter:INTEGER;

BEGIN    {Symbols}

  WriteLn('How many symbols?');
  ReadLn(howMany);

  FOR       {Display symbols}
    counter:= 1 TO howMany
  DO
    BEGIN
      Write(symbol)
    END;
  {ENDFOR}
  WriteLn

END.      {Symbols}
```

Programs Ch4S12a and Ch4S12b show possible solutions. The former is preferable as it gives a sensible amount for the sum, even if the input data consists of the sentinel alone. Neither is adequate if negative marks are entered.

```
PROGRAM Ch4S12a(input,output);

{Calculates total of marks}

CONST
  sentinel = -1;

VAR
  mark,
  sum: INTEGER;

BEGIN    {Total marks}

  {Initialise}
  sum:= 0;
  WriteLn('Enter next mark');
  ReadLn(mark);
```

```
WHILE        {Sum marks}
  mark <> sentinel
DO
  BEGIN         {Process mark}
    sum:= sum + mark;
    WriteLn('Enter next mark');
    ReadLn(mark)
  END;          {Process mark}
{ENDWHILE} {Sum marks}

WriteLn('Sum is ', sum)

END.     {Total marks}
```

```
PROGRAM Ch4Sl2b(input,output);

{Calculates total of marks}

CONST
  sentinel = -1;

VAR
  mark,
  sum: INTEGER;

BEGIN    {Total marks}

  {Initialise}
  sum:= 0;
  WriteLn('Enter next mark');
  ReadLn(mark);

  REPEAT        {Sum marks}
    BEGIN         {Process mark}
      sum:= sum + mark;
      WriteLn('Enter next mark');
      ReadLn(mark)
    END           {Process mark}
  UNTIL
    mark = sentinel;
  {ENDREPEAT} {Sum marks}

  WriteLn('Sum is ', sum)

END.     {Total marks}
```

ise 4.13

```
PROGRAM Ch4S13(input,output);

{Calculates total of marks}

VAR
  howMany,
  mark,
  sum,
  counter: INTEGER;

BEGIN     {Total marks}

  {Initialise}
  sum:= 0;
  WriteLn('How many marks?');
  ReadLn(howMany);

  FOR       {Process marks}
    counter:= 1 TO howMany
  DO
    BEGIN     {Process mark}
      WriteLn('Enter next mark');
      ReadLn(mark);
      sum:= sum + mark
    END;        {Process mark}
  {ENDFOR} {Process marks}

  WriteLn('Sum is ', sum)

END.        {Total marks}
```

se 4.15 See Figure S4.15.

RE S4.15

Chapter 5

```
PROGRAM Ch5S1(input,output);

{Foodstuffs trial: groups of pigs to be
weighed,and weight of each pig recorded.
Calculates average weight of pigs in
each group, and average weight of all
pigs.  Assumes no empty groups.}

CONST
  sentinel = -1;

VAR
  groupIndex,
  nmrGroups: INTEGER;

  weight,
  groupWt,
  groupAve,
  groupTotal,
  sumTotal,
  sumWt,
  grandAve: REAL;

PROCEDURE PPig;
BEGIN
  groupTotal:= groupTotal + 1;
  groupWt:= groupWt + weight;
  WriteLn('Weight of next pig?');
  ReadLn(weight)
END;

PROCEDURE PGroupAverage;
BEGIN
  groupAve:= groupWt / groupTotal;
  WriteLn('Group: ', groupIndex:4,
    ' Average weight: ', groupAve:7:2)
END;

PROCEDURE UpdateTotals;
BEGIN
  sumWt:= sumWt + groupWt;
  sumTotal:= sumTotal + groupTotal
END;

PROCEDURE GroupInitialise;
BEGIN
```

```
  groupWt:= 0;
  groupTotal:= 0
END;

PROCEDURE PPigsInGroup;
BEGIN
  WHILE
    weight <> sentinel
  DO
    BEGIN
      PPig
    END
  {ENDWHILE}
END;


  PROCEDURE FinishWithGroup;
  BEGIN
    PGroupAverage;
    UpdateTotals
  END;

  PROCEDURE PGroup;
  BEGIN
    GroupInitialise;
    WriteLn('Weight of next pig?');
    ReadLn(weight);
    PPigsInGroup;
    FinishWithGroup
  END;

  PROCEDURE Initialise;
  BEGIN
    sumWt:= 0;
    sumTotal:= 0
  END;

  PROCEDURE PGroups;
  VAR
    groupNdx: INTEGER;
  BEGIN
    FOR
      groupNdx:= 1 TO nmrGroups
    DO
      BEGIN
        groupIndex:= groupNdx;
        PGroup
      END
```

```
      {ENDFOR}
    END;

  PROCEDURE PGrandAverage;
  BEGIN
    grandAve:= sumWt / sumTotal;
    WriteLn('Average weight of pigs: ',
      grandAve:8:3)
  END;

  BEGIN    {Porkers}
    Initialise;
    WriteLn('How many groups?');
    ReadLn(nmrGroups);
    PGroups;
    PGrandAverage
  END.      {Porkers}
```

Chapter 6

Exercice   6.1

```
  PROGRAM Ch6S1(input,output);

  CONST
    stringLength = 6;

  TYPE
    StrNdxs = 1..stringLength;
    String = PACKED ARRAY[StrNdxs]OF CHAR;
  VAR
    first,second,third: String;
    strNdx: strNdxs;

  {Note: this program could be written
  much more concisely by creating
  procedures GetString and FindSecond
  with parameters}

  BEGIN

    {Get first string}
    FOR
      strNdx:= 1 TO stringLength
    DO
      BEGIN
        Read(first[strNdx])
      END;
    {ENDFOR}
    ReadLn;
```

```
{Get second string}
{... similar ...}

{Get third string}
{... similar ...}

{Find first}
IF
  (first < second) AND (first < third)
THEN
  BEGIN
    WriteLn(first);
    IF      {Find second}
      second < third
    THEN
      BEGIN
        WriteLn(second);
        WriteLn(third)
      END
    ELSE
      BEGIN
        WriteLn(third);
        WriteLn(second)
      END
    {ENDIF} {Find second}
  END

ELSE
  IF
    (second < first)AND(second < third)
  THEN
    BEGIN
      WriteLn(second);
      IF      {Find second}
        first < third
      THEN
        BEGIN
          WriteLn(first);
          WriteLn(third)
        END
      ELSE
        BEGIN
          WriteLn(third);
          WriteLn(first)
        END
      {ENDIF} {Find second}
    END
```

```
        ELSE
          BEGIN
            WriteLn(third);
            IF       {Find second}
              first < second
            THEN
              BEGIN
                WriteLn(first);
                WriteLn(second)
              END
            ELSE
              BEGIN
                WriteLn(second);
                WriteLn(first)
              END
            {ENDIF} {Find second}
          END

      {ENDIF}

    {ENDIF}

END.
```

Exercise   6.2

```
PROGRAM Ch6S2(input,output);

{A sequence of "references" are entered
to test the design of this program}

CONST
  sentinel = -1;
  stackLength = 7;
  lengthExtended = 8;

TYPE
  StackNds = 1..stackLength;
  ExtendedStacks = 1..lengthExtended;
  Stacks = ARRAY[stackNds]OF INTEGER;

VAR
  stackPointer: ExtendedStacks;
  newRef: INTEGER;
  stack: Stacks;
  stackNdx: StackNds;
```

```
BEGIN

  stackPointer:= 1;
  Read(newRef);

  WHILE
    newRef <> sentinel
  DO
    BEGIN
      {Push stack}
      IF
        stackPointer > stackLength
      THEN
        BEGIN
          WriteLn('Stack full: ',
            newRef:3, ' not stacked')
        END
      ELSE
        BEGIN
          stack[stackPointer]:= newRef;
          stackPointer:= stackPointer +1
        END;
      {ENDIF}

      Read(newRef)
    END;
  {ENDWHILE}


  {Display stack}
  IF
    stackPointer = 1
  THEN
    BEGIN
      WriteLn('Stack empty')
    END
  ELSE
    BEGIN
      FOR
        stackNdx:= 1 TO stackPointer - 1
      DO
        BEGIN
          WriteLn('Position ',stackNdx:2,
            ': Stack element: ',
            stack[stackNdx])
        END
      {ENDFOR}
```

```
      END
      {ENDIF}

  END.
```

Exercise   6.3

```
  PROGRAM Ch6S3(input,output);

  {Demonstrates how elements can be popped
  from a stack}

  CONST
    stackLength = 7;
    lengthExtended = 8;
    testLength = 4;

  TYPE
    StackNds = 1..stackLength;
    ExtendedStacks = 1..lengthExtended;
    Stacks = ARRAY[StackNds]OF INTEGER;

  VAR
    stackPointer: ExtendedStacks;
    stack: Stacks;
    counter: StackNds;

  BEGIN

    {Initialise}
    stackPointer:= testLength;
    stack[1]:= 111;
    stack[2]:= 222;
    stack[3]:= 333;

    FOR
      counter:= 1 TO testLength
    DO
      BEGIN {Pop stack}
        IF
          stackPointer > 1
        THEN
          BEGIN
            stackPointer:=stackPointer - 1;
            WriteLn('Counter: ',counter:2,
                '. Popped element: ',
              stack[stackPointer]);
            WriteLn('Stack pointer now ',
              stackPointer:2)
```

```
            END
          ELSE
            BEGIN
              WriteLn('Counter: ',counter:2,
                   '. Stack empty')
            END
          {ENDIF}
        END
      {ENDFOR}

  END.
```

se   6.13

```
      PROGRAM Ch6S13(input,output);

      {Processes a file of entered queries}

      CONST
        noOfPupils = 2;
        noOfSubjects = 3;
        sentinel = -1;
        colon = ' : ';
        askPMarks = 'Enter marks for pupil ';
        askSMark = 'Enter mark for subject ';
        askQueries = 'Enter queries now';
        askPupilRef='Enter pupil reference: ';
        askSubjectRef =
          'Enter subject reference: ';
        tableHeading = 'Results table: ';
        pupilHdg = 'Pupil: ';
        pupilMsg = 'Mark for pupil ';
        subjectMsg = ' in subject ';

      TYPE
        PuplNdxs = 1..noOfPupils;
        SubjNdxs = 1..noOfSubjects;
        Marks = ARRAY[PuplNdxs,SubjNdxs]OF
          INTEGER;

      VAR
        pupilNdx: PuplNdxs;
        subjectNdx: SubjNdxs;
        mark: Marks;
        i,
        j: INTEGER;

      BEGIN
```

```
{Enter marks}
FOR
  pupilNdx:= 1 TO noOfPupils
DO
  BEGIN {Enter marks for a pupil}
  WriteLn(askPMarks,pupilNdx:2,colon);
    FOR       {Enter subject marks}
      subjectNdx:= 1 TO noOfSubjects
    DO
      BEGIN {Enter mark for a subject}
        WriteLn(askSMark,subjectNdx:2,
          colon);
        ReadLn(mark[pupilNdx,
          subjectNdx])
      END    {Enter mark for a subject}
    {ENDFOR} {Enter subject marks}
  END;   {Enter marks for a pupil}
{ENDFOR}

  {Process queries}
  WriteLn;
  WriteLn(askQueries);
  WriteLn(askPupilRef);
  ReadLn(i);
  WHILE
    i <> sentinel
  DO
    BEGIN
      WriteLn(askSubjectRef);
      ReadLn(j);
      WriteLn(pupilMsg,i:2,subjectMsg,
        j:2,colon,mark[i,j]:3);
      WriteLn;
      WriteLn(askPupilRef);
      ReadLn(i)
    END;
  {ENDWHILE}

  {Display array}
  WriteLn;
  WriteLn(tableHeading);
  FOR
    pupilNdx:= 1 TO noOfPupils
  DO
    BEGIN
      WriteLn(pupilHdg,pupilNdx:2);
      FOR
        subjectNdx:= 1 TO noOfSubjects
```

```
      DO
        BEGIN
          Write(mark[pupilNdx,
            subjectNdx]:10)
        END;
      {ENDFOR}
      WriteLn
    END
  {ENDFOR}

END.
```

se   6.15

```
PROGRAM Ch6S15(input,output);

{Transposes rows and columns of a square
array}

CONST
  sidelength = 3;
  noOfRows = sideLength;
  noOfCols = sideLength;
  askRowAll =
  ´Enter elements(one by one) for row: ´;
  askRowOne = ´Enter element for row ´;
  askCol = ´, column ´;
  heading =
     ´Transposed array (or matrix): ´;

TYPE
  RowNdxs = 1..noOfRows;
  ColNdxs = 1..noOfCols;
  Squares = ARRAY[rowNdxs,colNdxs]OF
    INTEGER;

VAR
  rowNdx: RowNdxs;
  colNdx: ColNdxs;
  square: Squares;
  copy: INTEGER;

BEGIN

  {Enter data}
  FOR
    rowNdx:= 1 TO noOfRows
  DO
```

```
    BEGIN
      WriteLn(askRowAll, rowNdx:2);
      FOR
        colNdx:= 1 TO noOfCols
      DO
        BEGIN
          WriteLn(askRowOne, rowNdx:2,
            askCol, colNdx:2);
          ReadLn(square[colNdx,rowNdx])
        END
      {ENDFOR}
    END;
  {ENDFOR}

  {Interchange rows and columns}
  FOR
    rowNdx:= 1 TO noOfRows
  DO
    BEGIN
      FOR
        colNdx:= 1 TO noOfCols
      DO
        BEGIN
          copy:= square[rowNdx,colNdx];
          square[rowNdx,colNdx]:=
            square[colNdx,rowNdx];
          square[colNdx,rowNdx]:= copy
        END
      {ENDFOR}
    END;
  {ENDFOR}

  {Display transposed array}
  WriteLn;
  WriteLn(heading);
  FOR
    rowNdx:= 1 TO noOfRows
  DO
    BEGIN
      FOR
        colNdx:= 1 TO noOfCols
      DO
        BEGIN
          Write(square[rowNdx,colNdx])
        END;
      {ENDFOR}
      WriteLn
    END
```

```
{ENDFOR}

END.
```

Chapter 7

The semicolons after the two Read statements, after 'count:= count + 1', and after WriteLn statement are all legal but redundant. The one after the WHILE condition, and the two inside the WriteLn parameter list (which should be commas) are illegal.

```
PROGRAM Ch7S2(pay,output);

{Prints payslips with information from
a file on backing store}

CONST
  oTimeRate = 1.5;
  taxFreePercent = 40;
  taxRatePercent = 33;
  sentinel = -1;
  strLength = 8;

TYPE
  String = PACKED ARRAY[1..strLength]
    OF CHAR;
  Employees = RECORD
    referenceNumber: INTEGER;
    name: String;
    date: String;
    flatRtHours: INTEGER;
    oTimeHours: INTEGER;
    payRate: REAL;
    nationalInsurance: REAL
            END{RECORD};
  PayFiles = FILE OF Employees;

VAR
  pay: PayFiles;
  payrollRecord: Employees;
  flatRtPay,
  oTimePay,
  grossPay,
  taxablePay,
  tax,
  deductions,
  netPay: REAL;
```

```
PROCEDURE Calculate;
  BEGIN
    WITH
      payrollRecord
    DO
      BEGIN

        {Calculate gross pay}
        flatRtPay:=flatRtHours* payRate;
        oTimePay:= oTimeHours * payRate
          * oTimeRate;
        grossPay:= flatRtPay + oTimePay;

        {Calculate deductions}
        taxablePay:= grossPay - grossPay
          *taxFreePercent / 100;
        tax:=taxablePay * taxRatePercent
          / 100;
        deductions:= tax
          + nationalInsurance;

        {Calculate net pay}
        netPay:= grossPay - deductions

    END
  {ENDWITH}
END;

PROCEDURE DisplayPayslip;
  BEGIN
    WITH
      payrollRecord
    DO
      BEGIN

        WriteLn(name, ´  Week ending  ´,
          date);
        WriteLn(referenceNumber:1);
        WriteLn(´Pay at flat rate:  ´,
          flatRtHours:3, ´ hours at ´,
          payRate:7:2, ´ per hour:  ´,
          flatRtPay:7:2);
        WriteLn(´Pay at overtime rate:  ´,
          oTimeHours:3, ´ hours at ´,
          oTimeRate:7:2, ´ per hour:  ´,
          oTimePay:7:2);
        WriteLn(´National Insurance:  ´,
          nationalInsurance:7:2);
```

```
      WriteLn('Income tax:   ',tax:7:2);
        WriteLn('Total deductions:   ',
          deductions:7:2);
        WriteLn('Net pay:   ',netPay:7:2);

    END
  {ENDWITH}
END;

BEGIN

  RESET(pay);

  Read(pay, payrollRecord);
  WHILE
    payrollRecord.referenceNumber
      <> sentinel
  DO
    BEGIN
      Calculate;
      DisplayPayslip;
      Read(pay, payrollRecord)
    END
  {ENDWHILE}

END.
```

cise   7.8

```
PROGRAM Ch7S8(input,output);

{Reads in the ages of fifty people and
displays the total numbers in each
decade between two given figures.}

CONST
  lowestAgeGroup = 0;
  highestAgeGroup = 9;
  noOfPersons = 50;

TYPE
  Decades =
    lowestAgeGroup..highestAgeGroup;
  Totals = ARRAY[Decades]OF INTEGER;
  Persons = 1..noOfPersons;

VAR
  start,
  finish: INTEGER;
```

```
PROCEDURE FindAgeGroups
(low,high:Decades);

VAR
  totalNdx: Decades;
  personNdx: Persons;
  total: Totals;
  age: INTEGER;

BEGIN

  {Initialise totals}
  FOR
    totalNdx:= low TO high
  DO
    BEGIN
      total[totalNdx]:= 0
    END;
  {ENDFOR}

  {Read in ages and accumulate totals}
  FOR
    personNdx:= 1 TO noOfPersons
  DO
    BEGIN
      Read(age);
      IF
        (age DIV 10 >= low)
        AND
        (age DIV 10 <= high)
      THEN
        BEGIN
          total[age DIV 10]:=
            total[age DIV 10] + 1
        END
      {ENDIF}
    END;
  {ENDFOR}

  {Report totals}
  FOR
    totalNdx:= low TO high
  DO
    BEGIN
      WriteLn('Total for group ',
        totalNdx:2, total[totalNdx])
    END
```

```
    {ENDFOR}

  END;

BEGIN
  Read(start,finish);
  FindAgeGroups(start,finish)
END.
```

```
    PROGRAM Ch7S9(input,output);

    {Reads a stream of digits, and reports
    the proportion of times in which each
    one appears}

    CONST
      sentinel = -1;

    TYPE
      Range = 0..9;
      Totals = ARRAY[Range]OF INTEGER;

    VAR
      digit,
      count: INTEGER;
      total: Totals;
      index: Range;

    BEGIN

      {Initialise totals}
      FOR
        index:= 0 TO 9
      DO
        BEGIN
          total[index]:= 0
        END;
      {ENDFOR}
      count:= 0;

      {Read in ages and accumulate totals}
      Read(digit);
      WHILE
        digit <> sentinel
      DO
        BEGIN
          total[digit]:= total[digit] + 1;
```

```
            count:= count + 1;
            Read(digit)
        END;
      {ENDWHILE}

      {Report totals}
      FOR
        index:= 0 TO 9
      DO
          BEGIN
            WriteLn('Proportion for digit',
              index:2,
              total[index]*100 / count:8:2)
          END
      {ENDFOR}

    END.
```

Chapter 8

```
PROGRAM Ch8Sl(input,output);

CONST
  noOfSubjs = 3;
  coursePassMark = 50;
  examPassMark = 50;
  space = ' ';
  reqdIncoursePasses = 2;
  reqdExamPasses = 2;
  sentinel = '****            ';
  nameLength = 15;

TYPE
  SubjCtrs = 1..noOfSubjs;
  Lists = ARRAY[SubjCtrs]OF INTEGER;
  NameNdxs = 1..nameLength;
  Names = PACKED ARRAY[NameNdxs]OF CHAR;

VAR
  courseResults,
  examResults: Lists;
  student: Names;

PROCEDURE PResults
  (VAR courseMark, examMark: Lists;
   VAR incoursePassCount, examPassCount:
```

```
    INTEGER);
VAR
  subjCtr: SubjCtrs;
BEGIN
  FOR
    subjCtr:= 1 TO noOfSubjs
  DO
    BEGIN {P subject}
      IF       {P incourse mark}
        courseMark[subjCtr]
          > coursePassMark
      THEN
        BEGIN
          incoursePassCount:=
            incoursePassCount + 1
        END;
      {ENDIF} {P incourse mark}
      IF       {P exam mark}
        examMark[subjCtr]
          > examPassMark
      THEN
        BEGIN
          examPassCount:=
            examPassCount + 1
        END
      {ENDIF} {P exam mark}
    END    {P subject}
  {ENDFOR}
END;


PROCEDURE ReadRecord
  (VAR name: Names; VAR courseMark,
   examMark: Lists);
  VAR
    nameNdx: NameNdxs;
    subjCtr: SubjCtrs;
  BEGIN
    {Read name}
    FOR
      nameNdx:= 1 TO nameLength
    DO
      BEGIN
        Read(name[nameNdx])
      END;
    {ENDFOR}

    {Read subjects}
```

```
      FOR
        subjCtr:= 1 TO noOfSubjs
      DO
        BEGIN {Read subject}
          Read(courseMark[subjCtr]);
          Read(examMark[subjCtr])
        END;  {Read subject}
      {ENDFOR}
      ReadLn
    END;


 PROCEDURE PCandidateRecord
   (VAR name: Names; VAR courseMark,
    examMark: Lists);
   VAR
     incoursePassCount,
     examPassCount: INTEGER;
   BEGIN
     incoursePassCount:= 0;
     examPassCount:= 0;
     PResults;

     {Display headings}
     WriteLn('Name':15, 'In-course':15,
       'Exam':15, 'Result':15);
     WriteLn(space:15, 'Passes':15,
       'Passes':15);

     {Display record}
     Write(name:15, incoursePassCount:15,
       examPassCount:15);

     {Display result}
     IF
       (incoursePassCount
         >= reqdIncoursePasses)
       AND
       (examPassCount >= reqdExamPasses)
     THEN
       BEGIN
         WriteLn('Pass':8)
       END
     ELSE
       BEGIN
         WriteLn('Fail':8)
       END;
     {ENDIF}
```

```
ReadRecord (name, courseMark,
    examMark)
END;

BEGIN {P assessments}

ReadRecord (student, courseResults,
    examResults);
{P File Body}
WHILE
    name <> sentinel
DO
    BEGIN
    , PCandidateRecord (student,
        courseResults, examResults)
    END
{ENDWHILE}

END.  {P assessments}
```

---

se   8.3   The input data structure, adding a sentinel record with a name field to indicate the end of the candidate records for a constituency, is given in Figure S8.3(a).

JRE S8.3

(a)

Noting that we cannot count on there being a candidate in every constituency the operations list is as follows.

1 Input record (ReadRecord)
2 Display constituency results
3 Set winner to dummy candidate name
4 Set winner's part to dummy part name
5 Set winning vote to dummy value of zero
6 Update name of winner
7 Update party of winner
8 Update votes of winner
9 Set number of constituencies

We need read-ahead within each constituency, using the procedure called ReadRecord. This is based on the structure of Candidate record. Asking our usual questions of 'How many times?', 'Beginning, middle or end?' leads to Tabl S8.3. Our complete structure diagram is given in Figure S8.3(b).

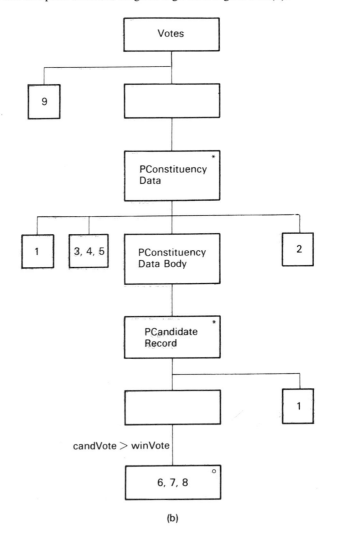

(b)

Table 8.3

operation	frequency	parent	position
2	Once/constituency	PConstituency Data	end
3, 4, 5	Once/constituency	PConstituency Data	beginning
6, 7, 8	Once/candidate	PCandidate Record	middle
9	Once/program	PVotes	beginning

:ise 8.4 For testing purposes, we can set the number of constituencies to 3 instead of 100. The risks of doing this include failing to discover that:

1 The program is too slow to execute;
2 the computer has insufficient store to cope with all the data;
3 integers may become too great and cause overflow errors.

None of these appears to be important in this example, and so we shall be safe to test the program using 3 constituencies. This is shown as Ch8S4.

```
PROGRAM Ch8S4(input,output);

CONST
  sentinel = '*            ';
  dummyWinner = 'No candidate        ';
  dummyParty = 'None        ';
  candLength = 20;
  partyLength = 12;

TYPE
  CandNdxs = 1..candLength;
  Names = PACKED ARRAY[CandNdxs]OF CHAR;
  PartNds = 1..partyLength;
  Parties= PACKED ARRAY[PartNds]OF CHAR;

VAR
  numberOfConsts,
  constituencyNdx: INTEGER;

PROCEDURE ReadRecord(
  VAR candVote: INTEGER;
  VAR candname: Names;
  VAR partyName: Parties);

  VAR
    candNdx: CandNdxs;
    partyNdx: PartNds;
    constNumber: INTEGER;
```

```
BEGIN
  WriteLn;
  WriteLn('Enter constituency number');
  ReadLn(constNumber);
  WriteLn('Enter candidate name');
  FOR
    candNdx:= 1 TO candLength
  DO
    BEGIN
      Read(candName[candNdx])
    END;
  {ENDFOR}
  ReadLn;
  WriteLn('Enter party name');
  FOR
    partyNdx:= 1 TO partyLength
  DO
    BEGIN
      Read(partyName[partyNdx])
    END;
  {ENDFOR}
  ReadLn;
  WriteLn('Enter votes cast');
  ReadLn(candVote)
END;


PROCEDURE PCandidateRecord(
  cVote: INTEGER; cName: Names;
  pName: Parties; VAR winVote:INTEGER;
  VAR winner: Names;
  VAR winParty: Parties);

BEGIN
  IF
    cVote > winVote
  THEN
    BEGIN
      winner:= cName;
      winParty:= pName;
      winVote:= cVote
    END;
  {ENDIF}
  ReadRecord(cVote, cName, pName)
END;

PROCEDURE PConstResults(
  constNdx, winVote: INTEGER;
```

```
      winner: Names; winParty: Parties);
   BEGIN
     WriteLn;
     WriteLn('Constituency number: ',
       constNdx:4);
     WriteLn('Winner: ', winner);
     WriteLn('Winning party: ',winParty);
     WriteLn('Votes cast: ', winVote:6)
   END;

PROCEDURE Initialise(
   VAR noOfConsts: INTEGER);
   BEGIN
     WriteLn('How many constituencies?');
     ReadLn(noOfConsts)
   END;


PROCEDURE PConstituencyData(
   cNdx: INTEGER);
   VAR
     candidateVote,
     winningVote: INTEGER;
     candidateName,
     winningCandidate: Names;
     nameOfParty,
     winningParty: Parties;
   BEGIN
     winningCandidate:= dummyWinner;
     winningParty:= dummyParty;;
     winningVote:= 0;
     ReadRecord(candidateVote,
       candidateName, nameOfParty);
     WHILE
       candidateName <> sentinel
     DO
       BEGIN
         PCandidateRecord(candidateVote,
           candidateName, nameOfParty,
           winningVote, winningCandidate,
           winningParty)
       END;
     {ENDWHILE}
     PConstResults(cNdx, winningVote,
       winningCandidate, winningParty)
   END;
```

```
{P votes}

BEGIN
  Initialise(numberOfConsts);
  FOR
  constituencyNdx:= 1 TO numberOfConsts
  DO
    BEGIN
      PConstituencyData(constituencyNdx)
    END
  {ENDFOR}
END.
```

Exercise 8.6 The Results box of Figure 8.8 is amended to the form in Figure S8.6.

FIGURE S8.6

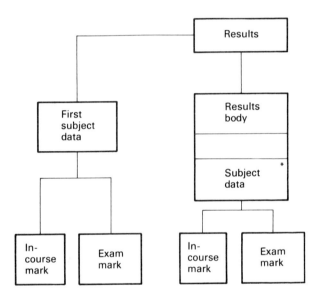

Exercise 8.10 First, let us deal with the batch preceding the first U-type record. This leads to data structure shown in Figure S8.10(a).

We can now amend the Stock movements file, as shown in figure 8.24, to co with the other types of records which may be present. The box reproduced in Figure S8.10(b) becomes as shown in Figure S8.10(c), and the box reproduce Figure S8.10(d) becomes as shown in Figure S8.10(e).

The additional operations required are:

set Pre U Record Count to zero;
increment Pre U Record Count;
print Pre U Record Count.

When these are allocated, we discover that the boxes called Other type record irrelevant, and may be omitted.

The changes required to the solution of Example 8.3 are shown as Ch8S10.

JRE S8.10

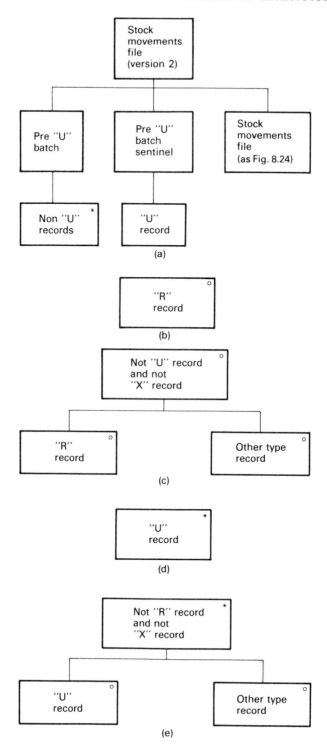

```
PROGRAM Ch8Sl0(input,output);

{Analyses file containing records of
type U, R and other (terminated by X).
Amendments indicated by {*} }

CONST
  utilisation = ´U´;
  replenishment = ´R´;
  sentinel =´X´;
VAR
  recordType: CHAR;
  rRecordCount,
  uRecordCount,
  beforeFirstURecord,            {*}
  largestUBatch: INTEGER;

PROCEDURE PPreUTypeRecord(       {*}
  VAR recType: CHAR;
  VAR preURecCount: INTEGER);
  BEGIN
    preURecCount:= 0;
    ReadLn(recType);
    WHILE
      recType <> utilisation
    DO
      BEGIN
        preURecCount:= preURecCount + 1;
        ReadLn(recType)
      END
    {ENDWHILE}
  END;

PROCEDURE PRRecord(VAR recType: CHAR;
  VAR rCount: INTEGER);
  BEGIN
    rCount:= rCount + 1;
    ReadLn(recType)
  END;

PROCEDURE PUBatch(VAR recType: CHAR;
  VAR uCount, longestBatch: INTEGER);
  VAR
    uBatchCount: INTEGER;

  BEGIN
    uBatchCount:= 0;
```

```
WHILE
  (recType <> replenishment) {*}
  AND                         {*}
  (recType <> sentinel)       {*}
DO
  BEGIN {P U Record}
    IF                        {*}
      recType = utilisation   {*}
    THEN
      BEGIN
        uCount:= uCount + 1;
        uBatchCount:= uBatchCount +1
      END;
    {ENDIF}
    ReadLn(recType)
  END;  {P U Record}
  {ENDWHILE}

IF
  uBatchCount > longestBatch
THEN
  BEGIN
    longestBatch:= uBatchCount
  END
  {ENDIF}

END;

PROCEDURE PFileComponents(
  VAR typeOfRecord: CHAR;
  VAR countOfRRecords, countOfURecords,
  mostUsInBatch: INTEGER);
  BEGIN
    IF
      typeOfRecord = replenishment
    THEN
      BEGIN
        PRRecord(typeOfRecord,
          countOfRRecords)
      END
    ELSE
      BEGIN
        IF                              {*}
          typeOfRecord = utilisation {*}
        THEN
          BEGIN
            PUBatch(typeOfRecord,
```

```
                        countOfURecords,
                        mostUsInBatch)
                  END
                {ENDIF}
              END
            {ENDIF}
          END;

    BEGIN {P Stock Movements File}

      PPreUTypeRecord(recordType,     {*}
        beforeFirstURecord);
      rRecordCount:= 0;
      uRecordCount:= 0;
      largestUBatch:= 0;

      {P File Body}
      WHILE
        recordType <> sentinel
      DO
        BEGIN
          PFileComponents(recordType,
            rRecordCount, uRecordCount,
            largestUBatch)
        END;
      {ENDWHILE}

      {Write report}
      WriteLn('Number of replenishments: ',
        rRecordCount:8);
      WriteLn('Number of utilisations: ',
        uRecordCount:8);
      WriteLn(
        'Largest batch of utilisations: ',
        largestUBatch:8);
      WriteLn('Number of records before ',
        'first utilisation: ',        {*}
        beforeFirstURecord:8)

    END.  {P Stock Movements File}
```

Chapter 9

Exercise   9.1

```
PROGRAM Ch9S1(input,output);

{Tests the procedure LinearSearch}
```

```
CONST
  noOfBranches = 5;

TYPE
  Branches = 1..noOfBranches;
  Lists = ARRAY[Branches]OF INTEGER;

VAR
  branchNdx: Branches;
  branchList: Lists;
  reqdBranch,
  pointer: INTEGER;
  targetFound: BOOLEAN;

PROCEDURE LinearSearch(target,noOfItems:
  INTEGER; VAR index: INTEGER;
  VAR found: BOOLEAN; VAR list: Lists);

  VAR
    pastIt: BOOLEAN;
    counter: INTEGER;

  BEGIN
    pastIt:= FALSE;
    found:= FALSE;
    counter:= 0;

    {Scan list}
    WHILE
      (counter < noOfItems)
      AND
      (NOT pastIt)
      AND
      (NOT found)
    DO
      BEGIN {Examine a branch record}
        counter:= counter + 1;
        IF
          list[counter] = target
        THEN
          BEGIN
            found:= TRUE
          END;
        {ENDIF}
        IF
          list[counter] > target
        THEN
```

```
                    BEGIN
                       pastIt:= TRUE
                    END
                 {ENDIF}
              END;  {Examine a branch record}
           {ENDWHILE}

           {Show index}
           IF
              (found) OR (pastIt)
           THEN
              BEGIN
                 index:= counter
              END
           ELSE
              BEGIN
                 index:= noOfItems + 1
              END
           {ENDIF}

        END;

     BEGIN

        {Set up branchList}
        FOR
           branchNdx:= 1 TO noOfBranches
        DO
           BEGIN
              WriteLn('Enter branch code');
              Read(branchList[branchNdx])
           END;
        {ENDFOR}

        WriteLn('Enter required branch');
        ReadLn(reqdBranch);

        LinearSearch(reqdBranch, noOfBranches,
           pointer, targetFound, branchList);

        IF
           targetFound
        THEN
           BEGIN
              WriteLn('Branch ', reqdBranch:3,
                 ' found at index ', pointer:3)
           END
```

```
      ELSE
        BEGIN
          WriteLn('Branch ', reqdBranch:3,
             ' not found; next index: ',
            pointer:3)
        END
      {ENDIF}

  END.
```

```
  PROGRAM Ch9S2(input,output);

  {Tests the procedure Insert}

  CONST
    maxNoOfBranches = 10;

  TYPE
    Lists = ARRAY[1..maxNoOfBranches]
      OF INTEGER;

  VAR
    noOfBranches,
    branchNdx,
    reqdBranch,
    branchList: Lists;
    targetFound: BOOLEAN;

  PROCEDURE LinearSearch(target,noOfItems:
    INTEGER; VAR index: INTEGER;
    VAR found: BOOLEAN; VAR list: Lists);

    {As in solution to Exercise 9.1}

  PROCEDURE Insert(itemReqd, howMany:
    INTEGER; VAR itemFound: BOOLEAN;
    VAR list: Lists);

    VAR
      ctr,
      pointer: INTEGER;

    BEGIN
      LinearSearch(itemReqd, howMany,
        pointer, itemFound, list);
      IF
        itemFound
```

```
          THEN
            BEGIN
              WriteLn(itemReqd:3,
                 ´ already present´)
            END
          ELSE
            BEGIN {Move other parts along}
              FOR
                ctr:= howMany DOWNTO pointer
              DO
                BEGIN
                  list[ctr + 1]:= list[ctr]
                END;
               {ENDFOR}
              list[pointer]:= itemReqd
            END
          {ENDIF}
        END;

    BEGIN

      noOfBranches:= 5;

      {Set up branchList}
      FOR
        branchNdx:= 1 TO noOfBranches
      DO
        BEGIN
          WriteLn( ´Enter branch code´);
          Read(branchList[branchNdx])
        END;
      {ENDFOR}

      IF
        noOfBranches = maxNoOfBranches
      THEN
        BEGIN
          WriteLn( ´List full´)
        END
      ELSE
        BEGIN

          WriteLn( ´Enter required branch´);
          ReadLn(reqdBranch);

          Insert(reqdBranch, noOfBranches,
            targetFound, branchList);
```

```
            IF
              NOT targetFound
            THEN
              BEGIN
                noOfBranches:= noOfBranches+1;
              WriteLn(´Number of branches now´,
                noOfBranches)
              END;
            {ENDIF}
            {Display branchList}
            FOR
              branchNdx:= 1 TO noOfBranches
            DO
              BEGIN
                WriteLn(branchNdx:4,
                    branchList[branchNdx])
              END
            {ENDFOR}

      END
    {ENDIF}

END.
```

```
PROCEDURE BinarySearch(
  target,noOfItems:INTEGER;
  VAR state:
    (found,missing,outOfRange,undefined);
  VAR position:INTEGER;
  VAR list: Lists);

  VAR
    low,
    mid,
    high: INTEGER;

  BEGIN

    {Initialise}
    low:= 1;
    high:= noOfItems;
    state:= undefined;

    {Perform range check}
    IF
      target < list[1]
    THEN
```

```
      BEGIN
        state:= outOfRange;
        position:= 1
      END;
    {ENDIF}
    IF
      target > list[noOfItems]
    THEN
      BEGIN
        state:= outOfRange;
        position:= noOfItems + 1
      END;
    {ENDIF}

    {Perform last element check}
    IF
      target = list[noOfItems]
    THEN
      BEGIN
        state:= found;
        position:= noOfItems
      END;
    {ENDIF}
  WHILE
    (state <> outOfRange)
    AND
    (state <> found)
  DO
    BEGIN
      {Scan part}
      WHILE
        (state <> missing)
        AND
        (state <> found)
      DO
        BEGIN {Check middle}
          mid:= Trunc((high + low)/2);
          IF
            target = list[mid]
          THEN
            BEGIN
              state:= found
            END
          ELSE
            IF
              high - low = 1
            THEN
```

```
                    BEGIN
                      state:= missing;
                      mid:= high
                    END
                  ELSE
                    BEGIN
                      IF        {Adjust range}
                        target < list[mid]
                      THEN
                        BEGIN
                          high:= mid
                        END
                      ELSE
                        BEGIN
                          low:= mid
                        END
                      {ENDIF} {Adjust range}
                    END
                  {ENDIF}
                {ENDIF}
              END;
           {ENDWHILE}

           position:= mid

      END
    {ENDWHILE}
  END;


PROGRAM Ch9S6(input,output);

CONST
  maxNoOfBranches = 10;

TYPE
  Lists = ARRAY[1..maxNoOfBranches]
    OF INTEGER;

VAR
  noOfBranches,
  branchNdx: INTEGER;
  branchList: Lists;

PROCEDURE LinearSearch(target,noOfItems:
  INTEGER; VAR index: INTEGER;
  VAR found: BOOLEAN; Var list: Lists);
```

se   9.6

```
      {As in solution to Exercise 9.1}

PROCEDURE Insert(itemReqd, howMany:
  INTEGER; VAR itemFound: BOOLEAN;
  VAR list: Lists);

      {As in solution to Exercise 9.2}
PROCEDURE InsertionSort(noOfElements:
  INTEGER; VAR list: Lists);

  VAR
    sortLength: INTEGER;
    targetFound: BOOLEAN;

  BEGIN
    sortLength:= 2;
    WHILE
      sortLength <= noOfElements
    DO
      BEGIN
        Insert(list[sortLength],
          sortLength - 1, targetFound,
          branchList);
        sortLength:= sortLength + 1
      END
    {ENDWHILE}
  END;

BEGIN

  noOfBranches:= 5;

  {Set up branchList}
  FOR
    branchNdx:= 1 TO noOfBranches
  DO
    BEGIN
      WriteLn('Enter branch code');
      Read(branchList[branchNdx])
    END;
  {ENDFOR}

  InsertionSort(noOfBranches,
    branchList);

  {Display sorted list}
  WriteLn('Index':10,'Branch code':12);
```

```
FOR
   branchNdx:= 1 TO noOfBranches
DO
   BEGIN
     WriteLn(branchNdx:10,
        branchList[branchNdx]:12)
   END
   {ENDFOR}

END.
```

Exercise 9.10 If 'target' is less than x[1], then the program fails to evaluate x [0] in the condition

```
WHILE
   (x[mid] <> target) AND (low <= high)
```

when mid = 0.

Oddly enough, the suggested change overcomes this difficulty, and shows how tricky a binary search can be.

Chapter 10

Exercise 10.1 See Figure S10.1.

FIGURE S10.1

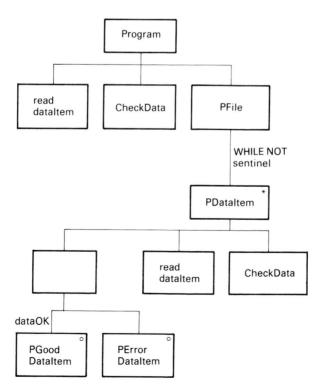

Invalid data would be a record which did not allow the sentinel to be recognised.

Exercise 10.2

```
BEGIN
  valid:= TRUE;
  FOR
    charIndex:= 1 TO charLength
  DO
    BEGIN
    Read(character[charIndex]);
    IF
        NOT(
    (character[charIndex] = space)
    OR
    (character[charIndex] IN ['0'..'9'])
            )
        THEN
          BEGIN
            valid:= FALSE
          END
        {ENDIF}
    END;
    {ENDFOR}
    WriteLn('Characters are ', valid)
END.
```

Exercise 10.3   Modify Program Ch10S2 as shown.

```
{....}
    2:BEGIN
        year:= date MOD 100;
        IF
          (year MOD 4 = 0)
          AND
          (
            (year MOD 400 = 0)
            OR
            (year MOD 100 <> 0)
          )
        THEN
          BEGIN
            valid:= day <= 29
          END
        ELSE
          BEGIN
            valid:= day <= 28
```

```
                    END
                  {ENDIF}
                END;
        {....}
```

(a) Yes.
(b) Yes.
(c) Yes.

```
PROGRAM Ch10S5(input,output);

{Tests linear search using backtracking}

CONST
  noOfParts = 5;

TYPE
  PartNdxs = 1..noOfParts;
  Lists = ARRAY[PartNdxs]OF INTEGER;

VAR
  part :Lists;
  partNdx: PartNdxs;
  present: BOOLEAN;
  reqdNumber,
  pointer: INTEGER;

PROCEDURE BacktrackLinearSearch(
  target, n: INTEGER; source:Lists;
  VAR found: BOOLEAN;
  VAR position: INTEGER);

  LABEL
    100, 200;

  VAR
    index: INTEGER;

  BEGIN

    {Posit Source Excludes Target}
    index:= 0;
    WHILE
      index < n
    DO
      BEGIN {P element}
        index:= index + 1;
```

```
                        IF
                          source[index] = target
                        THEN
                          BEGIN {Quit Source Excludes
                                    Target}
                            GOTO 100
                          END    {Quit Source Excludes
                                    Target}
                        {ENDIF}
                      END;  {P element}
                   {ENDWHILE}
                   found:= FALSE;
                   {Quit BacktrackLinearSearch}
                   GOTO 200;


         100:{Admit Source Includes Target}
             found:= TRUE;
             position:= index;



         200:
           END;

         BEGIN

           {Set up array}
           FOR
             partNdx:= 1 TO noOfParts
           DO
             BEGIN
               WriteLn('Enter part number');
               ReadLn(part[partNdx])
             END;
           {ENDFOR}

           WriteLn('Enter your required number');
           ReadLn(reqdNumber);

           BacktrackLinearSearch(
             reqdNumber, noOfParts, part,
             present, pointer   );

           IF      {Display result of search}
             present
           THEN
             BEGIN
               WriteLn(reqdNumber:6,
```

```
                ´ found at position ´,pointer:3);
        END
      ELSE
        BEGIN
          WriteLn(reqdNumber:6,´ not found´);
        END
      {ENDIF} {Display result of search}

    END.
```

se   10.6   *step 1* Assume that we can identify good and error records from the start. This leads to a data structure of Figure S10.6(a).

RE S10.6

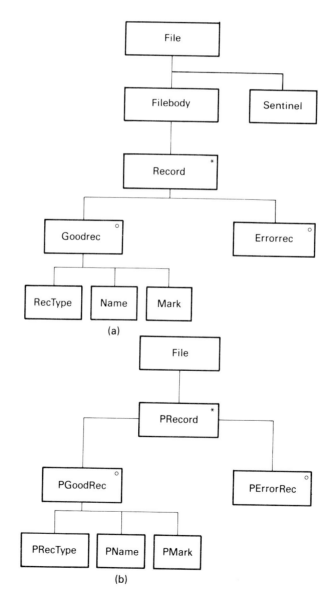

(a)

(b)

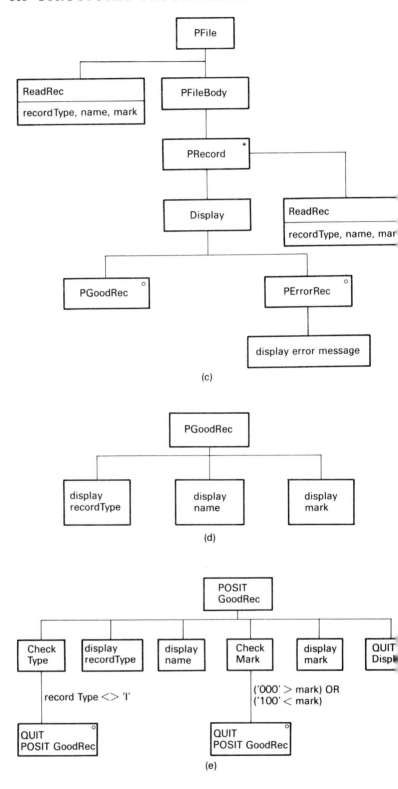

(c)

(d)

(e)

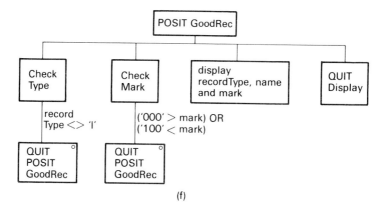

(f)

The program structure diagram is given in Figure S10.6(b), and the operations list is as follows.

1 Read record

2 Write error record

Allocating these gives the design of Figure S10.6(c), and PGoodRec is given in Figure S10.6(d).

step 2 Remove the selection between the two main processes, and POSIT Goodrec

Build in the CHECKS and QUITS, and be prepared to ADMIT Errorrec. Do not consider side effects.

PGoodRec becomes the design given in Figure S10.6(e).

step 3 Examine side effects of quitting POSITGoodrec, and deal with them.

As we do not wish to print an Errorrec as such, we reposition our checks to obtain the design given in Figure S10.6(f).

se 10.8

```
PROGRAM Ch10S8(oldMaster, transactions,
    newMaster, transErrors);

CONST
  sentinel = 'zzzz        ';
  dummy = 'z';
  stringLength = 12;

TYPE
  String = PACKED ARRAY[1..stringLength]
    OF CHAR;
  UpdateRecords = RECORD
                    surname: String;
                    transType: CHAR
                    {plus other fields}
                  END{RECORD};

VAR
  nextSurname: String;
  oldMaster,
```

```
      transactions,
      newMaster,
      transErrors: FILE OF UpdateRecords;
      oldRecord,
      transRecord: UpdateRecords;

   PROCEDURE Lower(a,b: String;
                      VAR nextString: String);

      BEGIN
        IF
          a <= b
        THEN
          BEGIN
            nextString:= a
          END
        ELSE
          BEGIN
            nextString:= b
          END
        {ENDIF}
      END;


   PROCEDURE PNextItem;

      LABEL
        100,200,300;

      CONST
        insertion = 'I';
        amendment = 'A';
        deletion  = 'D';

      BEGIN {P next item}

        IF
          (oldRecord.surname = nextSurname)
          AND
          (transRecord.surname <>
            oldRecord.surname)
        THEN
          BEGIN {Transfer OldMaster Record
                 to NewMaster}
            Write(newMaster, oldRecord);
            Read (oldMaster, oldRecord)
          END    {Transfer OldMaster Record
                 to NewMaster}
```

```
          ELSE
            BEGIN {P Transaction}
              IF
                (transRecord.surname =
                  nextSurname)
                AND
                (transRecord.surname <>
                  oldRecord.surname)
              THEN

      {<<<<<<<<<<}
      BEGIN {Revised P Insert}

        {Posit Good Insert}
        IF       {Check type}
          transRecord.transType <> insertion
        THEN
          BEGIN {Quit Posit Good Insert}
            GOTO 100
          END;  {Quit Posit Good Insert}
        {ENDIF} {Check type}
        BEGIN   {P Insert}
          Write(newMaster, transRecord);
          Read (transactions, transRecord)
        END;      {P Insert}
        BEGIN   {Quit P Next Item}
          GOTO 200
        END;      {Quit P Next Item}

      100:{Admit Error Insert}
        BEGIN
          Write(transErrors,transRecord);
          Read (transactions, transRecord)
        END

      END   {Revised P Insert}

    {>>>>>>>>>>}
            ELSE
    {<<<<<<<<<<}
    BEGIN {Revised P Deletion or Amend}

      {Posit Good Deletion or Amend}
      IF       {Check Type}
        (transRecord.transType <> amendment)
        AND
        (transRecord.transType <> deletion)
```

```
THEN
  BEGIN {Quit Posit Good Deletion or
         Amend}
    GOTO 300
  END;  {Quit Posit Good Deletion or
         Amend}
{ENDIF} {Check Type}
IF     {P Deletion or Amend}
  transRecord.transType = deletion
THEN
  BEGIN {P Delete}
    Read(oldMaster, oldRecord);
    Read(transactions, transRecord)
  END   {P Delete}
ELSE
  BEGIN {P Amend}
    Write(newMaster, transRecord);
    Read(oldMaster, oldRecord);
    Read(transactions, transRecord)
  END;  {P Amend}
{ENDIF} {P Deletion or Amend}
BEGIN {Quit P Next Item}
  GOTO 200
END;  {Quit P Next Item}

300:{Admit Error Deletion or Amend}
  BEGIN
    Write(transErrors, transRecord);
    Read (transactions, transRecord)
  END

END   {Revised P Deletion or Amend}
{>>>>>>>>>>}
        {ENDIF}
      END;   {P Transaction}
    {ENDIF}
200:
  END;


BEGIN {P Files}

  RESET(oldMaster);
  RESET(transactions);
  REWRITE(newMaster);
  REWRITE(transErrors);
  Read(oldMaster, oldRecord);
  Read(transactions, transRecord);
```

```
      Lower(oldRecord.surname,
          transRecord.surname,
          nextSurname);
    WHILE {P OldMaster/Transaction File}
      nextSurname <> sentinel
    DO
      BEGIN
        PNextItem;
        Lower(oldRecord.surname,
              transRecord.surname,
              nextSurname)
      END;
    {ENDWHILE} {P OldMaster/Transact File}
    oldRecord.surname:= sentinel;
    oldRecord.transType:= dummy;
    Write(newMaster, oldRecord)

  END.  {P Files}
```

```
    PROGRAM Ch10S15(output, custFile);

    LABEL
      100, 200;

    CONST
      sentinel = -1;
      deposit = 'D';
      repayment = 'R';

    TYPE
      CustomerRecords = RECORD
                          recType: CHAR;
                          accNo: INTEGER;
                          amount: REAL
                        END{RECORD};
      Files = FILE OF CustomerRecords;

    VAR
      custFile: Files;
      recBuff,
      rec1,
      rec2: CustomerRecords;
      current: INTEGER;

    BEGIN {P Customer File}

      RESET(custFile);
```

```
Read(custFile, recBuff);
WHILE {P File Body}
  recBuff.accNo <> sentinel
DO
  BEGIN {P Customer}
    current:= recBuff.accNo;

    {Posit valid customer report}
    IF
      recBuff.recType <> deposit
    THEN
      BEGIN {Quit valid cust report}
        GOTO 100
      END;  {Quit valid cust report}
    {ENDIF}
    rec1:= recBuff;
    Read(custFile, recBuff);
    IF
      (recBuff.accNo <> current)
      OR
      (recBuff.recType <> repayment)
      OR
      (recBuff.amount > rec1.amount)
    THEN
      BEGIN {Quit valid cust report}
        GOTO 100
      END;  {Quit valid cust report}
    {ENDIF}
    rec2:= recBuff;
    Read(custFile, recBuff);

    IF
      recBuff.accNo = current
    THEN
      BEGIN {Quit valid cust report}
        GOTO 100
      END;  {Quit valid cust report}
    {ENDIF}
    WriteLn(rec1.accNo:10,
  rec1.amount:10:2,rec2.amount:10:2);
    GOTO 200;

100:  {Admit invalid customer report}
    WriteLn(current:90);
    WHILE {Skip records for this cust}
      (recBuff.accNo <> sentinel)
      AND
```

```
        (recBuff.accNo = current)
     DO
       BEGIN
         Read(custFile,recBuff)
       END;
       {ENDWHILE}{Skip recs for this cst}
   200:
      END   {P Customer}
    {ENDWHILE} {P File Body}
   END.  {P Customer File}
```

Chapter 11

cise 11.8 The coding is given in C11S8. (Procedures ReadNamesLine and
WriteNamesLine are represented by their first lines as comments.)

```
PROGRAM C11S8(input,output);
{ This progam has P2 producing the
  report and calling P1 (procedure
  ProcessIn) as an inverted program,
  thereby removing the need for the
  intermediate file. The design of P1
  is unchanged from Fig. 11.13 but is
  implemented in a suitable way for
  Pascal. }

LABEL   100,200,300,310,400,
                    500,600,610;

{CONST, TYPE, VAR declarations as in
                    C11P3 }

 { PROCEDURE WriteNamesline; as C11P2 }

PROCEDURE ProcessIn(VAR name:NamesType);
LABEL 1,2,3,4,5,6,7,8,9,10;

 { PROCEDURE ReadNamesline; as C11P1 }
```

```
BEGIN { P1,inverted as procedure  }          {BEGIN |P1,principal code as Fig11.1
      {                 ProcessIn }
      IF qs=1 THEN GOTO 1;
      IF qs=3 THEN GOTO 3;
      IF qs=4 THEN GOTO 4;
      IF qs=6 THEN GOTO 6;
      IF qs=7 THEN GOTO 7;
      IF qs=9 THEN GOTO 9;
      IF qs=10 THEN GOTO 10;

1:    ReadNamesLine;                          {1: ReadNamesLine;
2:    name:=inNames[firstIn];                 {2: Write(interMed,inNames[firstIn])
      qs:=3;
      GOTO 10;

3:    name:=inNames[secondIn];                {3: Write(interMed,inNames[secondIn]
      qs:=4;
      GOTO 10;

4:    ReadNamesLine;                          {4: ReadNamesLine;

5:    name:=inNames[firstIn];                 {5: Write(interMed,inNames[firstIn]
      qs:=6;
      GOTO 10;

6:    name:=inNames[secondIn];                {6: Write(interMed,inNames[secondIn
      qs:=7;
      GOTO 10;

7:    ReadNamesLine;                          {7: ReadNamesLine;

8:    name:=inNames[firstIn];                 {8: Write(interMed,inNames[firstIn]
      qs:=9;
      GOTO 10;

9:    name:=inNames[secondIn];                {9: Write(interMed,inNames[secondIn
      qs:=10;
      GOTO 10;
10: END { P1, inverted } ;                    {END.

BEGIN { P2, Main program }
      qs:=1;



100:    ProcessIn(outNames[firstOut]);
200:    ProcessIn(outNames[secondOut]);

300:    ProcessIn(outNames[thirdOut]);
310:    WriteNamesLine;
400:    ProcessIn(outNames[firstOut]);

500:    ProcessIn(outNames[secondOut]);
600:    ProcessIn(outNames[thirdOut]);

610:    WriteNamesLine;

END { P2, Main program } .
```

The program to produce the intermediate file is as C11P1, except that if a name appearing in inLine is spacefilled, it is not written to the intermediate file. The coding of P2 is as given in C11S10.

```
PROGRAM C11S10(input,output,
                        interMed);
{ P2, consumes the intermediate file
 of names, which can be of any length,
 and produces the output. Backtracking
 has been used with a file of full
 lines  being posited. }

LABEL              1000,2000;

CONST
    nameLen        =4;
    spaces         = '    ';
    sentinel       = 'ZZZZ';

TYPE
    OutNamesPtrs   =(firstOut,secondOut,
                    thirdOut,dummyOutPtr);
    OutNamesType   =PACKED ARRAY
                    [1..nameLen] OF CHAR;
    OutNamesArray =ARRAY[outNamesPtrs]
                    OF OutNamesType;

VAR
    outNames       :OutNamesArray;
    outNamesPtr    :OutNamesPtrs;
    interMed       :FILE OF OutNamesType;
    name           :OutNamesType;


{ PROCEDURE WriteNamesLine; as C11P2 }
BEGIN { P2 }
 Reset(interMed,'intrMed');
 Read(interMed,name);
 BEGIN { Posit full line file }
 WHILE name <> sentinel DO
  BEGIN { Process full line out }
   outNamesPtr:=firstOut;
   WHILE outNamesPtr<= thirdOut DO
```

```
        BEGIN { WHILE used instead of FOR
               because of possible quit.
               Process name }
         outNames[outNamesPtr]:=name;
         outNamesPtr:=Succ(outNamesPtr);
         Read(interMed,name);
         IF (name=sentinel) AND
            (outNamesPtr>firstOut)
                          THEN GOTO 1000;
       END; { Process name }
     WriteNamesLine;
     END { Process full line out }
   END;{ Posit full line file }
   GOTO 2000;
   1000:
     BEGIN { Admit file with final
                         part line out }
       WHILE outNamesPtr<=thirdOut DO
         BEGIN
           outNames[outNamesPtr]:=spaces;
           outNamesPtr:=Succ(outNamesPtr)
         END;
       WriteNamesLine
     END; {  Admit file with final
                         part line out }

   2000: END { P2 } .
```

Exercise 11.11   The coding is as given in C11S11.

```
         PROGRAM C11S11(input,output);
         { This progam has P1 reading the input
           file and calling P2 (procedure
           ProcessOut) as an inverted program,
           thereby removing the need for the
           intermediate file. The design of P2
           is unchanged from C11S10 but is
           implemented in a suitable way for
           Pascal. }

         CONST
           nameLen     =4;
           spaces      ='    ';
           sentinel    ='ZZZZ';

         { TYPE, Var declarations as in C11P2 }

         { PROCEDURE ReadNamesline; as C11P1 }
```

```
ROCEDURE ProcessOut(name:namesType);
ABEL 100,200,300,
        1000,2000,3000,4000,5000,
                    6000,7000,8000;

  PROCEDURE WriteNamesline; as CllP2
```

```
EGIN { P2, inverted as ProcessOut}        {P2, principal original code,        }
                                          {                     see CllSl0     }
IF qs=100 THEN GOTO 100;
IF qs=200 THEN GOTO 200;
J0:;                                      {   Read(interMed,Name);             }
 BEGIN Posit full line file  }            {   BEGIN | Posit full line file     }
)00: IF name=sentinel THEN GOTO 3000;     {   WHILE name<>sentinel DO          }
  { BEGIN Process full line out       }   {    BEGIN | Process full line out | }
       outNamesPtr:=firstOut;             {     outNamesPtr:=firstOut;         }
)00: IF outNamesPtr>thirdOut THEN         {     WHILE outNamesPtr<=thirdOut    }
                         GOTO 5000;       {                             DO     }
       { BEGIN Process name }             {     BEGIN | Process name           }
       outNames[outNamesPtr]:=name;       {      outNames[outNamesPtr]:= name  }
       outNamesPtr:=Succ(outNamesPtr);    {      outNamesPtr:=Succ(outNamesPtr }
       qs:=200;
       GOTO 300;                          {       Read(interMed,name);         }
J0:    IF (name=sentinel) AND             {       IF (name=sentinel) AND       }
          (outNamesPtr> firstOut)         {          (outNamesPtr>firstOut)}
                     THEN GOTO 1000;      {                 THEN GOTO 1000; }
       { END Process name   }            {     END | Process name           }
    GOTO 6000;                            {                                  }
J00:  WriteNamesLine;                     {     WriteNamesLine;              }
   { END Process full line out  }         {   END | Process full line out |  }
 { END Posit full line file     }         {   END; | Posit full line file |  }
GOTO 2000;                                {   GOTO 2000;                     }
```

```
)00:;{ BEGIN Admit file with final }      {1000: BEGIN | Admit file with final|}
           {   part line out       }      {                    part line out | }
)00:    IF outNamesPtr>thirdOut THEN      {    WHILE outNamesPtr<=thirdOut  DO }
                        GOTO 7000;        {    BEGIN                           }
        outNames[outNamesPtr]:=spaces;    {     outNames[outNmaesPtr]:=spaces: }
        outNamesPtr:=Succ(outNamesPtr);   {     outNamesPtr:=Succ(outNamesPtr) }
        GOTO 8000;                        {    END;                            }
)00:    WriteNamesLine;                   {    WriteNamesLine                  }
        { END; Admit file with final }    {    END | Admit file with final |   }
               { part line out      }     {                 |part line out  |  }
)00: ;                                     {2000: END  }
    GOTO 4000;                             {END.       }
)00: ;
J0: END { P2, inverted } ;
```

```
BEGIN { Pl, Main program }
  qs:=100;
  WriteLn('Enter names: ');
  WHILE NOT Eof DO
   BEGIN { Process line in}
   ReadNamesLine;
   FOR inNamesPtr:=firstIn TO secondIn
    DO
     BEGIN
      IF inNames[inNamesPtr]<> spaces
       THEN
         ProcessOut(inNames[inNamesPtr])
     END;
   WriteLn('Enter names: ')
   END; { Process line in}
  ProcessOut(sentinel)
END { Pl, Main program } .
```

Exercise 11.12 The coding is as given in C11S12.

```
PROGRAM C11S12(input,output);
{ This progam has P2 displaying the
  output file and calling Pl (procedure
  ProcessIn) as an inverted program,
  thereby removing the need for the
  intermediate file. The design of Pl
  is unchanged from C11P1 and C11S10
  but is implemented in a suitable way
  for Pascal. }

LABEL    1000,2000;

CONST
  nameLen      =4;
  spaces       ='    ';
  sentinel     ='ZZZZ';

TYPE
  InNamesPtrs  =(firstIn,secondIn,
                      dummyInPtr);

VAR
  name         :NamesType;

{ Other TYPE, VAR declarations as in
                            C11P3 }
```

```
{ PROCEDURE WriteNamesline; as CllP2 }

PROCEDURE ProcessIn(VAR name:namesType);
  LABEL      1,2,3,4,
             30,40,50,60,70;

  { PROCEDURE ReadNamesline; as CllP1 }

  BEGIN { P1, inverted as ProcessIn
              -see CllP1 and CllS10 }
  IF qs=1 THEN GOTO 1;
  IF qs=2 THEN GOTO 2;
  IF qs=3 THEN GOTO 3;
  1: WriteLn('Enter names: ');
  40: IF Eof THEN GOTO 50;
      { BEGIN Process an input line }
      ReadNamesLine;
      inNamesPtr:=firstIn;
  30: IF inNamesPtr> secondIn THEN
                              GOTO 60;
        { BEGIN Process names }
        IF inNames[inNamesPtr]= spaces
                   THEN GOTO 70;
          { BEGIN Return a name }
            name:=inNames[inNamesPtr];
            qs:=2;
            GOTO 4;
  2:;     { END Return a name }
  70:     inNamesPtr:=SUCC(inNamesPtr);
        GOTO 30;
        { END Process names }
  60:  WriteLn('Enter names: ');
       GOTO 40;
       { END; Process an input line }
  50: name:=sentinel;
      qs:=3;
      GOTO 4;
  3:;
  4:
END { P1, inverted } ;

BEGIN { P2, Main program }
  qs:=1;
  ProcessIn(name);
  BEGIN { Posit full line file }
  WHILE name <> sentinel DO
   BEGIN { Process full line out }
```

```
        outNamesPtr:=firstOut;
        WHILE outNamesPtr<= thirdOut DO
          BEGIN { Process name }
            IF name=sentinel THEN GOTO 1000;
            outNames[outNamesPtr]:=name;
            outNamesPtr:=SUCC(outNamesPtr);
            ProcessIn(name)
          END; { Process name }
         WriteNamesLine
       END; { Process full line out }
     END; { Posit full line file }
    GOTO 2000;
   1000:
     BEGIN { Admit file with final
                      part line out }
       WHILE outNamesPtr<=thirdOut DO
       BEGIN
        outNames[outNamesPtr]:=spaces;
        outNamesPtr:=Succ(outNamesPtr)
       END;
      WriteNamesLine
     END; {  Admit file with final
                      part line out }
   2000:
  END { P2, Main program } .
```

The operation called 'Process valve cycles' in Figure 11.19 becomes 'P valve cycle batch', in Figure S11.15. 'Write totalOpenTime' is repositioned.

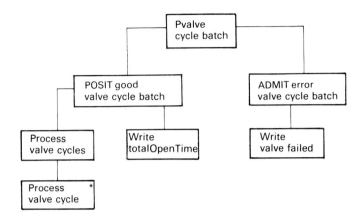

Index